THE BRITISH SLAVE TRADE AND PUBLIC MEMORY

The British Slave Trade
and Public Memory

Elizabeth Kowaleski Wallace

Columbia University Press *New York*

Columbia University Press
Publishers Since 1893
New York   Chichester, West Sussex

Copyright © 2006 Columbia University Press
All rights reserved

A portion of Chapter Two previously appeared under the title "Telling Untold Stories: Philippa Gregory's *A Respectable Trade* and David Dabydeen's *A Harlot's Progress,* in *NOVEL: A Forum on Fiction* (33 (2), Spring 2000). Copyright 2000 by Novel Corp.; reprinted with permission. An additional portion of Chapter Two appeared as "Transnationalism and Performance in 'Biyi Bandele's *Oroonoko*" in *Publications of the Modern Language Association* (119: 265–281, 2004). Reprinted by permission of the copyright holder, the Modern Language Association of America. Quotations from *Secrets & Lies* by Mike Leigh appear courtesy of Faber and Faber.

Library of Congress Cataloging-in-Publication Data
Kowaleski-Wallace, Elizabeth, 1954–
   The British slave trade and public memory / Elizabeth Kowaleski-Wallace.
      p. cm.
   Includes bibliographical references (p.   ) and index.
   ISBN 0-231-13714-1 (acid-free paper) — ISBN 0-231-13715-X (pbk. : acid-free paper)
   1. Slave trade—Great Britain—History—Public opinion. 2. Public opinion—Great Britain. 3. Slave trade in literature. 4. Slavery in literature.   I. Title.
   HT1162.K69 2005
   306.3′620941—dc22
                                                    2005053785

∞
Columbia University Press books are printed on permanent and durable acid-free paper.
Printed in the United States of America
c 10 9 8 7 6 5 4 3 2 1
p 10 9 8 7 6 5 4 3 2 1

Contents

List of Illustrations   vii
Preface   ix

Introduction: Millennial Reckonings   1

1. Commemorating the Transatlantic Slave Trade in Liverpool and Bristol   25

2. Fictionalizing Slavery in the United Kingdom, 1990–2000   67

3. Seeing Slavery and the Slave Trade   125

4. Transnationalism and Performance in 'Biyi Bandele's *Oroonoko*   179

Conclusion   207

Notes   213
Index   243

List of Illustrations

1. Tony Forbes, "Sold Down the River."
2. Pero Footbridge, Bristol.
3. "Queen Square."
4. Hakeem Kae-Kazim as Equiano from *A Son of Africa*.
5. Cover, paperback edition of *A Respectable Trade*.
6. Brenda Blethyn as Cynthia and Marianne Jean-Baptiste as Hortense in *Secrets & Lies*.
7. "A Negro Hung Alive by the Ribs to a Gallows" from John Gabriel Stedman, *Narrative of a five year's expedition against the revolted Negroes of Surinam*. Engraved by William Blake.
8. Mrs. Hartley as Imoinda.
9. Nadine Marshall as Imoinda.

Preface

On an untypical late spring Sunday in Bath, the sky is uninterrupted by cloud, pedestrians free from the threat of imminent drenching. The sun is relentless in its warmth and intensity, and the city is making the most of its cheer. Near North Parade, the operators of double-decker tourist buses are busy working the crowds, promising a narrated introduction to the city's historical and architectural highlights: the Roman Baths, the Pump Room, the Assembly, the Royal Crescent, and the Circus. If the events of September 11, 2001, have thinned the crowds of American tourists who have come to take in the sights, equally enthusiastic British tourists do their best to compensate for their numbers. Oversized tourist coaches, towering in the narrow eighteenth-century streets, carry excursioners who have come to Bath for the day, or perhaps the weekend. Among these are well-dressed women and men of a certain age with shopping bags, peering into shop windows. Many of these eschew the newly popular Starbucks in favor of Sally Lunn's traditional cream tea. Their numbers are supplemented by family groups who have come for the day by car. Ice creams melting in hand, they stroll through the Abbey Churchyard, past the benches where the city's homeless inhabitants soak up the warm sun, past the street musicians and painted human statues, past the Cornish pasty shop, past Cheap Street, and on up to Milsom Street, a route as popular in Jane Austen's time as it is now.

Just beyond the route of the tourist buses lies a very different kind of tourist event: Walcot Nation day. Walcot Street, the home of antique and retro-chic shops, curry shops and pubs, as well as new constructions designed to house trendier, high-tech industries, celebrates itself today with a massive all-day street party. Unlike the predominantly white crowds typically seen on the tourist routes in Bath, those on Walcot Street are multiracial, multiethnic, and multilingual. Their sartorial styles range from hippy to grunge, from dreadlocks to tattoos and piercings. One woman wears a T-shirt proclaiming, "This body is not a temple. It's an amusement park." The kids here are surfeited on sweets, their faces painted, as they clutch oversized helium balloons in the shape of exotic insects. Every few blocks a different band entertains the crowds. Near the Waitrose parking lot a swing band compensates for its less than perfect technique with overwhelming enthusiasm, apparent foremost in the lead saxophonist, who can't keep his feet on the ground. Around the corner, a large, multiethnic salsa band entertains an undulating Baby Boomer crowd dancing to the percussive music and singing along in Spanish. A little farther up the street the rhythm is American hip-hop, infused with a Caribbean beat, the crowd younger and dreadlocked. The air is thick with smoke from jerk chicken and rice and beans. Hip-hop yields to punk blaring from a speaker near an open-air pub, and so on up the street, where a rainbow nation strolls past the vendors of scented candles and brilliantly dyed sheepskins, jumbo hotdogs, and beer.

To visit Bath on a given day and to carry away either kind of tourist experience as a snapshot of England would no doubt be reductive: twenty-first century England can consist of both—or neither—of these scenes. Yet each scene also reflects a different understanding of and investment in Bath's history. For those who have come to tour the Roman Baths, sip tea in the pump rooms, or walk in the footsteps of Jane Austen, Bath is an important repository of what is best and most beloved about British history. As such Bath does not necessarily exclude diversity, but it distills Britishness into a series of recognizable attributes. For those who have come to Bath to party on Walcot Street, listen to world music, eat the spicy island food, or simply gather among a vibrant multicultural population sharing similar philosophies, Bath is the scene of possibility, the vision of what Britain might become and how it might embrace the best that the world has to offer, becoming stronger and richer in the process.

As an eighteenth-century scholar and a frequent visitor to Bath, I find myself intrigued by these coexisting investments in Bath because I believe they raise critical questions: how will England successfully constitute itself as a hybrid nation in the twenty-first century? How can it tell a comprehensive historical story that engages all of its citizens without being divisive? Yet perhaps Bath's landmarks remind us that the process of constructing a British metropolis, while conflicted and contested, can nonetheless result in livable and vibrant communities that endure for centuries. After all, beginning with Roman times, Bath's history is the story of people who have come from somewhere else, people who have succeeded, or failed, to make themselves at home. From the Roman baths to the assembly rooms, city landmarks commemorate social rites signifying who would belong and what it would take for them to do so. Thus, Bath's social history offers us one, encapsulated version of how a kingdom becomes "united." Indeed, one of Bath's major tourist attraction, the Roman Baths, is evidence of early intercultural contact, as Roman forms of worship displaced indigenous altars. During the Middle Ages, Christian Bath absorbed vagrants, the homeless, and the sick into its charitable hospitals, hostels, and spas. Then, in the eighteenth century, longer-residing citizens found themselves forced to accommodate newcomers, as older traditions and understandings encountered newer customs and social practices. Tobias Smollett, John Anstey, and even Jane Austen complained that newcomers brought disruption, noise, and disorder to the city. Yet, coming as they did from unknown backgrounds, and possessing different sensibilities, newcomers strengthened the fabric of social life in Bath. Bringing new economic potentialities, they also brought new perspectives. Their stately homes, ironically deemed architecturally insubstantial by Smollett in 1771, still testify to their impact on the emerging metropolis.

As an eighteenth-century coinage, the idea of Britain is a construction that simultaneously refers to a national orientation and a distinct local identity—not only the English, the Scots, and the Welsh, but also the Liverpudlians, the Mancunians, and the Glaswegians. But the word *British* also encodes a complex and fraught global history in which far-flung places and people were brought together under one flag. In the twentieth century, as the citizens of the Commonwealth began to relocate themselves on English soil, the mood has been tense, as those who have come home to "Mother England" have experienced resistance. Those hostile to these newcomers have unfairly charged them with fostering disorder. Yet, despite the forces working against them, and despite the fact that many have not been afforded the educational, social, or economic opportunities that should rightfully have been theirs as citizens of the British Commonwealth, Britain's newcomers have made significant contributions to the culture. If they lack the resources to build lavish architectural monuments, they nonetheless create other structures that will one day affirm their sustained impact.[1]

Moving easily between Milsom Street and Walcot Street on a cloudless day in June, a visitor can take heart from how comfortably two visions of England can coexist in Bath. However, if England is successfully to become a twenty-first century nation that embraces all its citizens, it will need to find occasions for dialogue between the excursioners in the Abbey churchyard and the salsa dancers on Walcot Street. The challenge is to find cultural forms that promote debate and dialogue and that actively engage individuals who become participants in the making of truly inclusive society.

This book was written with the generous assistance of people at my home institution, Boston College, and with the help of scholars and other individuals in the United Kingdom. At Boston College, my research was facilitated through a Research Incentive Grant in 2001 as well as subsequent Research Expense Grants. My colleagues Rhonda Frederic, Alan Richardson, Andrew Sofer, and Christopher Wilson read portions of the manuscript and provided helpful comments. In addition, the college's Transnational Reading Group provided me with thought-provoking discussion and bibliography. The staff of the Boston College Interlibrary Loan Department, under Margot McDonough and later Anne Kenny, could not have been more helpful. Stephen Veeder in Media Technology Services provided assistance with the illustrations. I also thank Pamela Bromberg, Vincent Caretta, Lynn Festa, Irene Fizer, Suzanne Keen, Erin Mackie, Susan Staves, and Beth Fowkes Tobin for their responses to work-in-progress.

In England, early encouragement for the project came from conversations with Ann Nunes and Barbara White at Advanced Studies in England. Anthony Tibbles generously shared information about the Liverpool exhibit and steered me in the right direction when I was just beginning my research One important fringe benefit of writing this book has been my acquaintance with Madge Dresser, who has been a terrific source of knowledge and wisdom, an insightful critic, and a good friend. My husband, Jim Wallace, has some right to feel this book is his as well as mine: without his willingness to listen to my ideas, to plow through drafts, and to patiently fix yet another computer glitch, there wouldn't be a book. To the extent that writing any book puts demands on a family that finds iself making trips to odd places or that tolerates living with towering piles of books and an inexplicably crabby mother, my children, Clarissa and Ian, can also claim this book as theirs.

Finally, this book is dedicated to Clare Hector and Ian and Charlotte Cutter, who have shared so much with me during the writing of this book—the pleasures of their spectacular garden in the summer and their hearth in the winter, many lovely meals, and long conversations on Anglo-American relations. Thank you for letting me become part of your family.

Introduction

Millennial Reckonings

"British tag 'coded racist'" read the lead headline of the Manchester *Guardian*, October 11, 2000. The article addressed the publication of *The Future of Multi-Ethnic Britain: The Parekh Report* by the Runnymede Trust.[1] Running to 417 pages, *The Parekh Report* was produced by a commission including academics, journalists, law-enforcement officers, social workers, educators, public policy researchers, and specialists. Its twenty-one chapters describe the current climate for multiethnic experience in Britain by reviewing existing social policies and surveying relevant issues in policing, the criminal justice system, education, arts, media, sports, health and welfare, employment, immigration and asylum, religion, government leadership, legislation, and organizational change. The report culminates with an eighteen-page checklist of recommendations.[2]

In the fall of 2000, the response to the report was wide-ranging. *The Parekh Report* attracted several weeks of media coverage and later provoked a debate in the House of Lords, as well as further consideration by the Home Secretary's Race Relations Forum and an All-Party Parliamentary Group on Race and Community. However, despite the commission's far-reaching recommendations, and its distillation of a long-standing conversation on the topic of inclusiveness, the initial media coverage focused on the report's discussion of racial terminology above all else. As the October 11 headline from the *Guardian* suggests, the perceived attack on the central concept of a "British identity" was predictably inflammatory. Although largely sympathetic to the report, the *Guardian* was one of many newspapers entertaining a lively debate on the meaning of the word *British*. One of its readers opined: "A piece of language does not have connotations. It is how we use it that counts." Another derided what appeared to be the upshot of the report, asking whether he should call himself a Teletubby. Yet another reader cited black British Olympic gold medalist Denise Lewis's wrapping herself in the Union Jack as proof of British inclusiveness.[3] Columnist Roz Coward weighed in to critique the concept of multiculturalism itself—although the title of the report clearly eschews the word *multicultural* in favor of *multiethnic*. To Coward, *multiculturalism* also "implies the absence of any dominant sense of a shared culture." She wrote, "Britishness has many positive as well as negative connotations: commitment to democracy, justice, moderation."[4] As the defenders of the report were quick to point out, the report actually asserted that the term *British* is *racial*, not racist—for instance, as in calling a Chinese population a racial group as opposed to a racist group.

Nonetheless, the media's focus on terminology effectively deflected attention from what were arguably larger and more important questions: why *this* report at *this* moment? What were the precipitating events leading to the publication of the report in 2000? What were the report's origins? For many Britons, the beginning of 2000 marked the end of a year in which a number of large-scale celebrations had failed to meet public expectation: the Millennium Dome flopped; the anticipated extravagant partying did not materialize; the Millennium Foot Bridge wobbled; even the Millennium Pyrotechnics, a river of fire designed to illuminate the Thames, did not light as planned. Nonetheless, the events associated with the turn of the millennium produced a great deal of national conversation in which many Britons reminisced about the source of the nation's strength, fascinated by historical events such as London during the Blitz, events that provided an opportunity to consider what Britain does best.[5] But this kind of historical retrospection inevitably led to further scrutiny of what Britain is now: what characterizes Britain in this moment, as it moves from its former position of imperial greatness to its newer position, first as member of a European economic community and then as a key player in a globalized world?

The Parekh Report explicitly engages with this question and tries to provide answers. It begins: "Britain is at a turning point, a crossroads. But was this not always so? Yes and no." What distinguishes the current moment, for the framers of the report, are "disparate but interacting forces" that have come together in an especially powerful and momentous way: "It is a coincidence but symbolically apt that the current confluence occurs simultaneously with the start of a new millennium."[6] Warning against a territorial view of Britain, "where people are divided and fragmented among the three separate countries and among regions, cities, and boroughs, and where there is hostility, suspicion, and wasteful competition," the authors propose an alternative: that Britain become a "community of communities."[7] In other words, the report unfolds as a millennial document with a specific agenda: to refashion Britain "as an outward-looking, generous, inclusive society."[8] Thus, in his contribution to the debate, Stuart Hall, one of the report's commissioners, tried to redirect the conversation away from the misperceived focus on racial terminology to what he argued was the report's main goal: a climate of social inclusiveness. "Belonging is truly a tricky concept, requiring both identification and recognition," he wrote. "If people from ethnic minorities are to become not only citizens with equal rights but also an integral part of the national culture, the meaning of the term 'British' will have to become more inclusive of their experiences, values and aspirations."[9]

In several ways, the main arguments of *The Parekh Report* can be traced to the discourse surrounding another end-of-century commemoration: June 22, 1998, marked the fiftieth anniversary of the arrival of the *Empire Windrush* at Tilbury Docks. Later understood as a symbol of postwar immigration, the decommissioned warship had originally been sent to islands of the British Commonwealth to collect soldiers at the end of World War II. With space remaining, passage to England was offered to anyone who could raise the fare of twenty-eight pounds ten. About three hundred West Indian men made the journey. In the media coverage of the *Windrush* anniversary, much discussion was focused on the difference between the experiences of the first trickle of immigrants and those of the waves that followed. It seems clear that no one in 1948 recognized the fullest implications of the arrival of the *Windrush*'s passengers. Nonetheless, it initiated a social shift that led on the one hand to vibrant new cultural expressions and on the other hand to such explosive political events as the Notting Hill Riots and the Stephen Lawrence Inquiry Report. For black Britons Mike Phillips and Trevor Phillips, "the spectacle of the *Windrush* has become a vital, necessary link between [their] nationality and the historical accident from which its springs, and for [them], the outline of the arrival and its consequences is also a journey which sketches out the shape of [their] identities."[10] However, the *Windrush* commemoration only testifies to larger shifts in British political and social life, changes that were brought on by the "coming home" of the "children" of the British empire. Sarah Lawson Welsh writes: "With the loss of her formal Empire, Britain was forced to confront a radically redrawn world map which had significant ramifications for her own role and self-image, shifting her sense of place on the map, as well as challenging those versions of national identity around which the Empire had been built."[11]

For the writers of *The Parekh Report*, above all it is important to refute the notion that postwar immigrants of color arrived to find a stable, homogeneous group of citizens who had previously not known conflict or ethnic strife. In many ways, this idea should not have been provocative to an audience living through an age of devolution.[12] In the wake of a movie such as *Braveheart*, the idea that "Britain is not and never has been the unified, conflict-free land of popular imagination"[13] should scarcely have seemed surprising. But the report went further to stipulate that "there has never been a single 'British' way of life.'"[14] In addition, "Britain is a land of many different groups, interests and identities, from Home Counties English to Gaels, Geordies and Mancunians to Liverpudlians, Irish to Pakistanis, African-Caribbeans to Indians."[15] Such statements reflect the legacy of a particular kind of late-twentieth-century history, one indebted to the academic left, one that recognizes that various kinds of diverse communities, with contesting religious, ethnic, economic, or cultural agendas, come together uneasily to contribute to a British identity. Cambridge University historian Raphael Samuel articulated one version of this understanding in 1989:

> There is no reason to suppose that British society in the past was more homogenous than it is in the present. Oppositions between town and country and between North and South are major themes in our literature. Militant particularism has been for some four centuries an organizing principle of religious life, nor is it less apparent in the history of trade unionism. One possible object of national history would be to identify the minority communities of which, at any point in time, the majority of the British was composed. Such a view is not necessarily inimical to the idea of a nation.[16]

Samuel's privileging of a heterogeneous British society, in which competing factions struggle for dominance, marks him as an important precursor for others interrogating the true nature of a "united" kingdom.

To return to the question of what circumstances led to the profound questioning of a British national identity in *The Parekh Report*, it is useful to survey several key developments in British intellectual life from 1970 to 2000, developments that centered on the history of one British ethnic group in particular: individuals of Caribbean, Afro-Caribbean, or African descent. These are drawn from a black revisionist history, accompanied by important emendations to the British literary canon; the emergence of black cultural studies and postcolonial studies; and an active debate about the idea of British heritage, with a serious consideration of the question "to whom does history belong?" Although retrospectively organized as separate events, these three developments were scarcely discrete or self-contained; the key players in one development are frequently also important to the others. Moreover, these developments defy strict chronology, as the dates of key publications and debates in each development significantly overlap. This survey allows us to see that, long before the popular media took up the topic of British involvement in eighteenth-century slave trade in the last decade of the twentieth century, scholarship on both the history of blacks in Britain and the legacy of slavery was readily available in the United Kingdom. The presence of such scholarship not only paved the way for the critique of British identity found in *The Parekh Report* but also anticipated key elements of its argument. However, as I will also argue, because this scholarship stayed largely within the British academy—without making its way with any regularity into school curricula or popular awareness—it remained possible to speak of the eighteenth-century slave trade and its aftermath as a "secret" history right up until the beginning of the current millennium.

Writing within a period of approximately twenty years, between 1970 and 1990, both James Walvin and F. O. Shyllon revise a white history that has either denied its own racism or given itself credit for liberating those whom it enslaved in the first place. Meanwhile, for Peter Fryer the point is to make a missing history of England's black population accessible to a broad audience. I note here the work being done by Walvin, Shyllon, and Fryer because they were among the first—although by no means the only—scholars to provide access to historical materials that later become crucial texts for the various cultural expressions that are under discussion in the rest of this study.

First, Walvin's *Black and White: The Negro and English Society, 1555–1945* (1973) provides a comprehensive survey of the black community in England since the mid-sixteenth century.[17] Walvin tells the history of how whites understood racial difference, beginning with "First Reactions" resulting from the sixteenth-century slave trade and culminating with the end of World War II. Although his aim is to identify black presence in English history, his emphasis necessarily falls on the devastating results of racism, on the ugliness of racial stereotyping and caricature, and on the distorted images of blacks as pets, enslaved workers, and sexual deviants—images that are then brought home by the book's illustrations. With an emphasis on white reaction to black presence, *Black and White* exemplifies both the strengths and the weaknesses of early revisionist history; while providing much-needed attention to the forgotten history of slavery, Walvin's perspective, by focusing on how a white population gradually revised its understanding of black humanity, remains Anglocentric, without critiquing the conditions that generated racist stereotypes in the first place.

Published nearly twenty years later, Walvin's *Black Ivory: A History of British Slavery* (1992) uses a changing historical method and focus that gives equal weight to black and white perspectives while telling a complicated story of intercultural contact.[18] Walvin locates the origins of the slave trade in an English domestic setting—the coffeehouse and the tea table—where the demand for coffee, tea, sugar, tobacco, and other commodities prompted transatlantic activity. He surveys the legal issues surrounding slavery in England but soon turns to the coast of Africa, and to the kingdom of Dahoumey in particular, to discuss African complicity. He examines conditions on slave ships, drawing on evidence of black writers (for example, Olaudah Equiano) and white writers (for example, Alexander Falconbridge). He covers the conditions of slave labor and plantation life in Jamaica and elsewhere in the Caribbean, with a separate chapter on conditions of women's lives under the slave system. A section entitled "Fighting Back" acknowledges how "slavery, conceived and nurtured in violence, naturally begat violence."[19] Although the book ends with a chapter on the abolition movement, it also returns to the legacy of slavery in Africa—and to current race relations in London, Liverpool, Bristol, and other places: "Was it mere accident that these cities should be plagued, long after slavery had died, for the sins of their fathers?"[20]

Like *Black and White In England*, *Black Slaves in Britain* (1974), by F. O. Shyllon, works within an Anglocentric paradigm but to different effect.[21] As a legal historian Shyllon (who is currently a member of the law faculty at the University of Ibadan, Nigeria) seeks to refute the idea, still circulating at the time of his book's publication, that slavery was "deleted" from the British Isles as a result of Lord Mansfield's judgment in the Somerset case. His larger stake, then, is to indict implicitly the white legal system for its long-standing tolerance of slavery. His book ends by citing Eric Williams's classic study *Capitalism and Slavery* (1944), for its focus on the gradually emerging economic reasons for the abolition of slavery. Shyllon's study provides a meticulous and compelling account of the major legal cases touching on the lives of slaves in England and the Caribbean during the second half of the eighteenth century and the early decades of the nineteenth century. With a focus on Granville Sharpe in particular, *Black Slaves in Britain* illuminates the complex and nearly always tragic ways in which black and white lives were interconnected by the slave trade. Yet in this book black lives are central to the narrative, as Shyllon pays significant attention to individual cases, including those of Jonathan Strong, Grace Jones, and James Somerset, without ignoring the intricacies of the legal system itself. Thus, *Black Slaves in Britain* simultaneously addresses individual intervention and takes up the larger institutional framework.

A related work by Shyllon, *Black People in Britain, 1555–1833* (1977), focuses exclusively on the "black experience" and provides a comprehensive survey of the various circumstances under which England's black population lived prior to the mid-nineteenth century, from "Princes, Students, and Scholars" to "Beggars, Mendicants, and Serenaders."[22] Particularly notable is his coverage of the economic conditions for blacks, as well as his discussion of the failed repatriation effort of the 1780s—an event in which Shyllon sees parallels to the effort to deport blacks in the 1960s. The last section, featuring brief biographies of notable eighteenth- and nineteenth-century black figures, from Ukawsaw Gronniosaw and Ottobah Cugoano to Ira Aldridge and Olaudah Equiano, predates by almost twenty years other scholarly efforts to create a more inclusive literary canon.

Peter Fryer opens his book *Staying Power: The History of Black People in Britain* (1984) with the bold assertion that "Black people—by whom I mean Africans and Asians and their descendants—have been living in Britain for close on 500 years,"[23] a statement also made by others, although not, perhaps, quite so effectively. Referring to black soldiers who were part of the Roman imperial army, Fryer maintains: "There were Africans in Britain before the English came here."[24] Fryer's strategy is to "denaturalize" the idea of an English identity by reminding his audience of the complicated and conflicted history of ethnic struggle leading to the creation of a specifically British nationalism. With chapters including "Britain's Slave Ports," "Eighteenth-century Voices," "The Rise of Racism," and (on twentieth-century topics) "Challenges to Empire" and "The Settlers," Fryer's book remains—and rightfully so—one of the best-known accessible popular histories surveying the long and ongoing history of blacks in England. Like Walvin's 1992 book, Fryer's *Staying Power* closes with a look at modern race relations, by examining the 1981 youth riots in Brixton, Southall, Liverpool, Manchester, Leeds, Bristol, and elsewhere. He reads such explosive violence as a "burst of youthful rage" proving that "the persistent bullying of black people was bound, sooner or later, to provoke rebellion."[25] But more important, he writes to counteract the removal of traces of black life from the British past, by way of ensuring that black people are part of the British future.

Taken together, these books suggest that a considerable body of work had been done in the academy to "remember" British involvement in slavery and the slave trade long before they became a topic for museum curators, television writers, screenwriters, and other cultural producers. The work of Walvin, Shyllon, and Fryer, as well as other historians,[26] was complemented from the 1970s to the 1990s by the research of literary scholars in England, most notably David Dabydeen and Paul Edwards, who were challenging the existing English literary canon in one of two ways—either by demonstrating how race was already depicted in English literature or by arguing for a revised and expanded canon, one that could acknowledge the contribution of early black writers such as Olaudah Equiano and Ignatius Sancho. As an example of the first category of challenge, in 1985 Dabydeen edited a collection entitled *The Black Presence in English Literature*, which, as Dabydeen writes in the Preface, resulted from a conference by the same title as the collection that had, ironically, taken place in Wolverhampton, a town famous for producing John Enoch Powell, a former Member of Parliament notorious for his incendiary, racist remarks.[27] Disputing the sentiment that the English school curriculum was "too crowded" to introduce the topic of multiculturalism, conference contributors argued that "reappraisal of the literature already taught in schools and used as sets for 'O' and 'A' level examinations would reveal its 'multi-cultural' content: it was merely a matter of making the black man visible."[28] With essays such as "Blacks in English Renaissance Drama and the Role of Shakespeare's *Othello*" (by Ruth Cowig) and "The Revelation of Caliban: 'The Black Presence' in the Classroom" (by Kenneth Parker), this collection anticipates the major shifts in emphasis, as well as new strategies for reading, that were later to characterize a postcolonial approach to English literature in the 1990s. Partly as a result of collections like this one, classic works—for example, *Othello*, *The Tempest*, and Aphra Behn's *Oroonoko*, the story of an African prince taken as a slave to Suriname—were given new critical scrutiny for both their representation of race and their capacity to provoke questions about the English empire. Dabydeen extended his project on the representation of blackness in two additional publications: *Hogarth's Blacks: Images of Blacks in Eighteenth-century English Art* and *Black Writers in Britain: 1760–1890, an Anthology*, which he coedited with Paul Edwards in 1991.[29] A second goal of literary critics such as Dabydeen and Edwards was to rethink not only the content but also the purpose and goal of literary study. Renewed attention to the autobiography of Olaudah Equiano, as edited by Paul Edwards in 1967 and then reprinted throughout the 1980s and 1990s, ensured the centrality of the abolition movement in literary scholarship of the eighteenth and nineteenth centuries.[30]

These early challenges to the eighteenth-century canon unfolded against the emergence of a field of black cultural studies in Britain that, although sharing several characteristics of a similar field in the United States, had its own dynamic. According to the editors of *Black British Cultural Studies: A Reader*, in the United States, black arts and black studies movements of the 1960s and 1970s were direct outgrowths of civil rights and black power politics. They were mass-oriented, with *blackness* itself the term that bridged the gap between a popular and an academic context:

> Blackness was defined in myriad ways. But it seems generally to have signified in the United States a congeries of historical, cultural, sociopolitical, and genetic properties shared by United States citizens of African descent. It was blackness that allowed disparate subject positions to converge under the sign of a politically engaged "we."[31]

However, in Britain, with very few direct descendants of slaves and no widespread civil rights movement, the term *blackness*, particularly in academic circles, was understood not as denoting shared properties but as signifying a condition of exclusion that was created through specifically racist discourses. "Black British cultural studies thus discovered that the supposed fixity of 'race' had generally been articulated in Britain through images of ethnic exclusion—'Britons' and 'aliens.' A convergence of race and ethnicity had produced what seemed to be clear national boundaries."[32] In other words, this difference meant that in Britain, from early on, race was de-essentialized—racial difference was understood to have been created in language, law, and politics, and then imposed on the human body, where it is continually "read" and imbued with powerful significance. Still, under this rubric of the politics of race, it "is difficult at times to say what is and what *is not* black British cultural studies."[33] In addition, according to the editors, it becomes difficult "to infer who precisely black British cultural workers intend when they say 'we'" in referring to people of color engaged in oppositional politics.[34]

Indeed, as the introduction to *Black British Cultural Studies* admits, the term "black" itself "alters in remarkable ways"[35] when used in the field. Who should be covered under this term? What histories does it encompass? For Prabhu Guptara, the term *black British* is delimited not necessarily by skin color but by terms of potential citizenship: "'black Britons' are those people of non-European origin who are now, or were in the past, entitled to hold a British passport and displayed a substantial commitment to Britain, for example, by living a large part of their lives here."[36] But Helge Nowak criticizes this definition as lacking in unity. Immigrants from the former British Empire do not share a common heritage but belong to ethnically and culturally diverse groups; they have immigrated from diverse regions of the world; they are not centered in a geographical region; they differ in settlement, housing situation, education, and economic performance; and, although some groups intermarry, others do not.[37] Moreover, according to a 1991 census, "'black' people taken together constitute only a minority within the minorities."[38] Yasmin Alibhai-Brown settles the issue by using *British black* as an umbrella term—"the political term embracing all non-white groups"—which she then supplements with a series of more precise terms, including British Asian (Hindus, Muslims, Sikhs, Chinese, Vietnamese, Sri Lankans, Indians, Bangladeshis, and Pakistanis), British black (Afro-Caribbeans and Africans), and mixed race/biracial (people of mixed ethnic or racial origins).[39] In this book, with its emphasis on people whose histories have been deeply affected by the eighteenth-century slave trade, the term *black* is used in Brown's sense of British black.

Still, for Fred D'Aguiar, the entire project of defining a specifically "black" culture is fraught with potential perils. Specifically, affixing the prefix *black* to any body of creative work "syphons off so-called blackness from the general drive of creativity in Britain."[40] Arguing that the term *Black British* is being burdened with "more weight than it can carry," D'Aguiar further maintains that "Britishness is not perceived differently by the prefix black so much as [by] the subject to whom it refers."[41] For D'Aguiar—as for historian Raphael Samuel—the term *Britishness* should already "conjure up a picture of a plural society." D'Aguiar continues:

> It can be argued that Britain has never been anything but plural in culture and race.... So rather than arguing for an animal called black British it became necessary to articulate another angle of what it is to be British, one markedly different from received notions of Britishness. It is *within* the arena of Britishness that battles of class and race and sex are being waged, not from those outside on some privileged inner circle.
>
> The creative imagination knows no boundaries. Border and passports do not confine it nor do attempts to hijack with neat terms said to be for the liberation of one section of it from the tyranny of another section.[42]

Later we see how, as a novelist, D'Aguiar negotiates the idea of English hybridity in novels that were published during a time of intense debate over and scrutiny of black political, social, and artistic life in the United Kingdom.

Surveying the various trends in black cultural politics during the 1980s and early 1990s, Stuart Hall maintains that the major shift during that period was "a change from a struggle over the relations of representation to a politics of representation itself." He provides a retrospective summary of the work I have discussed so far, by historians such as Shyllon, Walvin, and Fryer as well as by literary critics such as Dabydeen and Edwards:

> This analysis was predicated on the marginalization of black experience in British culture ... blacks have typically been the objects, but

rarely the subjects, of the practices of representation. The struggle to come into representation was predicated on a critique of fetishization, objectification, and negative figuration which are so much a feature of the black subject. There was a concern not simply with the absence of the black experience but with its simplification and its stereotypical character.[43]

But the shift that he describes—one that owes much to both poststructuralist and postcolonial theory—entails "the recognition that 'black' is essentially a politically *constructed* category, which cannot be grounded in a set of fixed transcultural or transcendental racial categories and which therefore has no guarantees in Nature." The consequences of this shift are far-reaching. For instance, "you can no longer conduct black politics through the strategy of a simple set of reversals, putting in the place of the bad essential white subject, the new essentially good black subject."[44] Hall's approach lessens the binary nature of black–white relations and insists instead that white and black are racial categories that are mutually constitutive. However, this understanding that race is constructed in language does not mitigate a political critique of British history. If anything, it makes it easier to locate and identify the origins and consequences of racism in the history of British imperial politics by showing how the growth of empire necessarily generated categories of "otherness" against which to chart its progress.

Indeed, one of the main contributions of Paul Gilroy's widely cited 1987 study *'There Ain't no Black in the Union Jack': The Cultural Politics of Race and Nation* is an argument for the necessity of a counternarrative to challenge existing notions about imperial benevolence. Writing against the backdrop of Thatcherism, Gilroy analyzes the dynamics of racism, arguing that it is as potent in statements not made as in its obvious expressions: the "capacity to evacuate any historical dimension to black life remains a fundamental achievement of racist society." Moreover, "racism rests on the ability to contain blacks in the present, to repress and to deny the past."[45] Gilroy's widely influential book defies easy summary, yet several of its key articulations are crucial for my project here. First, Gilroy weighs in on the preexisting discussion of the term *black* to argue that "it has moved away from political definitions of black based on the possibility of Afro-Asian unity and towards more restricted alternative formulations which have confined the concept of blackness to people of African descent."[46] However, at the same time, Gilroy, like Stuart Hall, writes against the idea of race as an essential category, arguing instead that it emerges as a discursive category in the context of a wider power struggle: "Races are political collectivities not ahistorical essences. 'Race' is, after all, not the property of powerful, prejudiced individuals but an effect of complex relationships between dominant and subordinate social groups."[47] This understanding of race as something not inherent but socially constructed leads, in turn, to a definition of racism not as "a unitary event based on psychological aberration nor some historical antipathy to blacks which is the cultural legacy of blacks and which continues to saturate the consciousness of all white Britons regardless of age, gender, income, or circumstances." Rather, continues Gilroy, racism "must be understood as a process."[48] In this way, he articulates a precise and clear goal for anyone engaged in the struggle against racism:

> What anti-racism must do if it expects to be taken seriously by the black settlers in whose name it claims to act is to transcend the sociologism [of imagining power relations as an eternal struggle between victims and perpetrators] and move towards the longer-term aims of demonstrating the historical dimensions of "race" and bringing blacks fully into historicity, as actors capable of making complex choices in the furtherance of their own liberation.[49]

Gilroy thus sets an important and precise agenda, one that I take seriously and aim to follow in this book.

Another concept that comes to light in *'There Ain't no Black in the Union Jack'* is that of a black British population as a diaspora, or a group dispersed, by historical circumstances not of their choosing, beyond the parameters of their homeland:[50]

> Black Britain defines itself crucially as part of a diaspora. Its unique cultures draw inspiration from those developed by black populations elsewhere. In particular, the culture and politics of black America and the Caribbean have become raw materials for creative process which redefine what it means to be black, adapting to distinctively British experiences and meanings. Black culture is actively made and remade.[51]

The introduction of the term *diaspora* into black cultural studies—a move that we can also see at this time in the work of other scholars, including Stuart Hall—accomplishes several purposes. First, it links black experiences across the globe, creating transnational connections and highlighting the fact that black culture is always "in process." Second, it emphasizes the "syncretic" nature of black experience in the United Kingdom. Rather than judging black culture in relation to white culture, a diasporic approach emphasizes how black culture develops on its own, in response to devastating historical circumstances, in creative and adaptive ways—through its music, for example. Gilroy's overall point is that "culture is not a fixed and impermeable feature of social relations. Its forms change, develop, combine, and are dispersed in historical processes. The syncretic cultures of black Britain exemplify this."[52] In 1993, Gilroy expanded considerably on this idea and coined the phrase "the black Atlantic" to denote the condition of black intellectuals, activists, writers, speakers, poets, and artists, all of whom "repeatedly articulate a desire to escape the restrictive bonds of ethnicity, national identification, and sometimes even 'race' itself."[53] An enormously influential, if somewhat controversial term, "the black Atlantic" has inspired new approaches to black culture, in which the emphasis most often falls on creative expression, intervention, and resistance to oppression.[54]

Work like that done by Hall and Gilroy unfolds against the broader introduction of postcolonialism, a term that is used to define both the social, political, economic, and cultural conditions of countries in the aftermath of their colonization and a body of social, literary, political, and cultural theory that has emerged to explain a wide range of related concepts including colonial subjectivity, ethnicity, and nationhood. As practiced by a range of scholars, from Frantz Fanon to Homi Bhabha, postcolonial theory permeated black cultural studies and ethnic studies throughout the 1990s.[55] For historian Catherine Hall, the importance of a "post-colonial moment" is precisely that it leads to questions such as "Who are we?" "Where do we come from?" and "Which 'we' are we talking about when we talk about 'we'?" Noting how traces of the British empire appear everywhere—from street signs to food—she argues for the necessity of imagining a British postnation that is not ethnically pure:

> This necessarily involves a re-working of the history of Empire for the Empire has been central to the ways in which British national identi-

ties have been imagined and lived. It matters, therefore, how the Empire is remembered and what kind of historical work is done. A reread, re-imagined imperial history, focusing on inter-dependence and mutuality as well as patterns of domination and subordination which are already inscribed in the relations between coloniser and colonised, might provide some resources from which new notions of twenty-first-century British cultural identities might be drawn.[56]

Hall's comments take us full circle, back to the publication of *The Parekh Report*, which—as in the following comment—can now be seen to synthesize thirty years of work on blackness, race, racial representation, and national identity:

> Britishness, as much as Englishness, has systematic, largely unspoken, racial connotations. Whiteness nowhere features as an explicit condition of being British, but it is widely understood that Englishness, and therefore by extension Britishness, is racially coded. "There ain't no black in the Union Jack," it has been said. Race is deeply entwined with political culture and with the idea of nation, and is underpinned by a distinctly British kind of reticence—to take race and racism seriously, or even to talk about them at all, is bad form, and something not done in polite company. This disavowal, combined with an "iron-jawed disinclination to recognize equal human worth and dignity of people who are not white," has proved a lethal combination. Unless these deep-rooted antagonisms to racial and cultural difference can be defeated in practice, as well as symbolically written out of the national story, the idea of a multicultural post-nation remains an empty promise.[57]

With its direct quotation of Paul Gilroy's work and its oblique reference to the eclipsing of black British history, as well as its allusions to a postcolonial discussion of nation, this paragraph translates key intellectual ideas for public consumption. Coming from an obviously leftist perspective, the claims made here are straightforward: the report does not simply assert that the term *Britishness* is "coded racist" but more precisely that certain individuals of color living in Britain have felt excluded or alienated from the idea of Englishness by means of persistent racism. In fact, *The Parekh Report* aims toward greater inclusiveness by encouraging a climate in which questions—and not statements—about British history might initiate broad public debate, possibly leading to an increased sense of social cohesion.

For example, in the chapter "Rethinking the National Story," the report poses a series of rhetorical questions designed to stimulate reflection:

> How are the histories of England, Scotland, and Wales understood by their people? What do the separate countries stand for, and what does Britain stand for? Of what may citizens be justly proud? How has the imagined nation stood the test of time? What should be preserved, what jettisoned, what revised or reworked? How can everyone have a recognized place within the larger picture? These are questions about Britain as an imagined community, and about how a genuinely multicultural Britain urgently needs to reimagine itself.[58]

Once again the report incorporates an existing academic discussion, with echoes of the debate over English heritage—and of Raphael Samuel's work in particular—but it also alludes to Benedict Anderson, best known for his book *Imagined Communities: Reflections on the Origin and Spread of Nationalism*.[59] The fact that the report merely synthesized existing work and yet managed to elicit such a widespread, and in many cases negative, response suggests that it functioned as a flashpoint for other, preexisting anxieties over issues raised by Britain's increasingly diverse racial and ethnic communities. Arguably, the report also made such an impact because of the persistent gap between academic and other circles, between an intellectual elite that had long before embarked on a process of revisionist history and a broader-based community that had not had much access to that history.

My own experience, talking to a range of British adults over the age of 35, is that neither slavery nor the British involvement in the eighteenth-century transatlantic slave trade was a subject regularly included in their school curricula. Even those growing up in Liverpool, Bristol, and other port cities, where the evidence of the trade lies all around, frequently report that the topic was not covered in their history classes. Although some might feel that the early nineteenth-century date for the abolition of slavery in Britain (1833) reasonably consigned the trade to an irrelevant past, others report feeling disadvantaged by their ignorance of such a crucial and potentially explosive event in their nation's history. Mine was an admittedly unscientific survey, and there are bound to be those whose personal experience contradicts my sense of this omission. However, it does seem accurate to state that what was remarkable about *The Parekh Report* is that it introduced a consolidated body of leftist academic work on the roots, issues, and consequences of multiethnicity into the British press, thereby ensuring a national consideration of a new historical agenda. To be sure, events such as the Liverpool and Bristol exhibits on slavery, opening in 1994 and 1999, respectively, predate the publication of the report. Still, similar to the city exhibits, *The Parekh Report* was written for broad outreach. It was designed to supplement, alter, or perhaps challenge what people might have learned in schools. Published at the end of the millennium, it articulates the need for a new kind of popular history incorporating the full aftermath of British imperialism, in which at stake is the reconstitution of Britain as a more diverse nation.

Like *The Parekh Report*, the cultural and artistic representations under discussion in this book belong to a moment of millennial reckoning. Also like the report, these representations aim for popular accessibility and education. Chapter One, "Commemorating the Transatlantic Slave Trade in Liverpool and Bristol," takes up civic efforts in two former slave-trading ports, Liverpool and Bristol, to explore how contemporary societies restore the slave trade to public memory. Here I examine two examples: the exhibit "Transatlantic Slavery: Against Human Dignity," which was still on display at the Merseyside Maritime Museum in Liverpool in 2004, and the Bristol Slave Trade Trail, a self-guided walking trail that winds its ways through the streets to mark the various places where the city's past involvement with the slave trade can still be seen. Arguing that commemorative sites work best when they position people to make meaningful connections between their everyday lives and a traumatic historical past, I also explore how ethnographic practices, as they have been redefined in the aftermath of a poststructuralist critique, are crucial and effective strategies for remembering the African holocaust. Thus, this chapter surveys the origins, foundational debates, structure, and major arguments of both the exhibit and the trail. It considers the cultural work of both forms of commemoration by asking what museumgoers and trail walkers "do" when presented with historical fact, and it makes an argument for helping individuals to understand that past and present are not discrete but rather are moments on a continuum. What we can learn from the legacy of the slave trade is the necessity of continual self-examination: where might we otherwise be currently complicit with invisible or hidden social injustices?

Chapter Two, "Fictionalizing Slavery in the United Kingdom, 1990–2000," takes up seven novels that feature representations of either eighteenth-century slavery or the slave trade. These novels were chosen for their engagement with the theme of hybridity, a theme that, as articulated by Hanif Kureishi and others, leads to a consideration of new ways of being British. Discussed under three rubrics, "Reading History," "Reading Pastiche," and "Telling the Untold Story," these novels, by Barry Unsworth, Fred D'Aguiar, Caryl Phillips, Philippa Gregory, and David Dabydeen, are all committed to exploring an "untold" story, yet they do so in different ways. Whereas some—Barry Unsworth's *Sacred Hunger*, D'Aguiar's *Feeding the Ghosts*, and Gregory's *A Respectable Trade*—aim to recover lost history and evince a belief that the past can be recovered and coherently narrated, the others—including Phillips's *Cambridge* and *Crossing the River*, D'Aguiar's *The Longest Memory*, and Dabydeen's *A Harlot's Progress*—deploy a postmodern style that foregrounds narrative issues—the inevitable biases of narration, the resistance of history to totalization, and the necessarily fractured and contradictory nature of human story-telling itself. These novels resist binary categories of thought, and they characteristically position the reader as proactive—as a crucial and necessary participant in the making of meaning.

Chapter Three, "Seeing Slavery and the Slave Trade," asks what it means to put the slavery and the slave trade on screen. It examines a biopic on Olaudah Equiano entitled *A Son of Africa*, the televised version of Philippa Gregory's novel *The Respectable Trade*, a four-part television documentary on the British slave trade, and Patricia Rozema's adaptation of Jane Austen's *Mansfield Park*. Despite the differences between the documentary and film media, all these projects are invested in the idea that it is better to "see" historical events like slavery. In this chapter, I argue that this is a complex and potentially problematic notion: where the project is to insert images of black agency, as in the case of the film biography of Equiano, important pedagogic work is accomplished. However, when the representation of slavery becomes scopophilic—that is, when the act of looking at the physical suffering of enslaved Africans becomes inadvertently tinged with eroticism and/or pleasure—as in Rozema's version of *Mansfield Park*—or when the representation of the "slave" elicits a romantic investment—as in *A Respectable Trade*—then a commitment to social justice becomes compromised. This chapter also addresses the treatment of slavery in the historical costume drama, a genre that, as Andrew Higson describes, conveys both liberal and conservative political messages. Finally, the chapter takes up the representation of the family on film as a means of visualizing circulating ideas about English hybridity.

In the last chapter, I look at a place where the eighteenth and the twentieth centuries come together in an especially compelling way, namely, in 'Biyi Bandele's 1999 adaptation of the story of Oroonoko for the Royal Shakespeare Company. Originally written in the late seventeenth century, Aphra Behn's tragic fiction about an African prince taken in slavery to Suriname was frequently reworked into dramatic form and performed throughout the eighteenth century. First, what explains the popularity of this play on the eighteenth-century stage? Second, what does it mean to revive the play at the turn of the twentieth century? Nigerian-born Bandele included in his version of the story of Oroonoko a "prequel" that provides an African context for the story. But in Act II the eighteenth-century script has been left more or less intact. He apparently takes seriously the idea that Aphra Behn's version was already an "authentic" expression of his culture. This chapter explores what Bandele might have seen in the eighteenth-century text by arguing for a "transnational" reading that places Aphra Behn and 'Biyi Bandele in dialogue. A transnational reading of Bandele's *Oroonoko* teaches us that the original story has always been an "improvised" text that tells a diasporic story. In addition, from this adaptation, we learn about possibilities of cross-cultural contact, as culture is understood as something to be jointly shared and constantly revised.

With its broadly interdisciplinary themes, this books taps work currently being done in several critical and cultural fields, including ethnography, museum studies, film studies, postcolonial literary criticism, and performance studies. In addition, I see much consistency between an emerging school of transnational studies, as practiced by, for instance Bruce Robbins, James Clifford, and Paul Gilroy, and performance theorists such as Joseph Roach and Julie Stone Peters: all these scholars share a commitment to exploring meaningful points of cultural contact occurring between groups whose relations are marked by a legacy of unequal power relations. Without ever underestimating the importance of difference or the nature of historical trauma, taking my cue from these writers, I hope to explore tropes of sameness that facilitate the possibility of interracial dialogue. As will also become clear in the following pages, my approach is indebted to several critics in particular: Marcus Wood and Saidiya Hartmann for their work on the representation of slavery and Vivian Patraka for her work on a "holocaust performative."[60]

As someone whose primary field of expertise and teaching has been, for the past twenty-five years, eighteenth-century studies, I believe it would be helpful to explain both the origins of this project and how I feel that I, as an American academic, can hope to make a meaningful intervention in a discussion about a culture that is not my own. First, as a scholar trained in an American university to teach eighteenth-century British literature and culture, I have witnessed vast changes in the content and approach of my discipline. When I began my professional career, the eighteenth century was often known and taught as "the age of Pope, Swift, and Johnson," that is, as a century most easily accessed through a handful of masterful, male writers known for their formal expertise in poetry, satire, prose, and the novel. History, when used in the classroom, was the backdrop against which the works were read. Although certainly those writers are still taught, students are now more likely to encounter eighteenth-century studies under a wide range of rubrics that incorporate not only literary masters but also a much broader range of writers, of both sexes and from a wider range of socio-economic and even national backgrounds. Now, themes such as "gender construction," "labor," "travel," "empire," "colonialism," "slavery," and "nationalism" are used to anchor classroom discussions of eighteenth-century texts. The focal point has shifted as well—the "British" eighteenth century is now understood to touch on the "circum-Atlantic," a phrase used to incorporate both the coast of North America and the Caribbean into the field. This changing focal point has facilitated new scholarship in which the histories of Britain and the Americas are more intertwined than ever. A transatlantic reading of the eighteenth century connects British colonial events to domestic life in England, and it illuminates how emerging imperial policies abroad affected the development of local sensibilities at home.[61]

Witnessing this wide-scale canon revision and revising my own teaching practices to incorporate this new scholarship have led me to be uncomfortable with the idea of the eighteenth century as a discrete or bounded historical period. Increasingly, what matters are continuities, or connections that transcend the boundaries of century markers. In several ways, I am arguing that the eighteenth century is not "over," and that the proof of this assertion lies, for example, in the fact that David Dabydeen rewrites Hogarth, or that 'Biyi Bandele revises an eighteenth-century play, or that the city of Bristol encourages its citizens to find traces of its eighteenth-century trade. As influenced by postcolonial studies, the "new" British eighteenth century emerges as a time of key political conflicts that led to racial and ethnic divides still operating today. But it also emerges as a historical moment offering some hope. If promising new work on the as-yet-unfixed status of race in the earlier eighteenth century (by Roxann Wheeler and others) proves accurate, then returning to the earlier period might allow us to imagine possibilities beyond our current political impasse. Thus, by examining contemporary literary and cultural texts against the background of eighteenth-century studies, I aim to provide both a broad historical context for contemporary political issues and a sense of how those issues might still evolve.

Certainly there are potential pitfalls in returning to such persistently dark topics as colonialism and slavery. Arguably, such an approach provides fewer opportunities to celebrate what is significant, notable, or praiseworthy in a British past. Moreover, the project can seem divisive, as it might seem to promulgate a "good guys/bad guys" approach to history. It is equally possible, as Fred D'Aguiar describes in "The Last Essay about Slavery," to create the circumstances for "slavery fatigue." Yet D'Aguiar also eloquently addresses the need to acknowledge "the future in the past": "It is not enough to direct someone to a large body of research on slavery as a mean to assuage [the] hurt [of slavery]. A vocabulary is needed to furnish the custom-made emblems that cope with pain." After stating that the talent to articulate black experience need not belong only to black artists, he further maintains

> This is part of the power of the story [of art]. In essence it denies the exclusivity of any one group or individual experience. It seeks to communicate against that privatizing zeal in us all, that impulse to say: "This is mine and no one else's." It posits ways of linking one person to the next, one strange group to another, by revealing aspects thought to be exclusive as resident in the other, and by showing difference as bridgeable.[62]

Thus, a discussion of British colonialism or involvement in the slave trade need not be discordant, and it does not have to pit oppressor against victim, white against black. If the emphasis falls on what we share as human beings, such a discussion may advance a broadly community-building agenda.

Second, it is important to state that I do not intend to suggest that the United States holds the higher moral ground for its more frequent discussions of slavery and its legacy. True, the American Civil War is replayed daily—both figuratively and literally—in battlefields across the country.[63] Moreover, during the last decades of the twentieth century, Americans have grown accustomed to the representation of slavery in popular culture. Toni Morrison's *Beloved*, to take just one example, received unqualified praise when it was published in 1987, and it now enjoys the status of a classic American work. Also, as historian Steven Mintz wryly points out, "Once a decade, like clockwork, Hollywood takes on the subject of slavery. In the 1970s, there was *Roots*; in the 1980s, *Glory*, and in the 1990s, there [was] *Amistad*."[64] Still, these examples do not mean that the topic has already been adequately "covered" in the United States or that the requisite work of reconciliation or healing has been achieved. At the time of this writing, several efforts are underway to continue a public American discussion about the legacy of slavery. These include the public acknowledgment of Brown University and other schools that considerable endowments rest on a history of slave trading and a wide-ranging and lively debate about national commemorative sites, including museums, that have yet to be completed.[65]

Thus, although this book focuses on contemporary British historical and cultural expressions, it is also written for an American audience that takes an interest in the broader topic of slavery and its aftermath, as I aim to contribute to a wider discussion about the possibilities and impossibilities of historical memory. The several similarities in the British and American context—for instance, the fact that in the United States, as well as Britain, notable cultural institutions can trace their founding to monies garnered from the slave trade and the fact that here, as in Britain, the pace to uncover such foundations has been slow—suggest the ongoing need for work in the United States as well as Britain on recuperation and commemoration. In either national setting, at stake is an exploration of human agency in history, with the ultimate goal of generating truly inclusive multiethnic and multiracial societies.

Needless to say, the project of constructing successful twenty-first-century communities is also currently in process globally, and around the world the commemoration of slavery has become a pressing topic. To take one instance, Dutch scholar Gert Oostindie describes recent efforts to commemorate the European slave trade as indicating a *fin de siècle* or millennial mood. She also argues that "the African diaspora has moved on and into Europe."[66] Her collection, *Facing Up to the Past: Perspectives on the Commemoration of Slavery from Africa, the Americas, and Europe*, is a revised version of her earlier Dutch publication, financed in the Netherlands by the Prince Claus Fund, a publication that included twenty-six essays originating from the Netherlands and the former Dutch Caribbean colonies. Oostindie describes how she formally presented her book to the Dutch government on June 30, the day on which Antilleans and Surinamese commemorate slavery, at the site of the former Dutch parliamentary building. (Later, a Dutch monument dedicated to the victims of slavery in Amsterdam's Oosterpark was commemorated on July 1, 2002.) Her 2001 collection, published in Kingston, Jamaica, contains essays by scholars from all over world, including Ama Ata Aidoo, Carl Niehaus, and James Walvin. It discusses the traces of slavery in Africa, the Americas, and Europe and includes photographs of national monuments to slavery throughout the Caribbean. Oostindie also includes more than forty full-color plates of artwork, from many countries, representing the subject of slavery and the slave trade.

Such a collection suggests how, as world politics respond to the inevitable fact of globalization, it is more important than ever to take up this history, to initiate debate, and to decide on effective forms of commemoration, but also to settle on the possibilities for the multiracial communities that are certain to exist in the world to come. It has been argued that the transatlantic slave trade was one of the earliest forms of globalism: European slavery put vast numbers of people into motion, under brutal and often deadly conditions and without their consent, for economic reasons, precipitating vast economic, political, and cultural shifts in the process. But this is scarcely the end of the story. If the catastrophic movement of transatlantic slavery wrenched people from their homelands, other kinds of modern movement—including immigration, migration, and travel—bring people together in places where their conversations are bound to be face to face and their discussions, if painful, nonetheless honest, with little left unspoken. Echoing the Caribbean scholar Edward Brathwaite, Yasmin Alibhai Brown writes:

White and non-white Britons may resent the cards that were dealt out by history—slavery and colonialism for us, Black migration for them—but no one in this drama can put the clock back or deny that the same history which caused such pain has also been a creative encounter, making both sides not only different but better than we might have been if we had never met.[67]

Writing from the perspective of someone who is not British, I can appreciate Brown's sentiment only from afar and hope that history repairs itself in the creative efforts of those who struggle to maintain a dialogue. With a new century underway, it is difficult to know whether the ten-year period that is the focus of this book will mark an anomaly, a moment when the discussion was intense and focused but short-lived—and soon forgotten—or whether this decade marked the beginning of a turning point, a moment when Britain's national conversation turned not only to the topic of the slave trade but also to the topic of a socially just and truly representative multicultural society.

Chapter One

Commemorating the Transatlantic Slave Trade in Liverpool and Bristol

How does a contemporary society restore to its public memory such a momentous event as its own participation in transatlantic slavery, especially when that event has been virtually unrecognized in public account for nearly two hundred years? What are the stakes of once more restoring the eighteenth-century slave trade to public memory? For whom? What can be learned from this history?

For Bristol and Liverpool in the 1990s these questions had special urgency. As ports that saw significant expansion and enrichment in the eighteenth century, both cities faced increased civic pressure to acknowledge that past municipal wealth resulted from a lucrative yet sinister trade that had "made fortunes for a few but a living hell for many."[1] In Bristol in 1996, municipal preparation to recreate John Cabot's 1497 voyage to North America sparked controversy when some residents viewed the failure to remark that Cabot's journey also initiated New World colonialism, as well as the genocide of Native Americans, as grievous and unforgivable. For some, this failure coincided with racial tensions that had been apparent since at least 1980, when a police raid in a cafe in the city's St. Paul district provoked a series of street disturbances.[2] If no one singular event marked Liverpool's increased attention to its slave-trading past, the city had long been urged to rethink its history in a more inclusive way. As the home of Britain's largest continuous black population,[3] the city had already been compelled to consider the fact of social and economic injustices affecting the daily lives of its black citizens: the July 1981 Toxteth riots had raised pressing questions concerning police treatment of a black and mixed-race population that was already beset by chronic unemployment, bad housing, and inadequate education. In both Bristol and Liverpool, the idea that current political tensions between the city's black and white populations ought to be traced to a missing history of slavery prevailed. Both cities faced pressure to articulate and address the consequences of the slave trade and the legacy of unequal racial relations that still existed. As one historian phrased it, "During the seventeenth century, sugar planters created one of the harshest systems of servitude in Western history, the repercussions of which continue to be felt as we move towards the twenty-first century."[4]

Bristol's first effort toward acknowledging its involvement in the Atlantic slave trade was the constitution of the Bristol Slave Trade Action Group, or BSTAG. Then, in 1998, three researchers—historian Madge Dresser and community activists Caletta Jordan and Doreen Taylor—working under the auspices of the Bristol City Council and with the sponsorship of the Society of the Merchant Venturers, published a pamphlet, *The Slave Trade Trail around Central Bristol*. This pamphlet, produced partly in response to the need for a civic history with an African-centered perspective, consolidated popular lore concerning the traces of slavery in Bristol and archival work proving that the legacy of the slave trade was indeed appreciable. Following the publication of the pamphlet, an exhibit at the City Museum and Art Gallery entitled "A Respectable Trade? Bristol and Transatlantic Slavery" ran from March 6 to September 2, 1999. When the exhibit closed, curators moved a few of the displays to an upstairs gallery in the Bristol Industrial Museum.

For many in Liverpool's historically black population, an attempt in 1987 by the Merseyside Maritime Museum to broach the topic failed to convey deep civic commitment. Moreover, the black community was understandably suspicious about the motives of the museum as an institution that had failed to offer employment opportunities for black members of the community and that had seemed unwelcoming.[5] Having recognized the limits and inadequacies of the exhibit, the museum received backing from philanthropist Peter Moores for a second exhibit, opened by Maya Angelou in 1994. "Transatlantic Slavery: Against Human Dignity" remains open at the time of this writing. In the meantime, community activists in Liverpool also continue to remap their city streets through frequent guided tours of a "Slave History Trail," under the auspices of the Merseyside Maritime Museum.

This chapter concentrates on the Liverpool exhibit and the Bristol Slave Trade Trail. Rather than compare the apparently similar efforts of the two cities (thereby perpetuating the unfortunate notion that somehow the two cities compete to remember slavery), I look at two different approaches to teaching a public audience about the slave trade.[6] While aiming to give consideration to the separate and complicated civic histories encapsulated in Liverpool by the exhibit and in Bristol by the slave trade trail, I argue in this chapter that commemorative sites work best when they position people to make meaningful connections between their everyday lives and a past trauma. This is especially the case when the trauma is not their own. Participants in commemorative events understand most when they are able to see that another person's humanity rests in more than his or her status as victim.

In approaching this topic, I have found it useful to consider what Vivian Patraka calls a "holocaust performative." In particular, I am persuaded by her eloquent assertion that "in a museum of the dead, the critical actors are gone, and it is up to us to perform acts of reinterpretation to make meaning and memory."[7] I stress that the point here is not simply to relate the African holocaust to the Jewish holocaust, nor to suggest that the two historical events somehow belong to the same category of catastrophe. Nonetheless, as Marcus Wood writes, "comparisons between the history of Atlantic slavery and the Nazi holocaust are precarious and frequently wrong but not always impossible or improper."[8] In the current political climate, both the Jewish holocaust and African slavery have led to wide-scale and contested discussions about appropriate forms for commemorative art: what should be memorialized in such art? For whom? To what effect? How does art best convey the deeply personal nature of individual experience, particularly when, as in the case of the slave trade, those individuals leave no record? How does such art honor their memory without appropriating their experience? To anticipate part of my argument, I propose here that one goal of commemorating the African holocaust might be to situate moral agents—individuals who learn from historical trauma how personal choices have invisible repercussions on a global scale and who become both more self-reflective and politically proactive as a result.

Among other scholars who have addressed these questions, Marcus Wood is most notable for his two invaluable books: *Blind Memory: Visual Representations of Slavery in England and America, 1780–1865* and *Slavery, Empathy, and Pornography*. Wood's main assertions that "the experiences of millions of individuals who were the victims of slavery is not collectable; it is unrecoverable as a set of relics" and that "there can be no archeology of the memory that corresponds to an emotional identification with a lost reality"[9] have been echoed in the work of French scholar Christine Chivallon. For Chivallon, "the violent tearing-away from Africa resembles all persecution, in that it prohibits maintenance of the subject as a producer of the subject's own history."[10] Thus, both Wood and Chivallon raise fundamental questions about the nature of any effort to represent the historical trauma of slavery. In addition, both initiate larger conversations about the ethical implications of such representation and ultimately the nature of a historical evil itself.

To be sure, historians of American history and culture have also taken on the task of representing the African holocaust in general and American slavery in particular. In *Standing Soldiers, Kneeling Slaves*, for example, Kirk Savage explores how monuments designed to commemorate the Civil War, "tested the limits and possibilities of collective consciousness." If, as he maintains, "more than any of the other arts, sculpture was embedded in the theoretical foundation of racism that supported American slavery and survived long after its demise," how did this medium carry the burden of helping a nation to define itself in the wake of the Civil War?[11] Similarly, in *Representations of Slavery: Race and Ideology in Southern Plantation Museums*, Jennifer L. Eichstedt and Stephen Small explore how plantation museums in the southern United States "reflect, create, and contribute to racialized ways of understanding and organizing the world." A concentration on significant features of plantations tours, and in particular on the narratives of tour guides, leads Eichstedt and Small to discover a symbolic annihilation of African Americans from white southern history, a pattern suggesting that "slavery and people of African descent either literally were not present or were not important enough to be acknowledged" in the discursive formation of a genteel white southern history.[12] Also worth mentioning in this context is the larger discussion concerning the representation of race at Colonial Williamsburg, Virginia. Among other scholars writing on the topic, Richard Handler and Eric Gable have been critical of the museum's past failure to incorporate social justice into its mission. They charge that commercialism had won out over the important task of conveying the actual conditions of slavery—for instance, the fact that miscegenation was a regular fact of plantation life.[13]

Similar to these studies in American cultural history, this project also draws on current museum studies, especially those pertaining to the politics of exhibition and display.[14] In addition, I borrow from a vocabulary occurring at the point where ethnography and performance studies intersect, as can be seen in the work of Dwight Conquergood, Michel de Certeau, and Richard Schechner. In what follows, I extend their work by arguing that an effective practice for remembering the African holocaust is analogous to recent ethnographic practice as it has redefined itself in the aftermath of a poststructuralist critique. To paraphrase Conquergood (who in turn summarized Clifford Geertz), whereas ethnography prior to poststructuralism located itself closer to the metropolitan center or capital (even while seeking out hinterlands and frontiers), delimiting its subject, and attending to the "whole" subject, ethnography after poststructuralism moves to the periphery or margin, dealing with what has been dispersed and what may therefore be fragmentary. Most important, after poststructuralism, ethnography no longer perceives identity as discrete, singular, integral, or stable. Or, as Conquergood writes, "The major epistemological consequence of displacing the idea of solid centers and unified wholes with borderland and zones of contest is a rethinking of identity and culture as constructed and relational, instead of ontologically given and essential."[15] Conquergood surveys the usefulness of a performance-inflected vocabulary for ethnography, as seen in the work of Victor Turner. As Conquergood explains, the appearance of this vocabulary marks another shift in ethnographic practice:

> The performance paradigm privileges particular, participatory, dynamic, intimate, precarious, embodied experience grounded in historical process, contingency, and ideology. Another way of saying it is that performance-centered [ethnographic] research takes both as its *subject matter* and *method* the experiencing body situated in time, place, and history.[16]

As I will demonstrate, the Liverpool exhibit simultaneously combines older and newer forms of ethnographic practice, with mixed results. In several ways, it attends to the notion that its subject—the enslaved African—was an "experiencing body situated in time in place." Yet older ethnographic practices of display that essentialize the "Africa" from which enslaved Africans would have come undercut this notion. In addition, although curators are clearly committed to the idea that the museumgoer must become "an experiencing body," therefore providing the opportunity for the viewer's imaginative participation in the African holocaust, arguably they misidentify the nature of the event in which the viewer can meaningfully participate. As Marcus Wood has persuasively argued, no one can "experience" the suffering of enslaved Africans, but viewers can be encouraged to situate themselves as moral agents in relation to historical atrocity.

In Bristol, in contrast, the idea of a walking trail is, from the inception, deeply indebted to ethnographic practice—akin to other forms of what historian Rafael Samuel categorizes as "living history," walking trails rely on the active participation of individuals whose embodied experiences are never far from consideration. Walking trails require a high degree of participation from individuals who are asked to make connections and to read the details of the city they know in light of new information. Yet while the trail engages with ethnographic method by engaging its walkers, the trail overlooks the embodied status of its subject—the historical men and women of the city of Bristol who were either involved or implicated in the slave trade. When it downplays the idea of historical citizens themselves as "experiencing bodies situated in time, place, and history," the trail narrative misses an opportunity to link past and present behaviors. Nonetheless, the Bristol Slave Trade Trail, like the Liverpool exhibit, demonstrates the relevance of an ethnographic understanding of subjectivity to civic discourse.

Transatlantic Slavery: *Against Human Dignity*

In his 2000 publication *The Atlantic Sound*, Caryl Phillips describes a visit to Liverpool, a place where slavery, although absent from official civic accounts, is nonetheless present in the city's streets, architecture, and public memorials. He comments on a square called the Exchange Flags, where, during the eighteenth and nineteenth centuries, trading was conducted on the "current prices of cloves, sugars, rum, spices, and other exotic commodities." He describes a fountain built to represent one of Nelson's sea victories, in which four figures seem reminiscent (or so Herman Melville remarked) of the slaves of Virginia and Carolina. He observes its Town Hall decorated with a frieze depicting the images central to Liverpool trade, including a llama, cocoa pods, a Native American woman with a bow, an African face, and a rhinoceros. Later Phillips visits the Maritime Museum and discovers what he calls "a collection of material relating to the African slave trade." Nonetheless, as Phillips departs from the city by train, he muses that he is glad to be leaving: "It is disquieting to be in a place where history is so physically present, yet so glaringly absent from people's consciousness. But where is it any different? Maybe this is the modern condition, and Liverpool is merely acting out this reality with an honest vigour."[17]

Although Phillips deplores public unawareness of the historical slave trade in Liverpool, academic efforts to make that history accessible can be traced to at least the late 1970s, when the subject was broached in *Liverpool, the African Slave Trade, and Abolition: Essays to Illustrate Current Knowledge and Research*, edited by Roger Anstey and P. E. H. Hair. According to their introduction, "the Atlantic slave trade is studied in our day and age, though from many different angles of interest, basically as the longest and largest migration in history which was both wholly involuntary and sufficiently recorded."[18] With its avowed commitment to quantitative research ("in the conviction that the 'clinical' approach to the human past is of more lasting value than the 'passionate'"),[19] the collection covers a range of topics from the volume of the slave trade during parts of the eighteenth century to the average duration of the whole triangular voyage to factors in slave mortality. On the subject of Liverpool itself, the collection includes essays on how local merchants financed their ships and the season for departure from Liverpool. Among the scholars contributing to the collection was David Richardson, whose work has, since the 1970s, continued to be notable, both for its thorough and careful recourse to statistical analysis and for its effort at making the fruits of that analysis accessible to a broader audience.[20]

Although Bristol's involvement in the slave trade was earlier than Liverpool's, in Liverpool the scope of the trade increased rapidly. As Richardson writes, "Between 1780 and 1807 over three quarters of all English ships involved in the English slave trade were fitted out in the port [of Liverpool]. Thus Liverpool was not only the largest single slaving port in the eighteenth-century. After 1780, it was also the undisputed slaving capital of England and by far the largest slave port in the Atlantic world," ultimately far surpassing Bristol.[21] Although slave trading was only one of several commercial enterprises in the city, "the traffic in enslaved Africans was the corner-stone of Liverpool overseas trade from 1730 to 1807." Moreover, "it appears that the African and related trades may have occupied at least a third and possibly up to a half of Liverpool shipping tonnage in the half century before 1807."[22] Thus, as in Bristol, the slave trade increased economic opportunities for many, by creating jobs for those who built, fitted out, and manned the ships, for example. Quite simply, contends Richardson, the African slave trade "was a vital pillar of the eighteenth-century Liverpool economy."[23]

That facts that Richardson brings forth demand to be read alongside recent cultural and literary discussion of eighteenth-century Liverpool. Indeed, Phillips might be interested in the poetry of eighteenth-century laboring-class writers who took up the slave trade as their topic. In a recent essay, Tim Burke finds evidence in Thomas Clarkson's history of abolition that in eighteenth-century Liverpool "fear and complicity kept lips sealed."[24] Nonetheless, Burke uncovers a lively intellectual debate that was in full swing in the abolitionist poetry of Edward Rushton, who had gone blind as a teenage sailor by contracting ophthalmia by tending to sick slaves on his ship, and in the work of John Walker, who defended slavery. Archival work such as Burke's reminds us that Liverpool had in fact had a public tradition of debating the slave trade, even though more recent events have eclipsed that tradition.

The poetry of Rushton and Walker might also be of interest to philanthropist Peter Moores, who in the foreword to the catalog published to accompany the transatlantic slavery exhibit traces his decision to initiate the project to a more recent public amnesia concerning the slave trade:

> During forty years of work and travel in Europe and America, it became increasingly clear to me that slavery was a taboo subject, both to white and to black people. Forty years ago, most Europeans had managed to suppress any acknowledgement of their connection with the slave trade. It was something in the past. In the United States, where it was impossible to ignore the results of the slave trade, there was segregation, later bussing and recently something like integration, but never any mention of how black people came to be in America in the first place. We can come to terms with our past only by accepting it,

and in order to be able to accept it we need knowledge of what really happened. We need to make sense of our history.[25]

Notable in Moores's comment is not only the announcement of a public forgetting but also the communal agreement that initiates the remembering: the plural pronoun *we* both constructs a unified group committed to telling the truth about slavery and glosses over the question of who the *we* might cover. Whose history will be unveiled? Whose past will be made sense of?

Such questions soon rose to the fore as the Maritime Museum—under the auspices of the Peter Moores foundation and with additional funds from the Tourist Development Project—initiated the project of creating a gallery on transatlantic slavery, beginning with a two-day seminar in 1992. Ultimately the museum decided that eleven guest curators, including British, American, Canadian, Barbadian, and Nigerian academics, would contribute to the exhibit. The ensuing struggle to create a meaningful civic display testifies to Ivan Karp's assertion that "decisions about how cultures are presented reflect deeper judgments of power and authority and can, indeed, resolve themselves into claims about what a nation is or ought to be as well as how citizens should relate to one another."[26] The curators' first task was to find a language, for both the catalog and the exhibition labels, that would convey responsibility for the slave trade in a straightforward manner without representing Africans as passive victims. Helen Coxall documents in detail the meticulous writing and rewriting process:

> The [exhibition] texts went through several stages. First, the exhibition briefs: two draft briefs were drawn up after discussion with the 11 guest curators/writers. The preferred one was edited seven times after discussion with advisors. Second, the exhibition text: the guest curators produced researched essays about the individual topics outlined in the brief. Third, this material was edited into the form of draft summaries by curators. Fourth, professional copywriters reduced the information into panel-sized format. Fifth, these panels were further edited and shortened by museum staff. Sixth and last, the final information panels were written after consultation with guest curators and advisors.[27]

Coxall further describes the elaborate rewriting process that eliminated an "institutional voice" characterized by "an unidentified authoritative voice which utilizes sweeping generalizations, euphemisms, model auxiliaries (would, might, will), the deletion of personal pronouns, names, and dates, and the persistent use of the agentless passive construction." For example, "Most enslaved people were captured in battles or were kidnapped" became "Portuguese and English slavers imprisoned Africans in forts."[28] Overall, the exhibition writers tried to avoid "Eurocentric" ideas in favor of "Afrocentric" concepts, a strategy that entailed scrutinizing the concept of evidence itself. In the matter of the number of lives lost to the slave trade, for instance, could ships' logs be considered adequate testimony?[29]

However, in addition to issues of language, two larger questions of representation emerged. First, how should the exhibition represent the African individuals whose lives were directly impacted by the slave trade? What vocabulary would give respect, dignity, and depth to their experiences? As Coxall writes, curators identified the term *slave* as problematic. As a shorthand, or naming device, the term *slave* robs Africans of an identity by omitting sex, age, nationality, and status: "Calling them *slaves* from before they were captured and repeatedly thereafter unconsciously perpetuates the common Eurocentric terminology that is taken for granted, due to the familiarity by those people of a Eurocentric view."[30] The writers chose instead the more historically precise *enslaved Africans*, a term that not only deessentializes the more common term *slave* but also moves closer to acknowledging Africans as embodied subjects in the terms given to us by Conquergood. Once *enslaved* becomes an adjective, the noun *African* denotes a geopolitical agent.

Yet the exhibit would need to go further to foreground the issue of individuated African agents. Curators therefore decided to create narratives for four fictional Africans, each of whom was given an individual story involving different ethnic, tribal, and class backgrounds. The first room introduces the viewer to the "characters," who are represented by life-size cardboard cutout figures draped in cloth. Sideboards explain how they were captured and sold and where they labored. As viewers make their way through the exhibit, they are meant to monitor each of the characters, following their stories and learning their individual fates. "Oyeladun" is a Yoruba woman who is put to work in the sugar fields of the Caribbean. At the time of abolition she is left impoverished and hungry, without a way to provide for herself. "Kofi," a young Fanti boy, is nephew to a court drummer: "Everyone else has been taken to shore. The Captain says he will take me as a servant to England." After abolition, he leaves England and goes to New York to become a clerk. "Kwame," an Asante goldsmith, works on a sugar plantation and is renamed Peter; at the time of abolition, he has died from the brutal conditions of his labor. "Okechukwu" is an Igbo whose father was a brassworker. He is renamed Bristol and becomes a blacksmith: "They say we are in a place called Virginia." Eventually he runs away and lives with a community of freed blacks. This use of narrative clearly attempts to locate displaced Africans in a variety of settings, emphasizing a wide range of experiences and circumstances under slavery. Still, some viewers expressed disappointment that the device was not taken further. In particular, at least one reviewer asked why curators resorted to made-up stories, especially when recent research furnishes real-life histories.[31]

In addition, more traditional museum display techniques that downplay the idea of performative subjects in favor of older ethnographic representations undercut the effort to create multiple and fluid African identities. Among such techniques is the use of the diorama. For example, in a room entitled "European Slaving in West Africa" the viewer is drawn to a scene of diminutive sailors trading for equally diminutive captives on the coast of Africa in the late eighteenth century. If the doll-size figures engage and focus the viewer's attention, the overall effect of the diorama is "comprehensive, extensive, commanding, aggrandizing," as Barbara Kirshenblatt-Gimlett has argued; "in its more problematic manifestations, the panoptic model has the quality of a peep show and surveillance—the viewer is in control."[32] The diorama freezes the more complicated and variable narrative being told elsewhere into one easily mastered and knowable moment—the moment in which Africans become slaves. The small, mute, and frozen statues have no story to tell on their own behalf, whereas the viewer is reassured by a scene that is perhaps all too familiar from a range of traditional representations of the slave trade. The life-size diorama has the same effect, as when Kofi's carefully individuated story is undercut by a full-scale diorama depicting him in a drawing room in Bristol. Frozen in a pose ironically evoking the popular black jockey lawn ornament of postwar America, with a candle rather than a lantern in his hand, Kofi-as-mannequin moves through neither historical time nor space.

Throughout the exhibition, the articulation of agency verges on paradox: how is it possible to convey the horrific nature of the slave trade, its utterly dehumanizing and debilitating impact on real human beings, while simultaneously thematizing the idea that enslaved Africans were not all passive, silent, and meek victims? How best to convey the brutal power of slavery as an institution while also showing that it did not always extinguish human dignity? To begin, the catalog text provides many examples of African resistance and rebellion. For example, according to curator Mary E. Modupe Kolawole

> The erroneous impression is often created that African women took enslavement, like subjugation and subordination, for granted as a normal fact of their reality and so did not resist transatlantic slavery. On the contrary, documents show us that they resisted European subjugation just like men. Slave revolts, insurrections in Africa, *en route* and on plantations in the Diaspora did not exclude women. Women were involved directly or indirectly in resistance against King Afonso I in the Congo (1529), Guinea slave traders (1556), in Sao Tome (1560) and the Macingo rebellion (1570).[33]

Similarly, in the inexpensive brochure designed to accompany the exhibit, a paragraph describing the horrific conditions of the middle passage ("The air in the hold was foul and putrid"; "Seasickness was common and the heat was oppressive") is directly followed by a paragraph describing African rebellion: "Africans resisted their loss of freedom by individual acts of resistance and by organized revolts. Most of these revolts were unsuccessful and were punished with brutal ferocity."[34] Although the missing transition between the paragraphs leaves a gap between the two ideas, it also indicates a powerful inclination to move the reader's attention immediately from a scene of African degradation to one of African agency. This inclination counters a tradition of representing enslaved Africans as mute, and very often kneeling, figures—as in the famous abolition medallion with the caption "Am I not a Man and a Brother," an image featured in the last display case of the exhibit ("The Abolition of Slavery"). While the famous icon advanced the abolitionist cause, arguably it perpetuates the notion that the freedom of enslaved Africans was given to them by whites, without whose assistance they would have been helpless.

There is no question that the curators were committed to conveying a sense of Africa as a complex continent with multiple histories. As Anthony Tibbles explains, "One of the main intentions [of the exhibit] was to get across the point that Africa should not be portrayed only as a place where Europeans got 'slaves.'"[35] Or, as curator Peter Manning wrote in his essay for the catalog, it is necessary to remember that Africa "was far more than a reservoir from which enslaved people were taken."[36] Display cases organized under the rubric "West African Life before European Slaving" paradoxically both undercut and confirm stereotypes about Africa, as the exhibit seems to waver between older and newer ethnographic understandings. The first room challenges the notion that "Africa had no past" by offering showcases with a variety of spectacular objects, many of them on loan from the British Museum, including hollow gold castings of three elephants and an eighteenth-century gold-dust box, both from Asante, Ghana. Also visually riveting are the gold "limb dippers," described as part of a kit used by wealthy individuals to prepare limb powder, which was chewed with cocoa leaves as a mild drug. West African music plays in the gallery, while sound sticks attached to listening posts allow the viewer to hear an African folktale narrated in Yoruba. The impression gathered is that, prior to contact with western Europe, indigenous cultures of Africa and the Caribbean were not only stable and enduring (witness the rare pre-Columbian Taino stool) but complex and urbane.

A second room attempts to move the viewer forward in time and reflects the evolution and development of African cultures. But here the plurality of objects, culled from very different African locations and time periods, contributes to an atmosphere of ahistoricity, as objects from disparate African homelands and time periods are displayed together. A ceremonial sword and stool from Ghana appear alongside masks from the Ivory Coast, and a man's embroidered gown from the twentieth century is displayed in the vicinity of a West African iron anklet that might be from the eighteenth century. Nineteenth-century musical instruments—gong, drum, and calabash—contrast with an intricate carving of a woman and child and a beautiful comb (the latter two are reproduced in the catalog).[37] Very few of these objects are precisely dated, unlike most of the objects elsewhere in the exhibit. Instead, they belong to an Africa that the viewer experiences as exotic and distant, as "out of time." Because Western ethnography is unable to place the objects within a Western time frame, it is as if the objects belong to no time in particular, with no mention of the possibility that African history, although often resistant to Western temporalizing, is nonetheless real and fully differentiated.[38]

If—as Svetlana Alpers argues—"everything in a museum is put under the pressure of a way of seeing,"[39] the pressure here is to see Africa from a consistently Western point of view. The display of artifacts fails to help viewers understand Africa on its own terms. It fails to communicate important national, tribal, religious, linguistic, and social differences on the African continent. In addition, the display fails to convey how "whether fractured or continuous, exclusive or interwoven with that of other groups, the past development of all surviving societies has the same time-depth."[40] The problem of representing Africa is further complicated by the fact that several of the items on display were taken as colonial booty. As such, they belong to a contested struggle of representation. Or, as anthropologist George Stocking reminds us, "objects viewed by museum observers are 'survivals' not only of the past from which collection wrenched them, but from those later pasts into which any given act of exhibition has placed them."[41] His assertion proves especially apt in the case of the exhibit's two "Benin bronzes," or plaques—one depicting a European with a gun and the other a Bini soldier surrounded by Portuguese soldiers with manilas.[42]

As Annie E. Coombes has demonstrated, these artifacts were originally trophies taken during a "punitive expedition" by the British to retaliate for the murder of several British officers who tried to enter Benin City without the king's permission. The artifacts were thus associated with the bloody events leading up to their acquisition. Once the bronzes were in England, their extraordinary nature posed a problem for British curators, who were hard pressed to explain the evidence of remarkable skills that were inconsistent with circulating beliefs about Benin society as a degenerate society in need of intervention from a "civilizing" British presence. In the words of one late-nineteenth-century commentator, "The wonderful technical skill displayed in the construction of the metal objects, their lavish ornamentation, much of which is deeply undercut, and in nearly every case, the highly artistic excellence of the completed subjects, have been a surprise and a puzzle to all students of West African ethnology."[43] Finally, when more than three hundred bronzed plaques were exhibited at the British Museum in 1897, the nature of their accomplishment, as well as the truly indigenous nature of their genius, was gradually recognized.[44] In the context of the Liverpool exhibit, the bronzes signify Benin workmanship and high cultural achievement, but they also encode a British struggle to control African representation.[45]

To summarize the argument so far, although the curators worked hard to counter the essentializing and dehumanizing notion of the African "slave," in the end they were hampered by a Western ethnographic temporalizing practice that persistently sees African history as out of time. At the same time, the necessity of representing life under slavery requires curators to walk a delicate line between depicting slavery's dehumanizing effects and preserving the human agents who somehow persisted through their ordeal. This dilemma becomes more pronounced in the second half of the exhibit, which depicts life under slavery. Here the paucity of artifacts from the period testifies to the fact that curators have traditionally had little choice in what they choose to represent. As Tibbles points out, "There are relatively few objects directly associated with the lives of slaves. Many of these are instruments of torture or punishment. Slaves themselves had few possessions. In maroon communities craftsmen produced a wider range of items that were necessary to sustain everyday life."[46] In the section of the exhibit called "Life in the Americas," music and colorful murals are used to fill the void; as visitors walk along a corridor where live sugar cane grows, they hear nineteenth-century black music. Yet even here, where the human voice tells a story of resistance, what draws the visitors' attention are not the sounds but the sights, particularly the instruments of torture—not only the shackles, chains, and branding irons but also a "punishment collar," a cast iron brace designed to keep the head torturously upright.

Yet, as Marcus Wood argues, these artifacts of torture can create "interpretative traps." In particular, when the object of torture is displayed as an abstract item, one divorced from a narrative context in which the human being who suffered is made apparent, the slave emerges as "an object afflicted, not as object capable of describing his or her affliction."[47] In other words, "The artefacts which were applied and attached to the bodies of slaves, and were then preserved either in museums or in printed representations in books, are not a gateway to knowledge of the events that produced them, or a substitute for the experience of anyone, white or black, involved in the process of their use."[48] Although Wood's critique seems appropriate, his comment also raises an important question: what might constitute a "gateway to knowledge about the events producing slavery?" If there can be "no substitute for the experience," then what can and should an exhibit like this one accomplish?

This is a crucial question when we consider the representation of the Middle Passage, the infamous transatlantic journey bearing enslaved Africans to the Caribbean and the coast of North America. For many whites and blacks alike, the Middle Passage remains the defining moment—the most horrific and yet somehow the most compelling moment of the entire history of the transatlantic slave trade. For many, the Middle Passage has become the ruling synecdoche of the worst aspects of the slave trade. As such, it exerts an extraordinary power over the imagination, and a range of contemporary writers and artists, from Toni Morrison to Stephen Spielberg, have taken up the challenge of its representation.[49] Yet at least since the time of the abolition movement, this notorious event has proven resistant to articulation. In the late eighteenth century, to make an argument about the dehumanizing conditions of the transatlantic passage, abolitionists circulated not only a drawing—the famous "Plan of an African Ship's Lower Deck with Negroes in the proportion of only One to a Ton" from 1789, depicting a myriad of small "slave" shapes lying crammed side by side in rigid rows in the hold of a ship—but also but also a small wooden model. The model fleshed out the flat illustration with three-dimensional figures—once again the minuscule enslaved Africans lie prostrate in the ship's hold, while the tiny figures standing on deck represent the white crew, as in one such model on view in the Liverpool exhibit. However, as Marcus Wood points out, both the illustration and the model support "an abolitionist cultural agenda which dictated that slaves were to be visualized in a manner which emphasized their total passivity and prioritized their status as helpless victims."[50] He further contends that this representation continues to influence contemporary representations, perpetuating the notion that enslaved Africans could not have been the agents of their own liberation.

Recent attempts to represent the Middle Passage have not been more effective in their representation of African agency, even when they eschew the diminutive and silent in favor of the life-sized and the voiced. The William Wilberforce Museum in Hull, for instance, was opened in 1983 to commemorate "the city's most renowned son, who worked tirelessly and successfully to bring about the abolition of the slave trade," thereby inextricably linking the history of slavery in Britain to the history of Wilberforce's life.[51] As visitors make their way through the small galleries of this house museum, they eventually come across a small passageway with a low ceiling. There they encounter a tableau of life-size plaster mannequins representing the "human cargo" lying on benches. As a simulacrum of human suffering, the tableau is designed to elicit shock and horror; the mannequins are contorted and grotesque. The viewer's entry into the room activates a recording of the sound of surf, over which the voices of invisible slave traders speak: "That's a sorry lot, this lot!" "Aye, there's another one dead over there. Get it out of the way. Aye, that'll do." In addition, the viewer hears the sounds of heavy breathing and vomiting. It should be noted that in the 1980s, when the exhibit was first created, this tableau would have been one of the earliest attempts to bring the fact of the slave trade into public view, and the curators deserve credit for their willingness to broach the topic at all. However, the tableau aims to depict how enslaved Africans were treated like animals, and so it depicts them as animals, thereby inadvertently playing into racist stereotypes; this representation thus fails to help its almost exclusively white audience understand either how Africans were complex and individuated or how their humanity would have survived their degrading ordeal.[52]

In the case of both the abolitionist drawings and models and the Wilberforce House tableau, the viewer stands outside the representation of suffering, looking on from the perspective of someone who pities the sufferer. At best, the viewer wishes to do something for the victim. At worst, perhaps, the viewer merely congratulates himself that such a thing has never happened to him. In neither case does the viewer truly see himself as being on a continuum with the sufferer. In the terms of performance-centered ethnography, the viewer understands neither the subject—the enslaved African—nor himself as "experiencing body situated in time, place, and history." Instead, it is the nature of this kind of representation, whether it is a tiny wooden doll or a full-size human mannequin, to create an object that is decidedly not human. However, in the Liverpool exhibit, curators represent the Middle Passage as an empty space, the simulated hold of a ship, creating the possibility of the viewer's embodied and imaginary connection with those who endured the Middle Passage.

Gallery visitors must walk through this room, which recreates the space in which enslaved Africans would have been stowed, in order to continue through the exhibit. The room is thus both literally and metaphorically the center of the exhibit. It was built to scale (although the ceiling, covered by wooden grating, has been raised six inches because of the fire code). The room is only partially lit, making it purposefully difficult to see the empty spaces—resembling narrow bunks or shelves—for the bodies that would have been enchained there. On entering the room, museum visitors must first adjust their eyes to the darkness, then strain to listen to a recording of surf, wind, and voices reading excerpts from several sources, among them John Newton's record of his time on a slave ship, Equiano's autobiography, and the logbook of a Liverpool captain. When the technology is working, the exhibit also features video clips on the back wall, indistinct black and white images of captives that aim not for realism but suggestion. On the floor is a dark sticky substance, perhaps suggesting human blood. The overall effect of the space is disorienting to visitors struggling to understand what they are experiencing. During the several visits I made to the space, people responded in various ways. Most often, they moved rather quickly through the space, with an apparent lack of interest in imagining themselves as "human cargo." Some seemed confused about the purpose of the gallery. On one occasion, rambunctious schoolboys were using the dark corners for a game of hide and seek. On another, an elderly couple seemed inclined to turn back rather than proceed through the dimly lit space.

In contrast to earlier representations of the Middle Passage, this one aims to shift the point of identification. Now viewers are no longer outside the experience. Instead, they are implicitly asked to put themselves in the position of the enslaved African, to "experience" something of the physical effects of the passage. This approach borrows from other current, ethnographically influenced museum practices; it resembles, for example, a current exhibit at the Imperial War Museum in which visitors enter a small space to undergo a simulation of London life during the Blitz. But the Middle Passage representation fails to accomplish its purpose, as curator Anthony Tibbles acknowledges: "We wanted visitors to use their imaginations and hoped to provide them with enough information and experience to do so . . . I have to be honest and say that this solution is not a 100% success. But I hasten to add that I don't think any solution would be perfect."[53]

However, if this representation of the Middle Passage is not successful, perhaps the reason lies not in its *strategy*—a tapping of performative theory to place the museum visitor in position of embodied identification—but in its *aim*. While, as Marcus Wood eloquently argues, one cannot and should not aim to identify with horrific human suffering, perhaps visitors can connect instead with eighteenth-century citizens who—whether or not they consciously acknowledged the fact—lived with the slave trade as a key factor of their daily lives. To identify with complex historical personages in this way is to begin to meditate on the origins and conditions of human suffering. It is to ask as well about how such suffering can persist and endure against the backdrop of the most mundane human experience. Thus, a number of everyday objects in the exhibit successfully bridge the gap between historical past and the museumgoer's present, encouraging viewers to see themselves in relation to historical subjects who participated in the trade. For example, a portrait of eighteenth-century Liverpool merchant and civic leader Thomas Golightly hangs in the exhibit to make a point about the number of eighteenth-century prominent citizens whose wealth directly or indirectly resulted from the slave trade. On one visit, the portrait, as well as its exhibition text, drew the attention of two elderly ladies who expressed surprise to discover this unsettling connection ("I thought it was the Yanks who had the slave trade," one commented).

Similarly, old coins, maps, and street signs, already familiar to most visitors to the exhibit, take on new meaning when they are placed within the history of the eighteenth-century slave trade. As the viewer is asked to consider such familiar objects within their broader context—to understand, for instance, that a "guinea" by its very name memorializes the African trade—he recognizes the role of the slave trade in a more familiar history. Thus, the experience being recreated is not one of someone else's unspeakable or unimaginable suffering—which, as Wood points out, is only reduced or cheapened in the moment of its representation—but one of living in a world where atrocity coexists with the most ordinary kind of human experience. When people are brought to reflect on how the history of enslaved Africans is inextricably interwoven into the story of their everyday lives, they not only awaken from the culture amnesia about which Phillips writes but—as we will see when we examine the Bristol Slave Trade Trail—they also potentially learn to reconsider the nature of their own responsibilities as moral agents.

The Bristol Slave Trade Trail

In the exhibition note to his painting "Sold Down the River," Tony Forbes refers to a citywide festival commemorating Bristol's maritime history in 1996:

> The centerpiece of the exhibition was the launch of John Cabot's ship The Mathew. His voyage in 1497 opened the way to the genocide of

FIGURE 1 Tony Forbes, "Sold Down the River."
Source: Reprinted with the permission of the artist.

Native Americans and colonisation. The festival, encouraged by the [Bristol City] Council, funded by big business, and hyped by our media, was a slap in the face to the black community and an insult to the intelligence and sensitivity of many Bristolians. It was the weekend that Bristol broke my heart.[54]

Forbes's painting dramatizes his sense of betrayal: chained to a raft pulled by a sailing ship advertising three British media and bound by police tape, a central black figure is seated before a statue of Edward Colston, Bristol city father, whose participation in the slave trade is here commemorated, in this artist's rendering, by the skulls that lie at his feet. In the distance, silhouetted, exuberant festivalgoers cross the Clifton Bridge, oblivious to the situation in the foreground.

But if the painting records the artist's isolation from his native city, the placement of the painting puts the artist's experience right back in the middle of city politics; the painting now hangs prominently in the exhibition entitled "Bristol and Transatlantic Slavery: The Story of the City's Role in the 18th Century Slave Trade." Housed in an upstairs gallery at the Bristol Industrial Museum, this exhibition includes a small portion of a much larger exhibit, "A Respectable Trade? Bristol and Transatlantic Slavery," at the Bristol City Museum and Art Gallery in 1999. Like "Transatlantic Slavery: Against Human Dignity," the Bristol exhibit is directed at public education and outreach for a population that comes to the museum without much prior knowledge of its city's involvement in the eighteenth-century transatlantic slave trade.

On a visit in the summer of 2003, the remaining parts of the larger exhibit had begun to show signs of wear and neglect due to inadequate funding, and indeed the long-term future of the exhibit is in question. Meanwhile, Bristol's other major commemorative site—the Slave Trade Trail—continues its work. With its attention to the twin ideas of seeing and experiencing history, the trail reflects a movement to create "living history," a late-twentieth-century form of historical interpretation explained by Cambridge historian Raphael Samuel in this way:

> [Living history] eschews epic and grand narrative in favor of personal observation and local knowledge.... It pins its faith in surface appearances, visible artifacts, "evidence ... which can be seen, touched, and photographed," rather than aggregates and abstractions. For a

history of master narratives, or evolutionary theories of growth, it substitutes one of moments which can be intercepted and arrested—as in the postmodern novel—at any point in time.[55]

Although Samuel is alert to the potential misuses of this kind of history, in the end he becomes its staunchest defender. Rejecting the idea that historiography is the prerogative of the historian, Samuel argues instead that history is "a social form of knowledge . . . [not] the work of the individual scholar, nor yet rival schools of interpretation, but rather the ensemble of activities and practices in which ideas of history are embedded or a dialectic of past–present relations is rehearsed."[56]

Thus, similar to the idea of "resurrectionary movements" once invoked by the French historian Michelet, living history depends on active, interpretative subjects who participate in the making of meaning. Living history aims not only to retell a historical story but also to reexamine the conditions under which history is made in the first place. In its organization, focus, and structure, it asks: Whose history? Who tells? Under what circumstances? This section examines the Bristol Slave Trade Trail as an example of a "living history" that embeds an ethnographic understanding of human subjectivity. As an attempt to rewrite and remap civic history, walking trails create citizens who engage in commercial activities, people who can learn to ask questions and actively to forge links between past and present behaviors. Here I argue that such projects as the Bristol Slave Trade Trail can situate people not merely as voyeurs or passive recipients of their city's heritage but as informed and active interpreters who can learn to see themselves as capable of critical inquiry and informed choices.

However, to arrive at this argument, it is necessary to ask about the nature of a *walking* trail: why is the physical experience of being on-site crucial to the act of civic remembering? Moreover, who is the subject created by the trail? What opportunities are offered to this subject? After briefly surveying the eighteenth-century background of the slave trade, this section engages these questions. First, it considers early efforts to create civic participation at one site of particular importance to Bristol: the Georgian House, also known as the Pinney House, once the home of a prominent local sugar merchant. As we will see, this historic site, understood as a *place* of historical events, becomes—in the terms of Michel de Certeau—a *space* of multiple understandings and reckonings. Second, this section explores the ethnographic work of the trail itself. Along the way, it critiques a binaristic account of the slave trade—one that divides historical subjects into speaking or silent, present or absent, not guilty or guilty—in favor of a performative understanding of human subjectivity, one recognizing that the idea of "the experiencing body located in time and space" is crucial to any process of historical reckoning.

First, however, what are the events to which Forbes refers? Once again the work of historian David Richardson provides the backdrop. Along with London and Liverpool, Bristol was once "one of the first outports to show a regular interest in the slave trade." He estimates that between 1698 and the abolition of the trade in 1807, over 2000 ships from Bristol were involved in the slave trade off the coast of Africa. "Bristol traders were responsible therefore," writes Richardson, "for carrying probably half a million blacks from the African coast."[57] Although only a very few of those enslaved Africans were ever brought to Bristol, having been sold either in the Caribbean or on the coast of North America, the trade had a notable impact on the local economy, as ships left Bristol for the first leg of the highly lucrative Triangle Trade loaded with local goods. Richardson explains:

> The demand for trade goods for shipment to the African coast, for example, encouraged both the expansion of local industries such as brass, copper, glassware and gunpowder, all of which experienced notable growth during the eighteenth century, and the strengthening of Bristol's commercial links with various parts of Europe.[58]

Similarly, in her definitive study *Slavery Obscured: The Social History of the Slave Trade in an English Provincial Port,* Madge Dresser explores the profound economic impact of the slave trade on the Bristol economy. She writes, "Few realize today that for a brief period, from around 1723 to 1743, Bristol was the nation's number one slaving port, eclipsing London as well as Liverpool."[59] Like Richardson, Dresser provides convincing evidence of the many levels of local involvement in the lucrative trade, and she provides ample examples, from the captains, ship owners, mariners, and surgeons to those provisioning the ships, from the shareholders to those making money from the slave trade—those hoping to make a profit selling textiles, glassware, umbrellas, "Negro hats," beads, cooking pots, bangles, brandy, guns, knives, and other goods on the Guinea Coast. Yet, despite the overwhelming evidence that virtually no one in eighteenth-century Bristol was untouched by the trade, the role of slavery in the city's history had largely disappeared from public conversation until late in the twentieth century.

This is not to deny, however, that at least some Bristolians had once been willing to consider the role of the slave trade in their city's economy. Alan Richardson argues that in the abolitionist poetry of four late-eighteenth-century Bristol writers in particular—Thomas Chatterton, Hannah More, Ann Yearsley, and Robert Southey—we find evidence of the widespread circulation of abolitionist sentiment. Moreover, during the Romantic era, "for the Bristol poet, the slave-trade was an all but unavoidable theme and Africa was at once an exotic and familiar locale."[60] Richardson concludes that "the Abolitionist campaign forced the average British citizen at least to consider connections between his or her daily life and the politics and economics of growing colonial and mercantile empire."[61] However, as we will see later, the issues of what people knew and when they knew it remain contested; what appears painfully obvious in retrospect—that no one's livelihood was untainted by "slave money"—may have been less clear in the moment. In what follows below, I argue that, from the fact of "slavery obscured," we stand to learn a great deal about current political situations as well.

With the successful abolition of the slave trade in 1807 and the end to slavery in 1834, the topic of the slave trade and its impact on Bristol society ceased to hold public attention—until, as the third millennium approached, pressures increased to put the legacy of the slave trade once more front and center in city politics. In 1997, the Bristol Slave Trade Action Group (BSTAG) was founded to consider "how and in what form should the City Council acknowledge the Atlantic slave trade and all its legacy in Bristol." The group was composed of university faculty, museum officials, and members of the city's black community, among them a local Trinidadian historian, a city librarian, and a city council member.[62] At first, the effort to make "absent" slavery "present" in civic accounts centered on the memory of one slave in particular: Pero, a West Indian native who spent his adult life in Bristol.

Several current Web sites (created by school groups, among others) tell the story of John Pinney, Caribbean plantation owner and later local sugar merchant, and his Bristol slave.[63] Pinney bought Pero and two siblings for 115 pounds. While in Nevis, Pero appears to have been educated as a barber, that is, "to shave and dress hair," as well as to pull teeth.[64] When Pinney left Nevis, he brought Pero back with him to be his servant. The relationship seems to have been fraught, particularly toward the end of Pinney's life, when Pinney wrote that Pero "has waited upon my person for upwards of thirty-two years, and I cannot help feeling much for him, notwithstanding he has not lately conducted himself as well as I could have wished."[65] Pero died at 45 in Ashton, Bristol, in 1798. Thus, for some, the Pinney house, at 5 Great George Street (number 40 on the Slave Trade Trail) serves as an important symbol of what some perceive as a "cover-up" of the historical facts of the trade: how is it possible to celebrate both Pinney's accomplishments and the historical feature of his architecturally notable house without foregrounding the origins and nature of the wealth that made the man and built the house?

On October 24, 1998, the issue of Pero's memory became crucial when a group of visiting African American actors, who were in town to perform at a nearby theater, attempted to dramatize the issues through a short piece of guerilla theater. The actors never finished their performance, because they were evicted from the premises after only five minutes. On a Web site commemorating the aborted performance, the house itself is imagined as having agency, the power to testify to the experience of enslaved Africans:

> If the Georgian House could speak would it depict the lies told on the walls in the room next to John Pinney's bedroom, or would it speak the truth about the Bristol slave trade? Would it gloss over the pain and humiliation of thousands of slaves brought over to Bristol on the bottoms of ships, or would it support the notion on the walls of the room which state that the conditions of slavery were unknown?[66]

In de Certeau's terms, the visiting actors' performance constituted an effort to make the Pinney House into a "place," a site for a prescribed performance of a particular interpretation of historical events.[67] This interpretation was structured around three binaries: the house is silent, not speaking, it leaves truths that ought to be present absent; and, although it assumes an air of "not guilty," it is in fact marked by guilt. However, according to de Certeau, it is the nature of "place" to delimit events, to narrativize in advance, and to offer them to the spectators, who then "receive" them.[68] Having occurred—and having been interrupted—in one specific time and place, the performance cannot be repeated.

In addition, the performance polarized, rather than united, a community committed to the full story of Pero's life. From the perspective of the house curators, the actors—outsiders who knew nothing of the delicate state of city politics—attempted to impose terms from a foreign context, and they alienated community members who might otherwise have been sympathetic to more moderate attempts at revisionist history. As it stands now, a small wall display on Pero and slavery currently hangs in an attic gallery in the house. Although to some visitors the exhibit may seem out of the way and perhaps too small, it marks a major shift in the city's willingness to concede that Pinney's life revolved around the slave trade. Furthermore, the prominent use of the interior of the Pinney House as the set for the 1998 BBC production of *A Respectable Trade*, the story of a slave-trading family in Bristol, marks a new era in the interpretation of this historical site.

Leaving Park Street, visitors to Bristol soon encounter another monument to Pero, one dedicated with much publicity in March 1999. The Pero Footbridge is a graceful pedestrian walkway that crosses from one side of a city quay to another. In the case of the footbridge, a "place" has become what de Certeau would call a "space"—a site for multiple performances of interpretation that situate the spectators themselves as historical subjects.[69] To begin, a bridge has different semiotic potential; whereas the Pinney house "locks up" city secrets, the bridge connects. It metaphorically spans older and new understandings of civic history, and it symbolically knits together a community torn apart by the history of slavery. To be sure, some might argue, walking across the bridge does not necessarily entail an act of political consciousness: the bridge is not "prescribed" or "delimited" in what it has to say on the subject of Pero or slavery, and it cannot bring someone to hear a story that he or she may want to ignore or resist. On the other hand, precisely because the bridge does not tell walkers what to think in advance, and because it leaves open questions of agency, complicity, and historical responsibility for walkers to consider, it provides the opportunity for individuals to question their own contribution to the city's racial politics.

In much the way, then, that a public space like the Pero Bridge retains the potential to stimulate ongoing reflection in participants, the Bristol

FIGURE 2   Pero Footbridge, Bristol.

Slave Trade Trail also creates active, performative participants in a rewriting of civic history. The trail is a "text," an inexpensive pamphlet that can be purchased at the City Museum and Art Gallery as well as other tourist venues in the city.[70] Published in 1998 by three researchers—Madge Dresser, Caletta Jordan, and Doreen Taylor, who worked under the auspices of the Bristol City Council and with the sponsorship of the Society of Merchant Venturers—the pamphlet maps out a walking trail for tourists wishing to discover Bristol's involvement in the slave trade. The pamphlet explains the relevance to the slave trade of 42 city sites, including architecturally notable buildings and city spaces, burial grounds, cathedrals, churches, pubs, and public monuments. Similar to (and indeed modeled after) Boston's Freedom Trail, the Slave Trade Trail takes its walkers through a variety of city settings.

Unlike the Freedom Trail, however, this trail is not marked on the pavement. Only the walker's footsteps connect the places into a coherent path. Beginning at the city dockside, the trail crosses an eighteenth-century square and winds its way through crowded business and shopping districts. Some sites have changed so much that they bear little resemblance to their eighteenth-century description; Marsh Street, "once a rough area near the quayside, the haunt of seafarers," gives little indication of its former color.[71] Other sites—for example, the Commercial Rooms on Corn Street, currently housing a pub—still retain their eighteenth-century flavor. Those seeking adventure are allowed a peek into the Redcliffe caves—rumored to have held incarcerated slaves—and a visit to the Hole in the Wall Pub, a dockside spyhouse linked to the business of press-gangs. After a detour to Bristol Cathedral, the trail ascends steep Park Street, now a thriving neighborhood of trendy restaurants and shops geared toward students, passes the Wills Memorial Building of the Bristol University library, and culminates at the City Museum and Art Gallery.

The pamphlet is addressed to a varied audience, including those in wheelchairs or maneuvering "pushcarts" (strollers).[72] They are assumed to know something, through local lore or legend or rumor, but not a great deal about the historical facts of the slave trade. In the pamphlet, strategically placed boxes alert walkers to places that might be mistakenly associated with the trade. "There is no evidence," for instance, "that slaves were sold on Blackboy Hill" at the top of Whiteladies Road.[73] It is expected that many walkers do not understand the vital connections between the eighteenth-century financial services of their city and the slave trade, and they need to be informed:

> The trade in Africans and in the slave-produced commodities from America and the Caribbean (such as sugar, chocolate, coffee and cotton) meant more money came to Bristol. This money had to be administered. Loans were needed, slaving and cargo ships had to be insured, as did the sugar refineries and warehouses where fire was a constant threat. Goods had to be sold off and commission needed to be paid. In this way, financial services could be said to have been stimulated by the success of the triangle trade.[74]

Walkers learn, then, that the evidence of the trade in their city lies not where they might expect but in far more complicated commercial practices. They further emerge as individuals who want to know and will not need to be persuaded that the project of the trail is necessary and appropriate.

Implicitly, walkers function as part of a collective and a contemporary "we," a group with the benefit of hindsight. This group is occasionally poised for judgment, even while it is very much in the process of learning the facts. For instance, consider number 22: All Saints' Church: "Colston helped to fund the restoration of the tower at All Saints' in 1716. This may account for the fact that inscribed on his tomb is a list of all his charitable bequests, but no mention of his involvement in the slave trade, nor of his trading interests in the sugar plantations in the West Indies."[75] I will return to the special case of Colston later, but for now it is notable what the trail intimates: the message on Colston's tomb appears to "cover up" his guilt. In this example, we have the first instance of how the trail asks the walker to position himself on one side—the side that knows slavery is wrong and that those who participated in it were "guilty." Before exploring further the implications of such positioning, however, it is necessary to return to the work of a walking trail.

For those of moderate fitness (and without small children in tow), walking the trail is not physically challenging. The weather—not likely to be ideal in most seasons—is less an obstacle than is the city traffic. Several sites are reached via hazardous pedestrian crossings, and in some places the heavy stream of buses, trucks, and cars plaguing the city center obstructs the view. These factors are worth mentioning because this trail is explicitly designed for pedestrians, in contrast to similar historical trails that are not exclusively designed for on-site pedestrians. For example, the guide to the Portsmouth Black Heritage Trail in New Hampshire describes sites in chronological order of their associated events so that "the armchair reader can follow Portsmouth's history through the centuries." As a result, "the corresponding numbers on the map do not follow a convenient walking route."[76] In Boston, the trademarked Black History Trail is first identified as "a walking tour that explores the history of Boston's 19th century African American community." But then the Web site notes that the historic homes "are private residences and not open to the public." Alternatively, this trail can be toured online, by clicking on the "footsteps" that bring you to each of fifteen sites, including the African Meeting House on the island of Nantucket.[77] The cynic might find in these examples further evidence of American laziness: why walk when you don't have to leave the comfort of your chair? But it is also possible to argue that a great deal more is going on here.

To begin, the Bristol Slave Trade Trail puts live bodies into action, and this makes good economic sense: only live, on-site tourists get hungry or thirsty or waylaid by tempting shopping opportunities. I will return to this point later, but for now I emphasize how trail walkers correspond to Conquergood's definition of the ethnographer after poststructuralism: here walkers are participatory, dynamic, intimately involved, precarious, and "grounded in historical process, contingency, and ideology." Most important, they are experiencing bodies "situated in time, place, and history." Conquergood's succinct and rich redefinition of ethnography opens up to explain much of the work that can be theoretically done by a walking trail. According to his rewriting, only when the body is put into motion, on site, in opposition to weather, traffic, and even consumerist diversions, can it actually make meaningful connections. The physical act of being present becomes the catalyst to understanding, as walkers are made into active participants who "confront" those who were alive during the time of the slave trade. As walkers "listen" to the voices of the past, they "encounter" those responsible for the city's history. Rather than see themselves as distanced from eighteenth-century citizens, they are implicitly enjoined to imagine themselves as "coeval," or as sharing the same time of city fathers, purveyors of the slave trade.[78]

Thus, on the one hand, walkers can pause to consider Thomas King, who traded with Africa (although not in slaves); looking down from Redcliffe Parade, they can imagine King watching his ships being built on the docks below. What were his thoughts as he watched his fortune take shape before his eyes? Would he have paused to consider the continent from which he made his fortune? Would walkers themselves have felt differently? On the other hand, they can imagine the first open meeting in Bristol on the abolition of the slave trade held in 1788 in the now-demolished medieval Guild Hall on Broad Street. Which citizens found their way to the meeting? What motivated their attendance? Would walkers have found themselves among them? Trail walkers are thus given the opportunity to learn about themselves from this ghostly encounter with Bristol's eighteenth-century citizens, and they are meant to go home as changed individuals—not unlike pilgrims—who have made a significant cultural journey. Yet, although a sense of "coevalness" is implicitly a goal here, obviously modern walkers only simulate the work of the ethnographer. Unlike actual ethnographers they do not exist at the same moment as the players they conjure up for dialogue.

Indeed, through their dialogue with the ghosts of the past, walkers can also be seen as "performers," not unlike other kinds of enactors who similarly engage in what performance theorist Richard Schechner has called a "restored behavior." Restored behaviors are organized sequences of events that exist separately from the performers who "do" the events, thus creating a reality that exists on a plane separate from everyday existence.[79] Schechner uses the examples of actors at Plimouth Plantation; civil war enactors furnish further examples, as did the "performers" in the historically based British reality television series *The 1900 House*. Although walkers on a trail are not quite performers in the same way as these participants who very self-consciously take on clearly defined characters, we can make the case for placing their actions within the context of "restored behavior." As walkers traverse modern city streets, they participate in the making of another historical reality. If, as Schechner writes, "performance consciousness is subjunctive, full of alternatives and potentialities,"[80] then walkers move toward an alternative political reality, one in which they both recognize the need for redress and become aware of a need for social action.

Like Conquergood and Schechner, de Certeau is also interested in the implications of embodied practices for understanding history. According to de Certeau, walking in the city is a "spatial practice" that helps us to read the haunted history of a place. Or, as he writes, "There is no place that is not haunted by many different spirits hidden there in silence, spirits which one can 'invoke' or not." Urban places are themselves, he explains, "fragmentary and inward turning histories . . . accumulated times that can be unfolded like stories held in reserve."[81] De Certeau's interest lies primarily in walkers whose paths follow no map, whose "bodies follow the thicks and thins of an urban 'text' they write without being able to read it."[82] Nonetheless, he offers a useful approach to the idea of urban walking, one in which footsteps are "a style of tactile apprehension and kinesthetic appropriation. Their swarming mass is an innumerable collection of singularities. Their intertwined paths give their shape to spaces. They weave places together."[83]

In other words, for de Certeau urban walking is like a linguistic speech act with an "enunciative" function: walking appropriates topography (the way a speaker appropriates language); it is a spatial acting out of the place (the way the speech act acoustically acts out language); and it implies relations among different places (the way a verbal enunciation, as "allocution," initiates contacts between interlocutors).[84] This comparison between the linguistic speech act and urban walking facilitates an understanding of how trail walkers can become agents of communication and meaning—their footsteps not only claim the territory but also make it legible by physically creating "relations" between trail sites. As they move from place to place, from numbered site to numbered site, they create meaningful links and connections, and theoretically they begin to see and articulate the relationships not only between and among the numbered sites, but also between two narratives about their city: the one they may have been taught as schoolchildren or as inhabitants of that place and the one that they are now being encouraged to construct about the history of their city.

We can see how walking weaves places together and makes the history of the slave-trade history legible—becoming a spatial "acting out" in the process—by considering the example of Queen Square (numbers 11 through 15 on the Bristol trail). The pamphlet describes the square as having been completed in 1727, "when Bristol's involvement with the slave trade was nearing its height. The square is a reminder of the genteel lifestyle of Bristol's merchants and officials that was made possible by the wealth of the Atlantic trade, much of which involved trading in slaves and slave-produced commodities."[85] Laid out as a series of graceful Georgian or Georgian-style (several of the original structures were bombed during World War II) town houses fronting a city park with a statue of William of

Orange in the middle, Queen Square is bound to be a very familiar site to those who drive through the city. But walkers stop and consider several notable sites, among them number 12, a house built for Alderman Nathaniel Day (who petitioned against a proposed tax on slaves) and later the home of one-time Bristol mayor Henry Bright, prominent slave trader and merchant-venturer. The building currently serves as regional headquarters of English Heritage. Farther along the trail is the site of the first American Consulate, about which the guide says, "Exports of largely slave-produced tobacco from the [U.S.] southern states featured prominently in the city's economy."[86] This reminder thus links this site to number 41, the Wills Memorial Building, Bristol University, the gift of a family "who made their fortune in the tobacco trade."[87]

The trail then sends walkers to number 15, the Custom House, whose function was "to oversee the trade of the port, and derive duties and other revenues from the ships leaving and coming to Bristol, including those ships involved in the African trade."[88] As Madge Dresser reminds us in her comprehensive survey of "gentility and slavery" in eighteenth-century Bristol, these are only a few of the possible connections that might be drawn between those who lived in this specific location and activities of the trade. She illustrates this nexus as a web, a representation in which information about the various historical inhabitants of Queen Square is superimposed in textual boxes on an eighteenth-century engraving of Bristol, with lines connecting persons to addresses. In this way, the historian's text covers up the eighteenth-century image and foregrounds "what we know now" rather than what we would otherwise see: a vision of eighteenth-century order, symmetry, and urban civility.[89]

However, this kind of educational tool differs in its visual and cognitive impact from the experience of walking up to the building and reading text that encourages the walker herself to weigh what she sees, as well as whatever prior associations the building may have had for her, against what she now learns. The physical act of moving from place to place, along and across the square, thus echoes the mental act of piecing together the fragments of a narrative that gradually becomes clearer. Or, as Felecia Davis writes about similar attempts to map African American history onto the streets of Manhattan, "to make and create a tour or structured narrative from the sites listed is to haunt and remember the city by moving through it, allowing story to cut across map or allowing map and location to structure narrative."[90] In the new narrative emerging as the

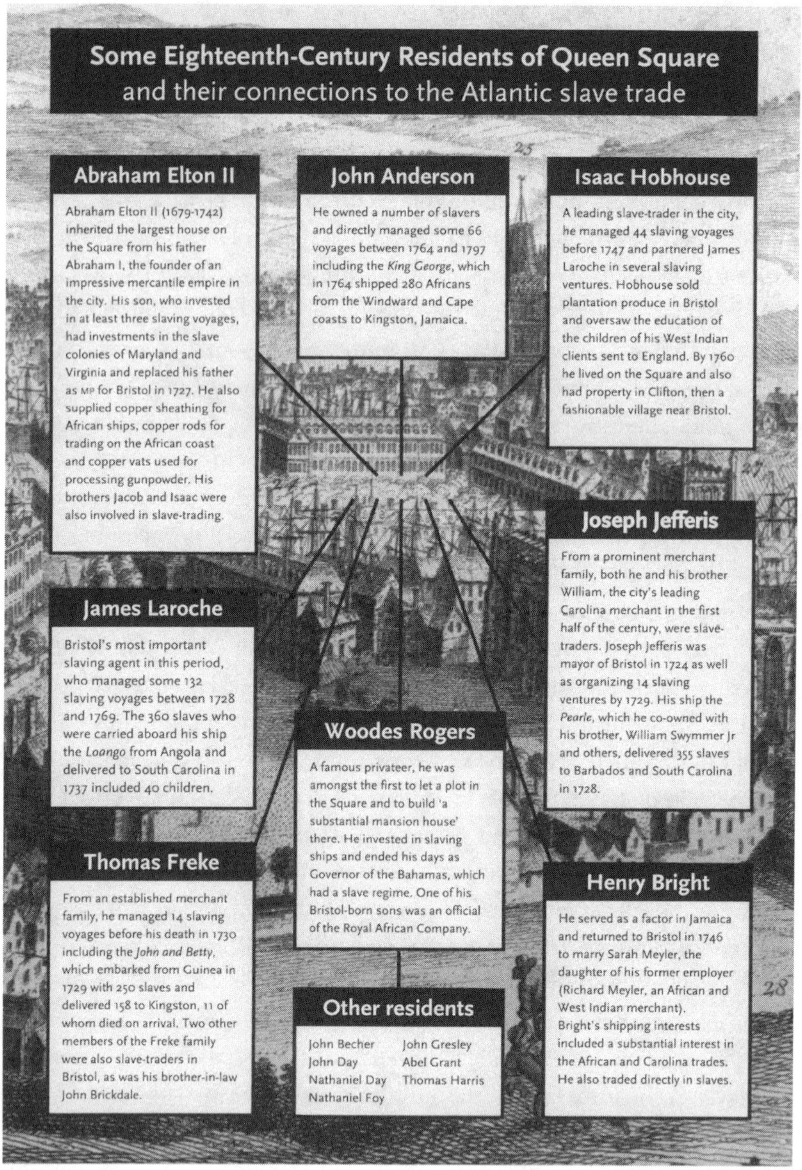

Some Eighteenth-Century Residents of Queen Square and their connections to the Atlantic slave trade

Abraham Elton II

Abraham Elton II (1679-1742) inherited the largest house on the Square from his father Abraham I, the founder of an impressive mercantile empire in the city. His son, who invested in at least three slaving voyages, had investments in the slave colonies of Maryland and Virginia and replaced his father as MP for Bristol in 1727. He also supplied copper sheathing for African ships, copper rods for trading on the African coast and copper vats used for processing gunpowder. His brothers Jacob and Isaac were also involved in slave-trading.

John Anderson

He owned a number of slavers and directly managed some 66 voyages between 1764 and 1797 including the *King George*, which in 1764 shipped 280 Africans from the Windward and Cape coasts to Kingston, Jamaica.

Isaac Hobhouse

A leading slave-trader in the city, he managed 44 slaving voyages before 1747 and partnered James Laroche in several slaving ventures. Hobhouse sold plantation produce in Bristol and oversaw the education of the children of his West Indian clients sent to England. By 1760 he lived on the Square and also had property in Clifton, then a fashionable village near Bristol.

James Laroche

Bristol's most important slaving agent in this period, who managed some 132 slaving voyages between 1728 and 1769. The 360 slaves who were carried aboard his ship the *Loango* from Angola and delivered to South Carolina in 1737 included 40 children.

Woodes Rogers

A famous privateer, he was amongst the first to let a plot in the Square and to build 'a substantial mansion house' there. He invested in slaving ships and ended his days as Governor of the Bahamas, which had a slave regime. One of his Bristol-born sons was an official of the Royal African Company.

Joseph Jefferis

From a prominent merchant family, both he and his brother William, the city's leading Carolina merchant in the first half of the century, were slave-traders. Joseph Jefferis was mayor of Bristol in 1724 as well as organizing 14 slaving ventures by 1729. His ship the *Pearle*, which he co-owned with his brother, William Swymmer Jr and others, delivered 355 slaves to Barbados and South Carolina in 1728.

Thomas Freke

From an established merchant family, he managed 14 slaving voyages before his death in 1730 including the *John and Betty*, which embarked from Guinea in 1729 with 250 slaves and delivered 158 to Kingston, 11 of whom died on arrival. Two other members of the Freke family were also slave-traders in Bristol, as was his brother-in-law John Brickdale.

Henry Bright

He served as a factor in Jamaica and returned to Bristol in 1746 to marry Sarah Meyler, the daughter of his former employer (Richard Meyler, an African and West Indian merchant). Bright's shipping interests included a substantial interest in the African and Carolina trades. He also traded directly in slaves.

Other residents

John Becher   John Gresley
John Day   Abel Grant
Nathaniel Day Thomas Harris
Nathaniel Foy

FIGURE 3   "Queen Square."

Source: *Slavery Obscured: The Social History of the Slave Trade in an English Provincial Port*, by Madge Dresser, 2001. Reprinted with the permission of T R&D T Clark, a Continuum imprint.

trail walker herself makes the connections, the origins of the city's wealth cannot be fathomed without reflection on historical circumstances. The concept of "English heritage" (the preservation of which is the mission of the current inhabitants of number 29) must be reconsidered in light of history. "Respectability"—what Dresser calls "gentility"—is now understood to cover a range of behaviors, attitudes, and positions, which must be scrutinized beneath their surface appearance. Trade itself is now understood to connect and adjoin both place to place and people to people, facilitating fortuitous gain for some and tragic loss for others.

As trail walkers take on the role of performers enacting a historical encounter, everywhere they confront the traces of those who have formerly performed their own role on the city streets—in other words, present-day walkers evoke absent historical players. But they also view signs that the past has been erased; pamphlet numbers refer not only to such long-dead citizens as Captain Woodes Rogers but also to warehouses, schools, and offices that have been demolished, sugarhouses that have been altered beyond recognition, and historical sites destroyed by riots or wars. However, what is persistently absent at certain sites reminds walkers how difficult it can be to confront events that were never prevalent in Bristol: there never were very many enslaved Africans living in the city, although history offers a few poignant examples of their presence. For instance, the biography of Bristol resident Hannah More includes an often-cited incident in which she witnessed firsthand the terror of a young girl being forced back into slavery. However, the most horrific aspects of the trade—the Middle Passage and the grueling labor of Caribbean sugar production—took place far away from the city.

It has been argued that some city residents—John Pinney among them—had firsthand evidence of the brutality of the trade, as well as an intimate knowledge of the unconscionable conditions under which slaves lived.[91] Yet many residents would not have had firsthand experiences with the horrors of the trade, unless they sought out or became abolitionists themselves. To many Bristolians, the actual conditions of slavery would have remained an "absence"—something only imagined, if considered at all—against the "presence" of everyday life. Yet this troubling historical fact establishes suggestive parallels between an eighteenth- and a twentieth-century circumstance, as the work of Vivian Patraka suggests.

In considering performative representations of the Jewish holocaust, Patraka isolates the complex relationship of "presence" in relationship to a historical "absence," particularly when that presence is performed or represented in a play or a museum exhibit. According to Patraka, under postmodern performance theory, the relationship between a "representation" and "something represented" is usually understood in terms of "presence" and "absence." (For example, the actor who takes on the role of Hamlet makes present an "absent" Hamlet, in the sense that that particular, dramatically rendered prince of Denmark never really existed except as the illusive product of Shakespeare's pen. Whether a real Hamlet existed is irrelevant, because Shakespeare's Hamlet is uniquely his alone.) However, Patraka suggests that, under the demands of a holocaust performative, we ought to shift the second term from *absent* to *gone*—any representation or performance of the Jewish holocaust makes present what was "gone." Patraka further substitutes the neologism *goneness* for *absence*.[92]

It is worth examining the implications of Patraka's coinage. First, unlike *absent*—a term that might play directly into the hands of those who would deny the actuality of the Jewish holocaust—*gone* acknowledges what was unarguably once there. Second, *goneness* acknowledges the impossibility of capturing what is lost, while never undercutting the historical fact of the wrong. Patraka explains that *goneness*:

> more completely reflects the definitiveness, the starkness, and the magnitude of this particular genocide by dictating the scope of what and who has been violently lost, including succeeding generations that cannot be. Murder and cruelty on a mass scale are what distinguish this goneness from the historian's problem of documentation and recovery. Goneness is inconceivable but its effects are palpable, particularly the inevitable desire to articulate, negotiate, mark, and define.[93]

In conclusion, she writes, "The Holocaust performative acknowledges that there is nothing to say to goneness and yet we continue to try to say it, identify it, memorialize the loss over and over."[94] Analogously, then, the African holocaust is "gone"—regardless of what we can prove about its presence in Bristol to begin with. Although historians seek to document what is missing from black history, the African genocide is not merely "absent," it was made "gone" through the agency of those who participated in the trade, as well as those who came after them. However (as Patraka's argument also reminds us) what is "gone" from the history of slavery nonetheless leaves palpable effects, and, like those remembering the Jewish holocaust, those remembering the African holocaust are similarly compelled to "say it, identify it, and memorialize the loss over and over."

When a population such as that in Bristol remembers slavery, it does not simply make "present" what has been absent—the past cannot be brought back. Instead, the nature of the project of historical reclamation becomes somewhat different, as thinking about "goneness" prompts a shift in focus not only to the enslaved Africans who are gone—whose histories and lives were lost as a result of the trade—but also to the local citizens who are also "gone," those who lived with and profited from the slave trade on a daily basis. In other words, shifting from *absent* to *gone* brings to the fore questions of complicity, as well as broader questions about the nature of any wide-scale historical evil. To paraphrase W. H. Auden, in a world where the torturer's horse scratches his innocent behind on a tree, how do we explain what those who are gone either knew or did not know or—perhaps worse still—refused to know about the slave trade?

This kind of questioning gathers relevance as walkers approach the statue of Edward Colston—number 32. As Forbes's contemporary painting suggests, Colston is a figure of great significance in Bristol history, and his name is familiar to all contemporary residents, not only because of the concert hall that still bears his name but also because of the many educational institutions, almshouses, and hospitals endowed in his name, including four extant charities set up in the eighteenth century. According to the trail pamphlet, "Colston was also a prominent sugar merchant with interests in the Caribbean island of St. Kitts." Madge Dresser points out that he was an official in the Royal African Company, and company minutes place him at meetings that "organized and approved the sale and transport of Africans to the Caribbean."[95] Yet his statue "is silent about his role as a member of the Court of Assistants, to the Royal African Company, which had the official monopoly on the slave trade until 1698."[96] Thus, Colston's statue raises questions for walkers. How should contemporary citizens weigh a powerful tradition of philanthropic benevolence against the tainted origins of Colston's fortune? What does the silence of his statue leave unspoken and unsaid?

Inhabitants of Bristol have asked similar questions elsewhere. For example, hanging in the exhibit in the Bristol Industrial Museum is a painting of Colston by Richard Jeffreys Lewis. Painted one hundred years after Colston's death, in the year that his body was exhumed and reburied, the work reconstructs a scene of racial reconciliation: a kneeling, distraught black female figure raises the dying Colston's hand to her lips, as if for a farewell kiss. This rendering resolves any question of Colston's culpability by showing the slave as grateful to her dying master. But Tony Forbes takes a different message: "When I look at the Colston statue I just think of dead children. I can handle the fact that the statue was erected in 1895 'by the people of Bristol.' Over a century later, isn't it time for Bristolians to express their feelings about today's multi-cultural society?"[97] As we have already seen, Forbes represents Colston in his own fashion, as holding the chains that tie black Bristolians to a racist heritage. In this way, the silence of the statue is explicitly tied to Colston's "guilt," whereas those who speak about the horrors of the trade, as well as those who listen, belong on the side of the "not guilty."

At a crucial stop on the Slave Trade Trail, the Colston statue challenges walkers to engage with a powerful representation. Here the pamphlet gives agency to the statue (rather than to those who raised the subscription for it, for instance)—the statue remains "silent" and refuses to engage in dialogue with us. It is "guilty" in its silence. But what if the statue is not silent? What if instead it has nothing to say? What if both to Colston and to those who later memorialized him, the slave trade was not a "topic" for discussion at all? What if, for Colston, the slave trade was simply "business as usual"? These questions are worth asking because they imply that Colston's statue may not be simply "covering up," repressing, or denying an absent historical truth that the walkers now recognize and make present. Instead, Colston's statue may demonstrate a fact much more troubling to consider, namely, that he might not have believed that he had any reason to feel that he was "guilty."

In other words, the attempt to create a binary opposition between contemporary walkers and Colston, between their "speech" and his "silence," is also a failure to afford him full status as performative subject. The historical figure is frozen in his perfidy in such a way as to make him categorically different from the walkers. The memory of Colston's own complicated life story, a living history that saw him as "participatory, dynamic, intimately involved" and "grounded in historical process, contingency, and ideology," is effaced in favor of a flat and one-dimensional understanding that makes him a "bad guy" to modern-day, liberal walkers. The point is certainly not to excuse Colston or to explain away his complicity; I do not deny that his actions resulted in historical atrocities. Rather, the point is to recognize how complex and multifaceted the circumstances were under which Colston drew his wealth from the trade—and then to encourage conversations about comparable contemporary situations, or to encourage the walkers to think of similar, contemporary situations in which such concepts as "guilt" and "innocence" may prove resistant to analysis. What commercial practices might *our* ancestors want to ask us about in the future, finding us to have been "silent" and morally unresponsive? Putting the question this way not only undoes the opposition between a past crime and a present consciousness but it also undoes the problematic tension between "guilty then" and "not guilty now."

Lessons drawn from Colston's statue can also be applied to site 25, the Corn Exchange, built in 1753: "Despite its name it was intended for merchants of all types, and a number directly involved in the Guinea and West Indian trade used it for business transactions."[98] Walkers are instructed to enter the exchange to see eighteenth-century plasterwork representing Asia, Africa, and the Americas, the reminders that globalization first occurred in relationship to early mercantile capitalism. But to enter the exchange is to find oneself in the middle of a thriving indoor market, where CDs, clothing, jewelry, candles, and sweets are sold from innumerable small stalls crowding the market floor. The plasterwork can only be viewed with the whole scene of tempting commodities in focus—and here parents are likely to find themselves distracted by their children's entreaties. In other words, the Corn Market continues its historical work as a place of exchange, and trail walkers find that here they are positioned to do the very thing that eighteenth-century citizens would have similarly done at this moment: to engage in commercial transactions involving goods brought in through global trade. Arguably, at this moment present and absent, the then and the now, collapse, because the trail walkers confront neither ghosts nor ancestors but contemporaries who carry on their business.

Yet, among all the sites on the trail, this is the one where connections are potentially most obvious, where links between past and present are strongest. Here too, of course, is where trail walkers fulfill their roles as tourists, adding money to city coffers as they stop to eat, drink, or buy candles or CDs. These tourist experiences do not necessarily distract from the task of reflecting on history. Instead, walkers alert to the theme of connections might make this stop into an important moment for reflection. Why do people buy and sell? What codes ought to govern what can be bought and sold? Under what circumstances does a particular form of commerce become unconscionable? What are the similarities between contemporary commercial practices and those that occurred during the eighteenth century?

Similar to taking a journey or a pilgrimage, walking the Slave Trade Trail can result in a radical readjustment of perspective; it can potentially denaturalize what seems natural and disrupt a sense of inevitability. Walking the trail can also provoke questions and lead to the insight that history does not just "happen" but is created by individuals who make choices for which they will one day, inevitably, be held accountable. I have argued that trail walking, with its ethnographically inflected vocabulary, as well as its privileging of the body as a site of knowledge, can be conceived as an exercise in understanding what has been made "gone." I agree with Vivien Patraka that it is fruitful to shift the discussion from what is absent from any historical account of the slave trade to what is gone, and I have also suggested that engaging in this shift can help walkers understand how the "then" and "the now" are not opposites but moments on a continuum, where the burden falls on all citizens to continually question their own complicity with the invisible wrongs of history.

But how can we be certain that any of what I have described actually occurs? What measurement might we use to chart changes in public opinion, or shifts in popular understanding, as a result of the Bristol Slave Trade Trail? These are questions that lie beyond the scope of my expertise, perhaps requiring access to cognitive methods. Although conceding that there will always be those for whom the message of the trail is not meaningful, I invoke the concept of "structure of feeling," originally coined by Raymond Williams, to describe a sense of how the particular activities of a given moment combine into a way of thinking and living. "Structure of feeling," writes Williams, "is as firm and delicate as 'structure' suggests yet it operates in the most delicate and least tangible parts of our activity." Structure of feeling is not necessarily "possessed in the same way by many individuals in the community," although it is deeply and widely possessed. It is not formally learned, but one generation may train its successors in aspects of that structure of feeling.[99] I have suggested that both the Bristol Slave Trade Trail and, in its best moments, the Liverpool exhibit gesture toward a new historical "structure of feeling," as Williams describes it. Operating delicately and intangibly, both the trail and the exhibit create participants who are encouraged to frame multiple meanings for themselves. If, as one museum educator has argued, "museums are places where people go to think and feel about what it means to be human,[100] then both the Liverpool exhibit and the Bristol Trail as an extension of museum practice address an urgent social mission—at stake in their cultural representations is not only the creation of self-reflective individuals but also the generation of a historical awareness that might form the basis for a movement toward social justice.

Chapter Two

Fictionalizing Slavery in the United Kingdom, 1990–2000

In Britain, the last decade of the twentieth century saw the publication of a series of novels taking slavery as their subject. A partial list includes Caryl Phillips's *Cambridge* (1991), Barry Unsworth's *Sacred Hunger* (1992), Phillips's *Crossing the River* (1993), Graeme Rigby's *The Black Cook's Historian* (1993), Fred D'Aguiar's *The Longest Memory* (1994), Philippa Gregory's *A Respectable Trade* (1995), S. I. Martin's *Incomparable World* (1996), D'Aguiar's *Feeding the Ghosts* (1997), and David Dabydeen's *A Harlot's Progress* (1999).[1] At first glance, so many novels point to a distinct trend among writers of a certain era. To Bénédicte Ledent, the novels of Phillips and D'Aguiar in particular suggest "the emerging tip of a body of historical fiction to be published in the years to come."[2] Without knowing how long this trend will continue into this century, we can say that these novels share an intense, end-of-the-century interest in "telling the untold story" of Britain's slave trade.

Nonetheless, with so much to distinguish them, it is certainly possible to question the gesture that places these works side by side and examines them as part of one historical development. First, differing in genre, the novels are written for different audiences, ranging from broadly popular (and most likely white) to more scholarly and elite. The most widely exposed of the novels is *A Respectable Trade*. Still circulating as both a mass-market paperback and an audiocassette, it is the only work that has been turned into a film: Gregory adapted her work into a miniseries broadcast by the BBC in 1998 and later by PBS in the United States in the fall of

1999. Although several of the novels have smaller audiences, they have been critically acclaimed and declared prizeworthy. *Sacred Hunger* was the joint winner of the 1992 Booker Prize. Phillips won the (London) *Sunday Times* Young Writer of the Year award for *Cambridge* in 1992, and *Crossing the River* was short-listed for the 1993 Booker Prize.[3] Both Dabydeen and Phillips write for more academically inclined audiences who will most likely recognize the range of literary and historical sources alluded to in their works. Meanwhile, S. I. Martin, who is also the author of *Britain's Slave Trade*, a mass-market book published by Channel 4 in the United Kingdom, writes to introduce a popular audience to a forgotten part of British history.

A second and more pressing reason to distinguish these writers from one another is their racial identity: most of the writers, including Martin, D'Aguiar, Phillips, and Dabydeen are black. Moreover, D'Aguiar, Phillips, and Dabydeen are often studied as Caribbean writers, and they hold special interest for scholars of postcolonial literature. For Ledent, the significance of D'Aguiar (born in London to Guyanese parents) and Phillips (born in St. Kitts) lies in their "post-migratory or displaced Caribbeanness," that is "the essentially cross-cultural, diasporic, and 'in-between' identity of Caribbean migrants living in the West though not of it."[4] Similarly, Gail Low cites these authors for their "specifically black British contribution to slavery." She asserts that "the positing and return to slavery as a mythic ur-text, the shaping, reconfiguring ... performs a distinctive transatlantic bonding of black diasporic identities."[5] Dabydeen, born in Guyana, also fits the profile of a Caribbean and diasporic writer. Martin, by nature of his British birth, falls into only the latter category. The black writers all appear to have taken their inspiration from the slave narratives that were reprinted in the United States beginning in the 1970s, and from Toni Morrison's *Beloved* in particular.[6] In contrast, both Unsworth and Gregory are white, although Gregory was born in Kenya. Both have an interest in local English history—Unsworth's novel unfolds partly in Liverpool, and Gregory sets hers in Bristol. Yet one rationale for examining this body of novels together is their common willingness to unsettle a myth of British whiteness that ignores a legacy of violent contact between blacks and whites and that represses a brutal history of unequal power relations.

In addition, these white and black writers alike engage with the notion of England as a "hybrid" nation. To be sure, the idea of hybridity has recently been much discussed and contested, particularly by postcolonial scholars. Robert Young explains that throughout the nineteenth century *hybridity* referred to a physiological phenomenon. However, "in the twentieth century it has been reactivated to describe a cultural one." *Hybridity* begins as a description of physical objects, specifically, "the making one of two distinct things so that it becomes impossible for the eye to detect the hybridity of the geranium or the rose."[7] But by extension it comes to describe an effect of a particular kind of cultural contact, in which what emerges is a distinctly new kind of identity, as theorized by Homi Bhabha among others.[8] According to Nikos Papastergiadis, "one of the 'achievements' of poststructuralist theory was to liberate the subject [of hybridity] from notions of fixity and purity in origin" in favor of other connotations. These depend on the social vision that generates the idea of hybridity:

> Whenever the process of identity formation is premissed [sic] on an exclusive boundary between "us" and "them," the hybrid, born out of the transgression of this boundary, figures as a form of danger, loss, and degeneration. If, however, the boundary is marked positively—to solicit exchange and inclusion—then the hybrid may yield strength and vitality.[9]

Thus, postcolonial theorists often debate the political nature of hybridity: does it challenge or reiterate existing power relations? Sara Ahmed takes the position that not all engagements with hybridity are necessarily progressive, and she expresses a fear that "encounters in global capitalism may involve restructuring of power relations *through* (rather than despite) the very forms of play, hybridity, and movement discussed by some postcolonial critics."[10] However, Stuart Hall has argued that questions of hybridity can "interrupt any 'return' to ethnically closed and 'centered' original histories. Understood in its global and transcultural context, colonization made ethnic absolutism an increasingly untenable cultural strategy."[11] This chapter considers instances in which a novelistic engagement with hybridity successfully opposes racism on both personal and institutional levels, but it also suggests where such an engagement fails to move beyond a current political impasse.

Thinking about hybridity often foregrounds the consequences of sexual relations. Several novels under discussion feature interracial love affairs, symbolic of transracial affiliation and connection. As D'Aguiar writes, "That one body is black and the other white ought to be irrelevant."[12] Several of the novels depict biracial children, characters whose tragic stories inevitably suggest the persistence of a powerful racist agenda, even while they hint that England may be less white than it believes itself to be. But hybridity is not only a theme; it is also a set of formal concerns, and the project of exploring England's hybrid roots puts pressure on the novelistic genre. An expressed need for multiple voices and tellings yields a variety of narrative styles, from realistic, first-person accounts that imitate eighteenth-century journals, diaries, and logbooks to postmodern forms that offer conflicting points of view and fractured and irresolvable story lines.

Along with their pairing of black and white partners, all these novels to some extent take up the idea of binary opposites, pairs of ideas, such as black and white, man and woman, oppressor and victim. However, the most successful novels in the group go beyond this kind of binary thinking to a place where several truths stand firm simultaneously, however painful and conflicted the resulting effect. Here Stuart Hall is helpful for his reminder that political binaries "do not (do not any longer? did they ever?) either stabilise the field of political antagonism in any permanent way or render it transparently intelligible."[13] Hall also asserts that a postcolonial perspective obliges us "to re-read the very binary form in which the colonial encounter has for so long been represented. It obliges us to re-read the binaries as forms of transculturation, of cultural translation, destined to trouble the here/there cultural binaries forever."[14]

Just as a postcolonial perspective leads to a healthy skepticism of binary oppositions, so too does it lead to a resistance to narrative closure—when novelists resist pressure to "finish" the story, they also resist the temptation to leave their readers with the sense that the story *has been told*, consigned to the past, that it has already been taken care of and can therefore now be forgotten. Thus, the most successful novels in this group encourage proactive readers, who are offered no easy solutions but rather are given the chance to make connections between apparently incongruous ideas, to ask questions of themselves, and to imagine a world that has not yet come into being.

Yet what is ultimately at stake in a discussion of these novels with their various attempts to engage, both thematically and formally, with hybridity? To answer this question, I borrow from novelist Hanif Kureishi, who has written eloquently about the necessity of articulating and coming to terms with "a new way of being British," a more inclusive cultural identity that might well result from wide-scale hybridity. He writes, "Much thought, discussion, and self-examination must go into seeing the necessity for this, what this 'new way of being British' involves and how difficult it might be to attain. The failure to grasp this opportunity for a revitalized and broader self-definition in the face of a real failure to be human, will be more insularity, schism, bitterness and catastrophe."[15] In addition, he maintains:

> The evil of racism is that it is a violation not only of another's dignity, but also one's own person or soul; the failure of connection with others is a failure to understand or feel what it is one's own humanity consists in, what it is to be alive, and what it is to see both oneself and others as being ends, not means, and as having souls. However much anodyne talk there is of "one's kind," a society that is racist is a society that cannot accept itself, that hates parts of itself so deeply that it cannot see, does not want to see—because of its spiritual and political nullity and inanition—how much people have in common with one another.[16]

In the discussion below, I focus on novels that foreground the eighteenth-century slave trade as a way of contributing to a broader public discussion of what it means to be British at the end of the twentieth century. All the writers cited attempt to understand English hybridity and to build a broader platform for fighting racism and constructing "a new way of being British." Yet not all are equally successful in their efforts.

Thus, I consider seven novels for their various strategies for engaging with history and their investment in the idea of telling an untold story about the slave trade. I place the novels in three groups for their similar themes, issues, and approaches rather than for their publication history. In the first section, "Reading History," I explore two novels—*Sacred Hunger* and *Feeding the Ghosts*—that feature images of history as recoverable text. Yet here, paradoxically, an avowed commitment to the authentication and documentation of the transatlantic slave trade leaves much unsaid. These two novels, although they aim admirably to offer a full recuperation of a "true" story, fail to convey the full complexity of black and white relations as they mutually constituted each other. In contrast, a second group of novels—*Cambridge*, *The Longest Memory*, and *Crossing the River*—here considered under the rubric of "Reading Pastiche"—distinguishes itself through its self-conscious manipulation of historical documents. As a technique, pastiche demands the reader's intense concentration and self-conscious distance from the narrative process. The reader who "gets it" is continually aware of writing as writing. Although he is denied the pleasure of being fully immersed in the story, or perhaps of "forgetting himself" in the details of the story, in recompense he gains a deeper understanding of how narrative always expresses a vested interest and how the best stories are those that leave final judgment for the reader. Finally, the section on the third category, "Telling the Untold Story," takes up two novels, *A Harlot's Progress* and *A Respectable Trade*. These novels not only deal with binary opposition in radically different ways but also respond differently to the pressures to "Tell" the story of the slave trade to an audience craving closure.

Reading History in *Sacred Hunger* and *Feeding the Ghosts*

Barry Unsworth's *Sacred Hunger* and Fred D'Aguiar's *Feeding the Ghosts* take us into the heart of the eighteenth-century slaving community. Both novels are realistic in style and acutely attentive to historical details. Both also foreground the idea of a recoverable history, a lost story to be discovered and told. Unsworth is concerned primarily with the effects of the trade on a range of white characters, from the owner of the slave ship through the sailors who are tricked or forced to serve aboard the ship. D'Aguiar takes up the story of a fictional African woman who survives an attempt on her life in the *Zong* incident—a notorious, actual event, in which Captain Luke Collingwood threw 132 sick and enfeebled enslaved Africans overboard in an attempt to claim insurance money as a result of their deaths.

Unsworth's novel—over six hundred pages long—is the more ambitious of the two stories. Written "in the tradition of conventional historical novels,"[17] it is set in two periods—1752–1753 and then in 1765—in various settings in Liverpool, on the slave ship itself, along the coast of Africa, and finally in a remote settlement in colonial Florida. This novel is organized to tell the intertwined stories of two main characters. The first is Erasmus Kemp, the son of William Kemp, a former cotton broker and merchant who builds a ship called the *Duchess of Devonshire* hoping to capitalize on the enormously lucrative African trade, only to commit suicide when it appears that his business will fail.[18] The second is Matthew Paris, an older cousin of Erasmus, a doctor who had formerly been disgraced and imprisoned for seditious writings on protoevolutionary topics.

Through Paris, who is given the position of surgeon on his uncle's slave ship, an intimate and detailed account of the African trade is conveyed. Paris is the moral center of the novel, a man whose gradually awakening conscience leads him to abhor the African trade both for its brutal and horrific treatment of the enslaved human beings and for its dehumanizing effects on the crew. One of the novel's strengths is its attempt to give names, backstories, and credible psychological motivations to the workingmen on the ship. Attention is given to the economic milieu from which they come. For example, after Blair runs up a large tab in an alehouse, his purse is stolen by a prostitute in league with the innkeeper, who then gives him a choice: to either to sign up for the slave ship or go to prison. Another sailor, Deakin, is a navy deserter who is evading execution by hanging. A friend's wife with a sick baby hands him over to a ship's recruiter in exchange for money. A third "recruit," Calley is a simpleton without any other prospects. He is lured on board by promises of "hot wimmen" willing to do anything he wants. Unsworth depicts in grim detail the reality of their working lives—the arbitrary and excessive exercise of corporal punishment; the inadequacy of their diet, leading to malnourishment; the brutal conditions of their everyday labor; and the overall depravity of the ship's ethos.

Later Paris becomes a key figure in a revolt against the ship's captain, who has relentlessly oppressed the crew and—in a scenario reminiscent of the *Zong* incident—jettisoned some of the weaker enslaved Africans. Having taken control of the boat, the crew and the newly freed slaves run aground off the coast of Florida, where they found a settlement based on the utopian principles described to them by a passenger on the ship, a visionary artist named Delblanc. The last hundred pages of the novel depict the efforts of the fledging interracial community to sustain itself. Not only do they set the principles for their society by freeing neighboring Indians from their would-be captors, killing the slavers in the process, but they also establish the fundamental laws, social practices, and myths necessary for social cohesion. Creating a lingua franca, they begin to raise the biracial children born into their midst. But several factors—including a shortage of women, requiring that men share their "wives" in uneasy alliances, and what appears to be human nature itself—undercut the utopian impulses of the community. As a leader, Paris is horrified to discover that one member of the community—formerly enslaved himself—plans to demand another member's servitude in revenge for that man's attempt on his life.[19]

Meanwhile, back in Liverpool, Erasmus Kemp lives the life of a rising mercantile capitalist. After his father's suicide, he marries into a "sugar family" and becomes consumed with the relentless pursuit of profit—in other words, he feels the "sacred hunger," as the utopian, anti-capitalist Delblanc facetiously terms it.[20] The plots of Erasmus and Paris come together when Erasmus, obsessed with the role of his cousin in the disappearance of his father's ship, goes to Florida following the discovery of the dead captain's logbook. With the assistance of British colonials in Florida (who are at the same time engaged in genocidal policies toward the American Indians), he raids the settlement, returning the formerly enslaved Africans to captivity and sending mutinous sailors to their fate back home. Paris dies on the way back to England, but his biracial son survives into the nineteenth century. Later called Luther Sawdust, he is an elderly "mulatto" of "dark amber" color haunting the streets of New Orleans in the 1830s and telling everyone, "My fadder a *doctor*. I born in a paradise place."[21]

Thus, Luther's story frames the novel with a picture of hybridity and provides a first image of the past as a recoverable story. In the prologue to the novel, the omniscient narrator—an unidentified and disembodied voice, unconventionally using the personal pronoun *I*—claims to have discovered the record of the elderly black man in the papers of Charles Townsend Mather, "a colorful and visionary character himself," who died in a Jacksonville sanitarium in 1841.[22] Although he initially doubts the veracity of the story, the narrator ultimately accepts it as truth. The frame suggests that the novel was a story only waiting to be found by the narrator, whose role is to be attentive to and uncover what is already there.[23] This image of history as recoverable and capable of being narrated is consistent with other images of history in the novel—for example, with Captain Kelso's logbook, which is eventually recovered and given to Kemp, or with the journal that Paris keeps. Paris's writing in particular provides a metacommentary on narrative process, as he philosophically considers the relationship between the act of his writing and the chaos of the events around him.[24] We receive yet another image of history as Paris observes Jimmy, "the linguister, " giving a history lesson to the settlement children. At Jimmy's prompting, the children participate in an apparently faithful recounting of the key events leading to the establishment of their community. At the appropriate moment, they all chime in to list their community's heroes. While Paris looks on, listening to the lesson and watching the teacher, his consciousness and memory of the past 12 years—containing details not available to the children—fill out the lesson and so provide necessary exposition for the reader.[25]

Unsworth seems to suggest, then that, when history is beyond contestation, it stabilizes a community's memory and creates a body of shared values. He further suggests that it is the role of the author to provide such a stabilizing historical effect by providing an "unusually strong authorial omniscience"[26] that occasionally, from an invisible vantage point, looks back over the story and makes moral pronouncements:

> On the line of the horizon there would sometimes appear the brief stain of another ship, like the breath on a distant mirror; but most of the time [the ship] could feel herself alone on the ocean, the sole trader of the world, instead of what she was, a member of a vast fleet sent forth by men of enterprise and vision all over Europe, engaged in the greatest commercial venture the world had ever seen, changing the course of history, bringing death and degradation and profits on a scale hitherto undreamed of.[27]

Similarly, when Erasmus meets with the English rulers in Florida, the omniscient narrator comments on the wider and deadlier repercussions of colonial practice: "In point of fact the Great White King was just then embarking on policies destined to lose him the whole of North America within two decades and to bring about the total destruction of the Creek nation."[28]

However, what is the narrative and political effect of such authorial intrusion? By way of answering this question, Paul Sharrad draws a distinction between novels that allow "the unspeakable a space in which to speak, uncovering gaps in discourse, and revealing hidden dialogue and intercourse" and novels that offer "the impression of *total description*, papering over gaps, and denying intercourse."[29] Here Unsworth engages in the latter practice: he tells the reader what he or she most likely already knows (the slave trade killed many individuals while making a few people rich; colonial policy was calculated to destroy indigenous populations), and he effectively consigns events to a knowable past that the invisible and detached narrator has "managed" and presented to us. In addition, his "total description" becomes a way to prevent further inquiry and discussion, as becomes apparent in a closer examination of the protagonist's consciousness.

Throughout the novel, anachronistic tendencies undermine the narrator's suggestion that history is recoverable, stable, and knowable. Such tendencies sometimes make the past strongly resemble the present, and the historical characters often appear to be versions of contemporary citizens, preoccupied with much the same issues and thoughts as those that concern people today. For example, one subplot puts Erasmus Kemp in the middle of an amateur production of Dryden and Davenant's Restoration version of *The Tempest, The Enchanted Isle*. Under the guidance of their "director" (an unlikely theatrical title in 1757), the group discusses Caliban's character in terms more likely to appear in a late-twentieth-century humanities classroom than an eighteenth-century setting; the director asks for an abject shrug, but the actor playing Caliban sees him as "proud and rebellious."[30] At other times, small details may cause the reader to question the presentation of eighteenth-century existence. Would an eighteenth-century doctor have diagnosed a patient as having "high blood pressure?"[31] Was it common for eighteenth-century Englishwomen to keep poodles as pets? Could Paris really have discovered a "European-style couch in worn red plush" (not a "settee" or another piece of furniture) on the coast of Africa? These are only a few examples of moments when images jar the illusion of mimesis.

Yet the accumulation of such details matters because, having set up the novel as a faithful representation of a knowable past, Unsworth inadvertently problematizes his own representation, by reminding his reader of the ultimate impossibility of knowing the past on its own terms. Instead, the novel's version of the past bears many traces of a present-day interpretation—while reading, we look for the past and find a reality that bears an unmistakable resemblance to the time in which we ourselves are living. In the process, the idea that the novel unproblematically reflects a stable and "knowable" past hides the role of the narrative art in any historical reckoning. Just when it seems urgent to ask, "Whose history is this? From whose point of view? Whose point of view is left out in this telling?," the reader is instead lulled into a false complacency, a too-facile sense that *the* past story has now been made accessible and comprehensible. In short,

Unsworth's political intentions to reveal the horrors of the transatlantic slave trade are subverted by his recourse to a narrative form that aims for an unsustainable historical verisimilitude.

To describe the trading coast of Africa, Unsworth borrows heavily from Joseph Conrad (as he himself acknowledges), giving us an eighteenth-century *Heart of Darkness* laden with metaphoric resonances from Conrad.[32] For instance, as Paris makes his way upriver to meet the slave traders, it seems to him that "disease lay like a tangible presence there on the river, that they were proceeding through the very exhalations of the plague."[33] But if *Sacred Hunger* shares Conrad's themes, it also brings up the many critical controversies surrounding the politics of Conrad's vision—including questions concerning the representation of Africa in the novel, the role of Marlow as narrator, and the possibility of Conrad's own complicity with both racism and colonialism.[34] In one form, the controversy takes the following questions: Can Conrad's overall narrative style, with its many layers of irony, be interpreted as a subtle criticism of the explicitly racist comments of his characters? Does Conrad subvert or support Marlow's own problematic statements about the native Africans?

In Unsworth's novel, Paris takes the place of Marlow as he is asked, in his position as the ship's surgeon, to scrutinize the "cargo" with a dispassionate medical gaze. Here Paris prepares to perform his medical duties on the first group of enslaved African being brought to the ship:

> Paris looked down at the bound figures in the waist of the long canoe. . . . There were ten of them, five men, two boys, two women, and a girl, all completely naked. They sat in silence, their arms bound behind them and their heads forced upright by means of a common yoke: it was the projections of this that had appeared so strangely ceremonial at a distance. They were lighter in color than the boatmen, who were coal black and heavy-browed, and had a muscular development of chest and arm such as Paris had never seen before.[35]

As Paris proceeds with his physical examination, Unsworth creates an excruciating sense of the physical intimacy between the two men:

> With the same sense of compulsion, like that attending some quest or mission in a dream, [Paris] met the dark and somehow impersonal regard of the negro, the eyes at a level with his own, fathomless and

shallow in the bony sockets. He faltered for a moment at the gaze of those eyes that did not see him, did not know what they were seeing—the man was stricken with the openness of the place, he was sightless at his own exposure.... With a slight grinding of the teeth, a simulation of savagery without which he could scarcely have proceeded, Paris seized the negro's lower jaw and forced it open. There was no trace of saliva in the mouth, but tongue and gums were perfect, the teeth immaculate.[36]

The passage continues to describe how Paris necessarily treats the man as a commodity to be inspected: "he peered at the negro's eyeballs and into the pink whorls of his ears. He prodded his chest and listened to the heart and felt the glands of his throat." Looking for evidence of disease, he finds only whip marks and the extensive contusions caused by the man's bonds. When urged not to "forget the cock," he discovers the man's circumcision.[37] When they later whip the man to make him dance, Paris sees that thick tears are gathering in his eyes.[38] Throughout this scene, Paris's deep discomfort is skillfully conveyed; the reader readily believes that Paris is struggling to perform as required, even as his awakening conscience tells him that the man is more than merchandise.

But what of the subjectivity of the inspected man throughout the scene? The choice of a third-person narration aligned with Paris's consciousness means that the other man's consciousness is eclipsed—the mimesis requires that the enslaved man's thinking be as impenetrable to the reader as it is to Paris, who can only dimly fathom the man's terror and humiliation. Although the point of the scene is to demonstrate how Paris struggles with his own racism, there is no reciprocity here. In this scene, African subjectivity is represented only as a cipher that advances the protagonist's moral awakening, and Unsworth's interest in a hybrid cultural identity is compromised by a narrative style that cannot move beyond a white perspective. Sara Ahmed's critique of unsuccessful engagement with hybridity in the 1990 film *Dances with Wolves* applies equally to Unsworth's novel. As in the film, here hybridization becomes "a technique for getting closer to strangers which allows for the reassertion of the agency of the dominant subject. The story remains organized around his ability to move and to overcome differences (his 'difference' from them)."[39]

The novel's politics are further complicated by its recourse to sugar metaphors as well as related tropes of consumption. For example, one of the more dubious moments in the narrative provides a protracted and graphic description of Erasmus Kemp's initiatory night of debauchery at a banquet for African Merchants off Chancery Lane. This phantasmagoric scene places Kemp in the middle of a pornographic spectacle, beginning with the display of "a three-foot high model of a negress fashioned in chocolate:"[40] "Except for bracelets, anklets and pearl collar, which were all made of sugar-crystal droplets, and a red sugar-paste rose in her hair, she was naked. . . . At her base was a plaque of chocolate with the letters picked out in spun sugar: THE SABLE VENUS." Needless to say, the merchants avidly devour the confection in a scene that is surely meant to highlight several themes—not only that their capitalism is a kind of cannibalism that preys on African flesh but also that their mercantile activities are nothing less than obscene.

However, this scene is quickly eclipsed by an even more prurient spectacle. Eight "scantily dressed and painted and high-stepping" women make their way into the room. One in particular, who is later designated Erasmus's sexual partner for the evening, unwraps a dildo—"a sugar penis, gleaming with crystals, heroically tumid, with a red tassel attached."[41] She then begins to masturbate with it, until it melts: "in accordance with hallowed custom it had been made of powder sugar, designed for quick melting in the hot spice of the vagina."[42] Perhaps the intention here is to link the merchants' moral depravity to their mercantile practice; one can imagine that the point is to highlight how the merchants get their sordid satisfaction by watching how the sugar trade "fucked people up." But the scene makes the sugar merchants into too-easy targets, cardboard characters lacking in depth, substance, and motivation. In addition, the graphic description draws the viewers into the debauchery as voyeurs. Here we are presented not with the horrifying vision of human labor on a Caribbean sugar plantation but with the titillating sight of a masturbating girl.

This scene is especially troubling when we consider the event to which it obliquely refers: the sugar boycott of the 1790s. Initiated by Quaker William Fox with his famous pamphlet *An Address to the People of Great Britain on the Propriety of Abstaining from Eating West African Sugar and Rum* (1791), the boycott reflected the political awareness and commitment of abolitionist consumers—many of them women—who denied themselves the pleasure of their sweetened tea, which they saw as tainted with the blood of Caribbean slaves. In the words of Quaker writer Mary Birkett, who was only seventeen when she penned this verse:

> How little think the giddy and the gay
> While sipping o'er the sweets of charming tea
> How oft with grief they pierce the manly breast,
> How oft their luxury robs the wretch of rest,
> And that to gain the plant we idly waste
> Th'extreme of human misery must taste![43]

However, for the image of conscientious female consumers, Unsworth substitutes an image of women being consumed—either literally, as in the case of the chocolate Venus, or metaphorically, as in the case of the masturbating woman consumed by sexual desire. This displacement plays to a prurient interest—and perhaps helps to sell the novel. The scene is indeed disconcerting, but in the end the reader registers the shock of the pornographic at the expense of any deeper understanding of what it meant for the British to consume sugar and other goods associated with the slave trade, or how a moral response to that consumption might have developed.[44]

In contrast to *Sacred Hunger,* with its focus on the historical experiences of different classes of white characters, Fred D'Aguiar in *Feeding the Ghosts* creates an African character to "write the Middle Passage" and to script "old age as a woman in the early nineteenth-century Caribbean."[45] The action of the novel takes place in three settings: the slave ship *Zong* in 1781, the courtroom of the Lord Chief Justice Mansfield in 1783, and Kingston, Jamaica, in 1833, when the British Slavery Abolition Act was passed. In the first part of the novel, Mintah is an enslaved African who is thrown overboard along with many other slaves so that the owner can make a claim to insurance money. But she manages to survive, eventually making her way back onto the ship. Befriended and hidden by the sympathetic cook's assistant, Simon, she eventually frees several of the slaves and leads them in a rebellion, which is soon suppressed. The captain punishes them by throwing other slaves overboard. In Part III, we learn the outcome of Mintah's story: sold into slavery in Maryland, she eventually earned enough money to buy her own freedom. She moved to Jamaica, the final setting of the novel. Mintah has become a woodcarver and sculptor, and has planted 131 trees to commemorate the dead from the *Zong*. She dies in a fire, the ironic counterpart to her watery first grave.[46]

Although Mintah is absent from Part II, D'Aguiar uses her history to foreground the idea of an "authenticating voice" that might have quelled the competing racist arguments, if only it had been allowed to speak.[47] During the trial to decide whether the owners of the ship can claim insurance money for the murdered slaves, Simon steps forward with an unpublished manuscript, a book that Mintah (having learned to read in a Christian mission) wrote while hidden on board. The book testifies in particular to the fact that the slaves were recovering from their illnesses and not beyond hope at the time the captain threw them overboard.[48] The counsel for the insurers, Mr. Wilkes, motivated by his clients' interests, supports her account and reasons that "were [Mintah] indeed sick she would not have been able to climb out of the sea and back up the side to conceal herself on board. How many others like her in good condition were simply unable to seize hold of a rope on time and so were left swimming in the sea until they drowned from exhaustion?"[49] But the counsel for the ship owners disputes the manuscript's authenticity, calling it a book "penned by a ghost."[50] Mintah's book thus becomes a trope, an opportunity to represent an alternative viewpoint, one thought to offer special weight and authority because it is grounded in the experience of an enslaved African. But Simon, dejected by the court's refusal to take Mintah's testimony at its face value and anxious about his own safety in light of the crew's hostility to its message, grabs the book and flees from the courtroom. Mintah's record is lost when Simon disappears onto a nameless ship, departing for an unspecified destination. Ultimately, then, Mintah's book is a paradox: it is the persistent image of a silenced or repressed truth but also a suggestion that, although historical truth is tragically elusive, it might, once upon a time, have nonetheless been recoverable.

The novel gives Mintah an intriguing backstory. In Part III she reminisces about the Danish missionaries who came to their village when she was a child, claiming that "there was one God and that Africans need not be slaves."[51] She recalls the very different responses of her parents, in particular her mother's eventual conversion to Christianity and her father's persistent fidelity to his African faith, even when the village is deserted. She remembers too how the missionaries proved that the cost of paying the African converts wages for their labor, yielding crops to be profitably sold, "would be less [expensive] than buying, transporting and keeping slaves and the profits better as a result."[52] After the death of the missionaries, she and her mother were sold into slavery. In fact, Mintah's recollection has a basis in an actual historical event, the arrival of Paul Erdmann Isert (1756–1789) on the west coast of Africa in the 1780s. Appointed chief surgeon on the fortified Danish settlement of Christianborg, Isert, a German national, became a thorough opponent of slavery. He established a plantation at the base of the Awapim Mountains after purchasing the land from the Asante king Osei Kwame on behalf of the Danish king. Isert's intention was to abolish slavery by paying African workers for their labor on sugar and coffee plantations. He may have been murdered in 1789—either by financiers of the slave trade and plantation owners in the Danish West Indies or by corrupt government officials in Christianborg.[53]

This relatively unknown history grounds D'Aguiar's story of Mintah's literacy and makes generally credible the idea of enslaved Africans who communicated with the oppressor in his own tongue. But historical grounding for Mintah's backstory also complicates the notion of her character. What sort of hybrid identity might have emerged in the case of a Fetu woman who was Christianized at a Danish mission? (Wouldn't Mintah have spoken Danish or perhaps German? Or should we assume that English was one of the many tongues to which she—like Gronniosaw—gained access?[54]) What kind of narrative might have been generated by this kind of complicated intercultural contact? Rather than explore the many layers of identity most likely to have been created under such complex cultural circumstances, the novel privileges Mintah's "African" (original?) identity by showing her return to her roots at the end of the novel, when she becomes a visionary woodcarver like her Fetu father, a man who stayed true to his roots and never left his native village:

> I made shapes with wood. Filled my hands with it. Woke and gave shape to whatever I dreamed. Saw my father instructing me in my dreams. Woke and followed his instructions. Sought out the grain in the wood. Found the shapes hidden there. The land showed me its secrets in that wood. My chisel unearthed them. I could almost close my eyes and carve with my father over my shoulder and the run of the grain as my guide.[55]

Here Mintah's story resolves itself in terms of a binary opposition. On one side lies her "colonized" and Christianized identity, an identity associated with her oppression and, curiously, her mother. On the other side lies her indigenous, African identity, associated with her discovery of an artistic gift and with her return to her father's way of life. But how real is the choice between the two identities? Does Mintah's story in fact need to resolve on one side or the other? What does she recover in returning to her paternal roots? What might she also lose in the process?

While Mintah's hybrid identity is eclipsed in favor of her essential African identity, the stories of the white characters fail to develop beyond one-dimensionality. For example, Mintah's paramour, Simon, is literally simple, having been dropped on his head as a baby.[56] To take another example, the real-life captain of the *Zong*, Luke Collingwood, becomes in this novel Cunningham; his fictional name puns on his incessant guile, but it also makes his motives transparent. "Are we to make a loss or a profit? Which is it to be, gentlemen?" he bullies the crew.[57] Yet, as Stuart Hall writes, "The differences, of course, between colonising and colonised cultures remain profound. But they have never operated in a purely binary way and they certainly do so no longer."[58] D'Aguiar gestures toward an awareness that the binary opposition between oppressor and oppressed and white and black may not hold absolutely in his portrait of the ship's first mate, Kelsal. Years before the *Zong* incident, having fallen ill and been taken in at the Danish fort, Kelsal had found himself being nursed back to health by Mintah. Mintah recalls how, as Kelsal recovered from his feverish delirium, he confused his own identity with that of his nurse:

"You are Kelsal?"
"No! You! You are Kelsal! I am Mintah!"
"I am Mintah?"
"No! I am Mintah! You are Kelsal!"
"Kelsal?"
"Yes! Kelsal!"
Why was I shouting? Because he seemed to be lost. The fever had knocked the common sense out of him so that I was him, he me.[59]

However, this confusion of identities, although intriguing for its suggestion that Mintah and Kelsal are more interdependent and interconnected than not, does not develop into a thematic statement. Instead, throughout the novel black and white characters are easily known and recognized for their stable and predictable identities. Thus, this novel—unlike *The Longest Memory*—fails to demonstrate the extent to which the slave trade mutually formed black and white identities.

In sum, both *Sacred Hunger* and *Feeding the Ghosts* take seriously the notions that official British history has omitted an important series of events and that the novelist's task is to listen for voices that have not previously been heard. Both are also invested in the idea that history ought ideally to be recoverable, that the past can be discovered and recaptured through the novelist's art. However, Unsworth's "recovery" reflects much of what the reader already knows, whereas D'Aguiar's paradoxical portrait of what has escaped historical recovery flattens out the probable complexities of intercultural contact. In addition, both novels close down too soon, leaving significant gaps in the process: Unsworth fails to bring his black characters into fruition, and D'Aguiar glosses over the likelihood of Mintah's hybrid identity and leaves his white characters undeveloped. Both novels are also limited by a narrative form that cannot accommodate multiple levels of truth simultaneously. For Unsworth to tell his story, enslaved Africans persistently figure only as "the other" to an awakening white consciousness. Even when they have become free, Unsworth's black characters fail to rise above stereotypes. For D'Aguiar to tell his story, the full import of black contact with white culture must be downplayed. As becomes apparent in the next section, the extraordinary nature of black–white relations during the eighteenth century often defied easy characterization and resulted in complicated, often contradictory, and even tortured identities. In contrast, another series of novels takes up hybrid forms. These novels allow for the simultaneous expression of multiple viewpoints and, rather than cover over their gaps in an attempt to tell a story, they leave them to be explored by the reader.

Reading Pastiche in *Cambridge*, *The Longest Memory*, and *Crossing the River*

In *Scenes of Subjection*, Saidya Hartman critiques the inclination to represent slavery as a "routinized" violence that risks inuring the reader to pain. She argues that "the barbarism of slavery did not express itself singularly in the constitution of slave as object but also in the forms of subjectivity and circumscribed humanity imputed to the enslaved." Hartman further suggests that the worst effects of slavery are not to be found in the obvious cruelty of the slave ship, the whipping post, or the coffle, but in the more mundane and quotidian sites of slave existence.[60] However, what narrative form best serves a history that forgoes the representation of the brutalized human body in favor of the daily ignominies of slave life? What kind of story can the mundane and quotidian site of slave existence yield? In the absence of more spectacular scenes of sufferings, how does a fiction engage its reader, elucidate historical atrocity, and mobilize a moral sentiment capable of becoming a political action?

In this section, I turn to fictions that register the farther-reaching effects of the transatlantic slave trade on the daily lives of black and white people. Thematically and formally similar, *Cambridge* and *Crossing the River,* both by Caryl Phillips, and *The Longest Memory*, by Fred D'Aguiar, are polyphonic novels offering multiple, overlapping, and often contradictory voices that represent human subjectivity—both black and white—under the slave system. The effect of all three novels is less to "recover" history and more to foreground history itself as a narrative process. All three novels thus involve the reader in a process of discovery and interpretation without necessarily closing down to clear moral statements. All three novels demonstrate how slavery's legacy constituted both black and white identities, and all three show how that same racial constitution still operates today. These fictions are circum-Atlantic stories; they are set along the Atlantic rim—along the west coast of Africa, the Caribbean, the east coast of America, and England—and they explicitly take up the theme of transatlantic connections. They unfold in a range of time periods, from the eighteenth century through post–World War II England.

To begin, the action in *Cambridge* unfolds in the 1830s on an unnamed Caribbean island in the West Indies. As the novel opens, one of the novel's two protagonists, a white woman named Emily Cartwright, is in transit across the Atlantic Ocean to visit her father's plantation. When she returns home, she must, according to her father's will, marry a 53-year-old widower with three children. The first part of the narrative—and indeed the majority of the novel, around 100 pages in all—is presented as if it were Emily's journal from her time on the island. The second part, a mere thirty pages or so, is the first-person narration of a slave named Cambridge—a man who was previously called Olumide in Africa, then Thomas, and who was then baptized a Christian under the name David Henderson. The name Cambridge marks his reentry to slavery. Having been freed after his initial enslavement, he was retaken by "Guinea-Men" while on a Christian mission on the African coast. At the time of Emily's residence at her father's estate, Cambridge has become a notable presence among the plantation's slaves, as she observes first from some distance and then at closer view. Emily and Cambridge live in separate yet intersecting worlds—especially when Cambridge murders a vicious overseer named Mr. Brown, a man who had been Emily's lover and by whom she had become pregnant. But a historical document detailing Cambridge's legal case in obviously biased and racist terms balances Cambridge's firsthand account of the events leading up to and including Brown's death. As Jenny Sharpe points out, the trick here is that this section reproduces an excerpt from an actual travel diary, Mrs. Flanigan's *Antigua and the Antiguans* (1844). Thus, "As a postmodern representation, fiction serves as a referent for factual evidence rather than the other way around."[61] The last section of the novel, an epilogue, returns us to Emily's world, this time presented in third-person narration. It tells of the burial of her stillborn child and of her bizarrely sentimental attachment to her black servant Stella.

Thus, the technique of the novel involves multiple stories that, in the words of Sylvie Chavanelle, reverberate, "refracting and diffracting various elements."[62] Those stories belong to the characters themselves, but they also belong to the historical personages whose narratives are alluded to through Phillips's extensive use of pastiche. The experience of reading the book is, as Evelyn O'Callaghan writes, "a disconcertingly echoic experience" in which "one constantly, and correctly, feels, 'I've read this before!'"[63] She traces the many original texts being imitated here, from Monk Lewis's *Journal of a West Indian Proprietor* to Lady Nugent's *Journal*. Traces of Janet Shaw's *Journal of a Lady of Quality to the West Indies* can be perceived as well.[64] As O'Callaghan argues, the effect of the pastiche is to focus "attention on the *connection* between the fictional and historical narratives."[65] In addition, the pastiche becomes a comment on "the essentially 'fictional' nature of [the original] texts, particularly in terms of the way conventional formal structures shape the manner in which the 'objective' narrator shapes and judges the 'facts.'"[66]

With the voices of other historical personages in the background, the reader moves back and forth between Emily's obviously biased views of Caribbean plantation life, which are themselves unstable and contradictory, and Cambridge's somewhat more objective perspectives, which are nonetheless deeply embedded in a flawed racial ideology. For example, when Cambridge is taken into a slavery a second time, he laments, "That I, a virtual Englishman, was to be treated as base African cargo, caused me such harmful pains as I was barely able to endure."[67] Although his comment implicitly condemns the slave trade, it also perpetuates the divide between Cambridge as an African "ennobled through Christianity" and his "base" African brethren. Cambridge's narrative also freely borrows from other historical texts, in particular from *The Interesting Life of Olaudah Equiano*, the life of James Gronniosaw, and other slave narratives.

In addition to forcing the reader to remain alert to the sound of "real" historical voices circulating through Cambridge's speech, Phillips also makes it difficult for the reader to sympathize with one character rather than another. Emily's narrative not only comes first but also occupies far more space in the book. Yet she is not necessarily more likeable or persuasive. According to Bénédicte Ledent, Phillips gives the reader a "soon-to-be undermined sense" of Emily's reliability, suggesting in the process how "the colonial enterprise was fraught from its inception with a mixture of good faith and conscious or unconscious delusion that resists any facile clarification."[68] Ledent demonstrates how, throughout Emily's narration, Phillips skillfully imitates a variety of colonial discursive practices, among them the differentiation and downgrading of the other and the compulsion to objectify.[69]

Ledent further explores how Phillips uses irony to undermine Emily—for example, how he makes her quick to condemn what she perceives as moral depravity among the black population, while making her oblivious to the more insidious and predatory behavior of the island's white men. At the same time, Cambridge's narrative ultimately serves to dispossess Emily of her superiority, since his intellectual and moral qualities surpass hers, as Chavanelle points out.[70] According to Ledent, "one senses [Cambridge] is slightly more trustworthy than Emily for he operates on a narrative rather than a merely descriptive mode."[71] In addition, the reader is likely to be drawn to Cambridge's greater flexibility and his avoidance of generalization.

However, the search for a center to the novel is further complicated by the fact that Phillips gives the elite white woman and the enslaved African man several important parallels in their stories, as several critics have noticed. First, both Emily and Cambridge experience the crossing of the Atlantic as a confinement and a "passage of loss."[72] Second, both are "at once opposed to and complicit with established power."[73] Third, whereas Cambridge is made into a "virtual Englishman" through contact with Christianity, resulting in an unstable identity, Emily is "creolized, neither at home in the Caribbean or in England."[74] But what is the effect of Phillips's drawing these parallels? By privileging the similarities between Emily and Cambridge, Phillips unsettles the binary oppositions between oppressor and oppressed, empowered and powerless, agent and victim. Yet his point is not the clichéd idea that female oppression and black oppression are both caused by white patriarchy. Rather, through the relationship between Emily and Cambridge, Phillips demonstrates the complicated and sometimes contradictory effects of power. Who is truly "free" in this novel? How does one come to meaningful forms of agency under the prevailing ideology?

The novel also de-essentializes racial identity, which is no longer fixed and stable but in flux. Cambridge, for example, is a black man who possesses the contradictory tendencies to rebel and yet to perpetuate the values of the established order.[75] Unlike Mintah, whose identity ultimately rests in an unambiguous return to her paternal, Afrocentric roots, Cambridge is a "decentered" subject. No doubt there are risks in the representation of a character who can seem too close to the master's position. Some readers wonder whether Cambridge has simply "sold out."[76] Or, as another critic asks, "Does Cambridge incarnate the fusion of two cultures, or is he a copier of patterns?"[77] Yet it seems important to Phillips's project to leave these questions in play rather than pin down the exact nature of Cambridge's identity.

In this novel, unlike in *Sacred Hunger* or *Feeding the Ghosts*, history is not a set of recoverable texts leading to a stable view of the past. To the contrary, historical archives—including the bits of journals, narratives, and other documents that frequently surface in the novel—are shown to offer only highly subjective, self-serving, and biased stories. If history has been "penned by a ghost," the ghost has no special access to the truth. There is no authentic untold story to be recovered or unburied. All history is a narrative that bespeaks someone's interest, and no one can tell his or her story without recourse to the master's discourse. Neither is history something that can be handed to a reader by a narrator in control. Instead, the reader must mediate among the various accounts, drawing his or her own conclusions in the process.[78] In an essay exploring the use of history in *Cambridge*, Gail Low cites Walter Benjamin's aphorism that "to articulate the past historically does not mean to recognize it 'the way it really was.'" She further argues that a novel such as *Cambridge* does not aim to capture a specific moment that can be understood and mastered. Instead, it elucidates history as ongoing process, as "the fulfillment of a potentiality which lies dormant in origin."[79]

In sum, in *Cambridge* the title character is a hybrid creation whose identity lies somewhere in between his African roots and Christianized Western identity. At the same time, the style of the novel is similarly hybrid, neither realistic nor fantastic, neither purely historical documentation nor fictional reconstruction. In much the same way, Fred D'Aguiar's novel *The Longest Memory*—published three years before *Feeding the Ghosts*—takes up the theme of diasporic identity while also experimenting with a hybrid form. In an interview, D'Aguiar said that his "wish is that the story is its own argument," and this novel, like *Cambridge*, accomplishes much through its method of narration.[80]

Set in Virginia in the early decades of the nineteenth century, the story centralizes the experiences of Whitechapel, an elderly enslaved African, who has "buried two wives and most of my children."[81] The main action of the novel unfolds as Whitechapel is forced to witness the brutal punishment of a young man named Chapel, his wife's son, whom he had raised as his own. Chapel has been brought back after trying to run away. The two hundred lashes he receives result in his death, and the other characters in the novel respond to the death, reconstructing the history that led to the tragedy and reflecting on its implications for themselves. The novel has ten narrators. After Whitechapel begins the narrative, the reader hears the voice of the reluctant and divided owner of the plantation, Mr. Whitechapel, who is trying to do his best to be a "good slave master." His narrative reveals that Sanders Junior, the overseer who administered the lashing, and Chapel were half-brothers. The third voice belongs to Mr. Sanders, the overseer, who had raped the cook, who was Whitechapel's wife and Chapel's mother:

> I grabbed Cook and pulled her into my room. She fought so much that both of our clothes were torn. She bit my hand. I was an inch away from cuffing her squarely on the jaw. I resorted to choking her until she virtually went into a faint. She was a statue for the duration of what, I don't really know, since I did not enjoy myself as much as relieve myself.[82]

His narration, given in the form of a journal, is followed by a brief response from Cook (she is not given another name) in which she remembers hearing her son Chapel reading. The fifth voice is that of Chapel, who speaks in poetry, having been taught to read by Mr. Whitechapel's daughter Lydia and punished for his efforts. He records how his mother's death precipitated his flight: "With her gone nothing could keep me there./Father, I am running. I feel joy; not fear."[83] The sixth voice collects the responses of anonymous plantation owners as they taunt and challenge Mr. Whitechapel over the death of his slave. The seventh belongs to Lydia, Mr. Whitechapel's daughter, who loved Chapel and who dreamed of running away to the north with him.

Lydia's narration is followed by editorial selections from *The Virginian*, in which a dispassionate yet racist journalist entertains a range of topics, from whether Christians should wield whips against slaves (the answer is yes) to what to do with a faithful old slave who is too old to work (treat him as a valued possession). In answer to the question whether mothers should be sold separately from their children, *The Virginian* reasons: "It is wise not to confuse such displays of attachment with habit and love. At the auction block, get the best price for your investment even if it means breaking up the capital into smaller holdings and selling each holding separately."[84] This section of the novel functions similarly to the historical document detailing Cambridge's legal case, although here the writing is constructed, not authentic. D'Aguiar relies on the reader to see through the pose of objectivity and recognize the heinousness of the argument. He offers his reader not merely the content of a racist ideology but also a sense of its strategy and method. The section brilliantly imitates the persona of a "reasonable" human being who uses condescension to disguise his bullying tactics. When a Miss L (Lydia?) writes to ask whether it would not be more profitable to pay slaves, he dismisses her query after a few cursory calculations: "It all sounds too rife with variables to be practical though I grant you it is an intelligent question from a lady."[85]

The granddaughter who discovers Whitechapel's dead body becomes the ninth voice in the novel. She is followed by Sanders Junior, who reflects on his own father while considering Whitechapel's death: "You yourself said I resembled him, that I was my father's young self. But my memory of him is sullied. He lacked your courage, Whitechapel. If you were white, I would have wanted you as my father."[86] Brief passages from Whitechapel, one called "Remembering" and the other "Forgetting," frame the other ten voices. Thus, D'Aguiar uses a variety of styles and genres to convey his characters, ranging from Chapel's lyrical couplets to Sanders Senior's staccato prose. Unlike Phillips, he does not foreground his art as pastiche, but like Phillips he uses irony and counterpoint to convey his message. For example, that *The Virginian* counsels its readers to religiously avoid the temptation of "young nubile slaves" comments obliquely on Sanders Senior's rape of Cook. Also similar to *Cambridge*, *The Longest Memory* uses polyphony, the technique of letting the story emerge through a combination of perspectives and voices.

In speaking about the creation of characters for this novel, D'Aguiar explains:

> The stereotypes of the black slave are easy to de-bunk. What's difficult is how to write a fully rounded character and reconcile that character with the belittling institution of slavery. How do you survive a life of slavery if you have a shred of dignity, insight, pride, ambition, and a capacity to love? It must have hurt to simply wake up and face another day as a slave with such consciousness. Yet it is the basis for humanity, a minimum requirement.[87]

The extraordinary demands of slavery on human consciousness are very much apparent in the detailed and complex portrayal of Whitechapel, a man who defies easy categorization. To all outward appearances a most compliant slave, Whitechapel rationalizes his own means of survival:

> There are two types of slave: the slave who must experience everything for himself before coming to an understanding of anything and he who learns through observation. The slave in the first category behaves as if he is the only slave in the world and is visited by the worst luck on earth. That type of slave is agitated, brings much trouble on his head and he makes the lot of the slave ten times worse. It is generally accepted that the slave in the second category is brighter, lives longer, causes everyone around him a minimum of worries and earns the small kindness of the overseer and master.[88]

The reader is given few clues about how to weigh Whitechapel's rationalizations. Is he a canny survivor, a profound realist who has learned how to bear up under the extraordinary psychological and physical pressures of slavery? Or does his compliance go too far? Do his rationalizations become excuses for cowardice? Does he owe it to himself or anyone else not to facilitate or resist slavery on a daily basis? Yet Whitechapel himself later alters his philosophy. He realizes the ineffectualness of his demeanor when, despite his stature in the slave community, he is unable to convince Sanders Junior to spare Chapel:

> Now when I hear insects at dusk each click, clatter, and croak is the voice of my blood asking for mercy. None was granted. My son, the last fruit of my wife's womb, her joy, was granted none. I who have worked my life for one estate under one family was shown no respect. I was granted none.[89]

Referring to the fact that he himself had told Saunders where the son was likely to have gone, he tragically admits, "I killed my son because I wanted him next to me when I died."[90]

To fully assess Whitechapel, the reader needs recourse not only to Whitechapel's own comments but also to those of the people who surround him. For example, to what extent does his "Uncle Tom" cheerfulness complement Mr. Whitechapel's self-serving yet morally reprehensible defense of himself as a benevolent master? To what extent does Whitechapel make possible the persistence of Mr. Whitechapel's obvious delusions? In this novel, each character emerges as a composite portrait of what the others project onto him or her. Lydia, for example, invests in the idea of Chapel as a romantic hero, with whom she will walk arm in arm in the abolitionist North, although his narrative does not convey a reciprocal investment in her love.

The imbalance of power means that the black characters in the novel are far more vulnerable to white psychological projection, and no doubt the consequences of such projection are direr for the enslaved Africans whose lives hang in the balance as a result. However, in this novel D'Aguiar is also interested in understanding how white racists see themselves not as "evil" or oppressive but as fully accountable, even rational. Mr. Whitechapel, for example, is duly horrified to hear about the death of Chapel, which occurred while he was away and had left the estate under the supervision of Sanders Junior. But he is most concerned that the event not compromise the integrity of his estate. He illogically blames Whitechapel, not himself, for failing to tell Sanders that Chapel was his half-brother and therefore forestalling the punishment: "Whitechapel should have reminded you. He must have thought that you knew, and did not care."[91]

This whole mess cannot be ended any more than it can be made as simple as it may have been at its inception. Your father's action and that of countless others before him and since ensured that. Whitechapel's longevity and living memory ensures that. Our consciences, for God's sake, ensure it too. We must not allow this trade to turn us into savages. We are Christians. God should guide us in our dealings with slaves as he counsels us in everything else.[92]

This is the voice of a man who is desperate to preserve a good self-image, despite every indication that he is involved in inhuman practices. His strategy is to deflect blame and to search for rationalizations within Christian doctrine itself for the system of slavery. In Part Six, Whitechapel's plantation-owning peers ridicule him for allowing Chapel's death to take place, despite his supposedly "liberal" slaveowning practices. Taunting him for being an "abolitionist," they charge, "We're all of us Christians of one sort of another. But you, Whitechapel, you promote the African at the expense of your own white Christian brother." In response he avows, "I promote the teachings of Christ and practice slavery. I do not practice slavery and hide my beliefs."[93] In this way, he differentiates himself from the other slaveowners. He reasons that they are the true hypocrites for failing to integrate Christian benevolence into their slaveowning practices. However, the effect of this false dichotomy is to heighten the tragedy of the novel: in the end, Mr. Whitechapel's "humanitarianism" is just as bloody as the obvious brutality of the other masters.

To some extent, Mr. Whitechapel's rationalizations are rooted in one kind of Christian ideology, as we realize from reading the pages of *The Virginian*. An editorial dated July 14, 1810, queries "Is Christianity incompatible with slavery?" It answers negatively: "It should be possible to treat a slave with Christian fairness and instruct him in the Christian faith as a just substitute for his pagan practices, without nullifying the relationship of master and slave." Through such passages, D'Aguiar's purpose is not to sway opinions against slavery but to "fathom and expose its complex mechanisms and so fight the racism it has given rise to."[94] In other words, if there is a mimetic impulse here, it seeks to reflect not a mirror image of "reality" but rather a mode of thinking, an emotional and discursive process of making *a* reality. This mode of thinking is often contradictory, and it permits two truths to uncomfortably coexist—for example, Mr. Whitechapel aims for benevolence while he denies other human beings their full rights. He practices a "humanitarian" Christianity that sees no conflict in oppressing Africans because of their religious practices. Ledent further argues that D'Aguiar's novel foregrounds "plurivocal relativity rather than reassuring binary or even monological certitude," adding, "for the 'either/or' epistemology which sustained the institution of slavery [it substitutes] the accumulative logic of 'both/and,' an appropriate echo of [its] diasporic ethos."[95] Yet no doubt a postmodern "plurivocality" has its risks. Such a strategy invests heavily in the idea of a reader who must herself do the work of sorting through the various messages and coming to some kind of interpretation. But readers can refuse to do the work. They can continue to hear one voice at the expense of another, missing the point altogether. At some point, the "reasonable" voice of the self-justifying racist may become too persuasive.

In interviews, D'Aguiar has addressed the issue of readerly projection and identification. He has cited Herder's term *Einfuhlen* (sympathetic understanding) to sum up his novelistic purpose, explaining that "fiction about history should be the act of feeling one's way into the past, not by holding a mirror but by stepping through the mirror into the unknown."[96] In "The Last Essay About Slavery," D'Aguiar elaborates:

> What is clear from reading novels about slavery and writing one myself ... is that "things" happen to all witnessing readers that affect their view of themselves and of the multi-racial world they inhabit. One of these effects is emotional: readers find that their coveted maps of empathy are redrawn by their engagement with these slave novels; redrawn in terms of their ability to experience fellow-feeling for someone of a different race, the opposite gender and the power-brokered relationships between and within such groupings. Readers emerge emotionally bruised, mentally reconfigured and, as a consequence, with deeper knowledge of those relations[97].

D'Aguiar's metaphoric "map of empathy" both reintroduces the idea of movement so crucial to the project of a walking trail (as seen in the previous chapter) and suggests a kinesthetic dimension to the reading experience. But the "emotional bruising" here should not be mistaken for the vicarious assumption of the enslaved Africans' suffering. Instead, what D'Aguiar posits is the painful but transformative power of the experience of reading fiction; the reader's mental reconfiguration is meant to include understandings that were previously elusive.

The advantages and risks of a postmodern plurivocality can also be seen in Caryl Phillips's *Crossing the River*. Here the many voices tell "stories of geographical and historical crossings,"[98] and they bring to the foreground diasporic themes, in particular the reconstitution of black identity after geographical dispersal. The four separate stories do not connect in immediately obvious ways, yet they cohere into a larger statement about human perseverance and the possibilities of redemption and reintegration. The novel is divided into four parts, each in a very different setting: Virginia and Liberia; the American West, and in particular Denver; a slave ship; and a small English village. Parts I and III most explicitly engage with the historical representation of slavery, and I turn to those first. Part I, "The Pagan Coast," resembles *Cambridge* in its use of pastiche, and it raises questions of readerly identification similar to those that arise in both *Cambridge* and *The Longest Memory*. This part of the novel tells the story of Edward Williams, a reluctant owner of a tobacco plantation in Virginia. Although he inherited a fortune from his father, he has "an aversion to the system which had allowed his fortune to multiply."[99]

As the story opens, he is embarking for Liberia in search of his former slave Nash Williams, who had been sent as a missionary and subsequently disappeared, apparently into the wild. The story is told through a combination of a third-person omniscient narration that tracks Edward from Virginia to Liberia and letters from Nash, sent to Edward sometime before he left for Liberia, in which pastiche is especially apparent. Nash's rhetoric and phrasing—and most of his convictions, contradictory though they may be—credibly imitate the discourse of a nineteenth-century African Christian who has thoroughly internalized the master's liberal discourse. For example, here Nash writes, from the position of a supplicant, to reassure Edward (and himself?) that as a black missionary in Liberia he is in the right place and performs a noble service:

> Perhaps you imagine that this Liberia has corrupted my person, transforming me from the good Christian colored *gentleman* who left your home, into this heathen whom you barely recognize. But this is not so, for, as I have stated many times over, Liberia is the finest country for the colored man, for here he may live by the sweat of his brow, though

everything remains scarce and high, such as provisions, clothing, etc. There are still many more arriving with each ship, who are not prepared for freedom, and who get on poorly because there is no one to act for them, and they are totally incapable of acting for themselves.[100]

As is the case in both *Cambridge* and *The Longest Memory*, the reader is left to judge and assess Nash's transparently flawed assertions. How do we weigh Nash's belief in the idea that he remains "transformed" against the condescending racism that awards him the label of a gentleman? How do we balance his overstated confidence in the power of his own labor against the obvious fact that he has been sent to Liberia without sufficient resources to survive? What do we make of his inclination to discredit the motives of others returning to Africa? Nash badly needs to believe in his mission, but it is obvious to the reader than he is up against insurmountable odds; climate and illness as well as a pressing lack of resources take their toll. Yet in his letters he avoids blaming Edward directly. Up until the very end of his correspondence, his subservience prevents him from writing in anger, even when it appears that Edward has most reprehensibly forsaken him. Instead, he tends to blame himself:

> Why, dear Father, you chose to ignore my previous letters, you do not indicate. I must assume that this represents your either not receiving them, or your finding their contents so ignorant and poor in expression that you rightly deemed them unworthy of response.[101]

The tension in this story arises as a result of important gaps between Nash's letters and the third-person, omniscient narration that describes Edward's journey. After Edward writes an initial letter to Nash, the narrator tells the reader that Edward's wife intercepted this response to Nash, apparently keeping Nash's letters from her husband as well: "Never again did Edward receive intelligence that his former bondsman Nash had either disobeyed his instruction, put himself in any mortal danger or done anything that might lead Edward once more to consider reaching for pen and composing lines for disapproval."[102] The result is that Nash struggles on, unsupported and beset by a series of tragic events that finally lead him to abandon his Christianity in favor of a more "primitive" lifestyle, as part of which he takes several wives and adopts other African practices. His last letter to Edward is dated January 3, 1842:

I believed fiercely in all that you related to me, and fervently hoped that one day I might be worthy of the name I bore, the learning I had been blessed with, and the kind attentions of a master with the teachings of the Lord fused into his soul. That my faith in you is broken, is evident.[103]

Gradually the reader understands that the story of the two men is further complicated by the fact that Edward is most likely a pederast. The novel does not foreground this fact but merely folds it into Edward's consciousness, where it rests uneasily mostly because of its consequences for his marriage.[104] Here the narrator conveys the tenor of Edward's troubled process of recollecting his wife:

> That she took it upon herself to sabotage her husband's relationship with Nash by destroying the colored man's letters was a painful discovery for Edward, but had he not found it in his heart to forgive her? Her accusation that in the wake of Nash's departure he was now making a fool of himself by lavishing an excess of affection upon a new retainer, was this not again met with forgiveness? That she had subsequently chosen to flee his home, then this mortal world at the instigation of her own hand, was a tragedy the responsibility for which could not reside at Edward's doorstep.[105]

Yet what is the aim of such characterization? Moreover, what is at stake in both the intertwined and complicated histories of Edward and Nash? Like Whitechapel and Mr. Whitechapel in *The Longest Memory*, Edward and Nash rely on each other for their self-definition. Like Whitechapel, Nash needs to maintain a sense of agency despite the crushing conditions of his life. Nash also needs to believe that he has made the right choice. He invests in the idea of Edward as a benevolent and well-intentioned master because he craves the respect he finds in the white man's investment in him. Nash may come across as self-deluding, but he is also courageous and resourceful. Phillips avoids turning him into the "victim" of a racist ideology. Nor does he flatten out the portrait. Instead, he leaves Nash's motives ambiguous. With a nod to Marlow's discovery of Kurtz in *Heart of Darkness*, the narrative passes no clear judgment on the bleak African settlement that Nash founds. Instead, it narrates Edward's utter incomprehension and profound sense of dislocation as he confronts Nash's legacy:

Everywhere he turned, Edward's eyes were assaulted by natives who squatted idly, their bodies resting awkwardly on their foundations, like their infantile shacks. Edward attempted to paint his face with a thinly benevolent smile, but realized that he was ill-equipped to disguise his true feelings of disgust in the midst of this specter of peopled desolation.[106]

In short, in Nash's portrait we are shown how a cultural hybridity such as his entails "the intricate processes of cultural contact, intrusion, fusion and disjunction."[107]

Edward is a similarly complex character. Phillips portrays him as a weak man who is not in control of himself or his own actions. Despite the utter blameworthiness of his actions, it is possible to feel some empathy for him. Edwards is often pitiful, as alienated from white society as he is from black. For example, when a black liveried servant inexplicably bars him from the club of the American Colonization Society in Monrovia, Edward "tarried a moment, scratched the skin under one eye, then realizing he was making little headway, turned on his heels, anxious that he should avoid having to suffer the ignominy of the door being slammed in his face."[108] Edward and Nash are hardly antagonists; rather, they are two men relatively positioned in a complicated human drama that defies a final assessment.

To see the full import of their story, the reader needs to look outside this narrative, to the other three narratives that compose the polyphonic message of the novel. Phillips's Virginian plantation owner shares the stage with another racist character, James Hamilton, the captain of a slave ship, who becomes the subject of Part III, ironically entitled "Crossing the River."[109] Here the main character writes home to his wife. His "professional," objective, and detached observations on the business of trading slaves contrast with his romantic letters to his wife, to whom he explains that the travails of the commerce "are, indeed, petty concerns when set against my love for you, for I can declare, with honor, that barely an hour of my past life comes to mind with any pleasure excepting valuable and precious time I have passed in your company."[110] Hamilton's letters are a pastiche of *John Newton's Letters to a Wife. Written during Three Voyages to Africa, from 1750–1754*, a fact that Phillips freely acknowledges. Yet this particular use of pastiche has generated some controversy.

For example, in *Slavery, Empathy, and Pornography*, Marcus Wood argues that it is difficult to tell the difference between Phillips's acts of creation and appropriation. He charges that Phillips fails to transform Newton's text into anything new and that Phillips's pastiche "reduces the complexities and complicities of the original." He further argues that we ought to protect the "ghastly authenticity" of Newton's text, Newton's voice being "more incredible and terrible" than Hamilton's. Finally, he asks: "What if the act of transposition exploits the power of Newton's historical specificity because the imaginative vision of the late twentieth century cannot invent anything more powerful than the words Newton has already made/written/invented/recorded?"[111] Thus, Wood implicitly argues the need to confront a horrific historical reality that is only distorted by what he perceives as a postmodern game.

However, Wood fails to take account of the formal integrity of the novel. Hamilton's letters are meant to be part of a series of interlocking pieces, each commenting on the other. As Gail Low says, "Hamilton's log book account of buying and selling, and the strategic maneuvers he undertakes to secure the slaves and commodities at the price he desires comes as a shock after the human pathos and tragedy of Martha's story,"[112] the story told in Part II. But Hamilton's logbook also contrasts with the omniscient narration that takes us inside Edward Williams's head and allows us to see how he explains away the responsibility for his own actions. Hamilton's voice counterpoints Nash's letters as well. Taken together, all three forms of narration comment on the process of turning events of the African slave trade into narrative. All three tell us how individuals attempted, in various forms, to "make sense" of their experience, often eliding the truly horrific in the process. All three forms of narration, in other words, expose the complicity of narrative in silencing or repressing something that resists being said. The content of the silenced or repressed may differ—for example, Nash may avoid speaking of the fact that he feels betrayed, and Hamilton may avoid speaking of the humanity of his "cargo." Nonetheless, the larger point is that the only "essential" truth is, paradoxically, the fact that truth is always embedded in some narrative process. Although there may be a "ghastly authenticity" to Newton's account, it is not diminished by a postmodern strategy that forces the reader to become self-conscious about the relationship between narrative and historical "reality."

Part II of *Crossing the River* expands the idea of the diaspora to the American West, during and after the Civil War. Martha is a runaway slave from Kansas who crosses the continent in an unsuccessful attempt to find her daughter, who had been taken from her and sold. The shortest of the novel's narratives, "West" places formerly enslaved Africans in an unusual setting and fleshes out a black history that is not often told—that of a black underclass of cooks, restaurant worker, and launderers, as well as the black pioneers who make up a "colored exodus"[113] of what Indians call "the dark white men" heading west.[114] But she dies in Denver, without anyone knowing her name. Gail Low argues that Martha "lies at the novel's heart and occupies a privileged position by being the figure who hears voices of other kinsfolk calling out not to be forgotten or forsaken."[115] Yet, although thematically central, Martha's story is more predictable and less compelling than other stories in the novel; that a man to whom Martha is attached is killed in a shootout suggests a myriad of stories of the Old West, for instance. Phillips covers more original ground in his portrayal of the novel's last protagonist, a white woman living in rural England during the Second World War.

Like Part II, Part IV, "Somewhere in England," is narrated from a female point of view. It tells the story of Joyce, a shopkeeper, who falls in love with a black American GI named Travis who is stationed in her small English village during World War II. She eventually conceives a child, and they marry while he is on furlough from the Italian front. When he dies in action, she is coerced into giving up her child as an orphan to the care of the County Council. The story ends with Joyce and her son about to become reacquainted in 1963. The particular brilliance of this story lies in the way it is narrated to show how racial difference is simultaneously invisible to Joyce yet utterly constitutive of her romance; although she initially does not see Travis as a black man, the fact that he is black determines every aspect of their love affair. In addition, the story of Joyce and Travis becomes the novel's ultimate comment on black and white relations. In particular, it shows how the African slave trade, although indisputably entailing massive human suffering, separation, and alienation, could also precipitate profound personal connections.

At first, Joyce only mentions the presence of the "bloody yanks," men who are outsiders by virtue of their nationality. Unlike her neighbors, Joyce is not bothered by their being there: "But our lot are quiet. They keep themselves to themselves, and when they meet us they seem polite. I see them going about their business."[116] An American officer visits to prepare her for the appearance of the black soldiers, saying apologetically, "It's just that they're different—We're not sending you a problem or anything,"[117] but Joyce still does not fully register the comment as racist, apparently thinking instead that the officer refers to national differences. Because Joyce does not pick up on the racial insinuation, at first neither does the reader, and so Travis's race is not specified for the first part of the narrative.[118] When he and a friend visit Joyce in the shop to invite her to a dance, she refers only to their relative heights (one tall, one not so tall but not short), their body types (stocky), and their demeanor (polite).[119] Later, when she and Travis start off the dance by venturing onto the dance floor, she is certain that everyone is staring at her, as someone who has always been at odds with local custom. Even when she is physically very close to Travis, what she notices is the unusual gap in his teeth in the middle of the bottom row.[120] Finally, her observations on his hairstyle, not his skin color, clinch the profile for the reader: "His hair is well-combed, with a sort of razor parting on the left. It's short, like thin black wool, but he puts some oil or something on it because it shines in the light."[121]

The effect of this narrative approach is to take the reader inside the mind of someone who is in fact color-blind, as well as to simulate the experience of color-blindness in the reader. Similar to the movie *Suture*, which presents a black actor whom none of the other characters seem to notice is black,[122] the narrative forces the reader to be "color-blind" and to consider what the world would look like if skin color were no longer the primary category of identification. Joyce narrates how she gradually comes to understand who Travis is:

> Most of the time I just listened, for he talked more than I did. He told me a bit about himself, and why he joined the army. Me, I didn't know much about Americans. Or Coloureds. I was sure that I was going to make a mistake. Bound to. So I said nothing. I just kept my mouth shut and listened to him talking in that sing-song accent of his. I like it.[123]

On the one hand, she is naive enough not to know that Travis will be beaten for being out with her. But on the other hand, she is courageous enough to go to the military base, confront the white officers, and seek out the truth concerning his punishment. The racism of other people seems truly mystifying to her, but then so do many of their other attitudes, and Joyce is profoundly alienated from her family, husband, and most of her neighbors. With few exceptions, Joyce paints the villagers as unsavory types, narrow-minded and self-interested people in whom the war has not brought out the best instincts. For example, Len, Joyce's husband, from whom she eventually obtains a divorce, spends most of the war in prison for profiteering. Len's friend, a soldier on the front, comes home on leave to brutally murder his wife, who has become pregnant by his best friend in his absence. Joyce is both socially and spiritually isolated from the other villagers, and this fact is her point of pride. At the dance, Travis asks her if she is "from around here." He then explains why he asked: "'I was just wondering. I don't know. I guess you don't act like them in some ways. Can't say how, but just different.' Inside I was smiling. That was just what I wanted to hear."[124]

Using Joyce as his narrator requires that Phillips limit his story to what she can and cannot see and to what she does and does not understand. However, Joyce's story is initially difficult to follow because of a narrative style that fractures the pieces of her life, breaking it into short vignettes, from one paragraph to several pages in length. Covering a period from July 1936, when Joyce was 18, to 1963, the vignettes limn the formative events of her adult life, including her first love affair, her abortion, her courtship and marriage to Len, her rapid disillusionment with him, her isolation as his wife in a provincial English village, and her attempts to make a new life once he is in prison. But these events are not chronologically arranged. For example, the first event, from July 1936, is located at the dead center of the story, directly after a scene from February 1941. As a result, readers must do the work of making the story cohere. As if constructing a mosaic, they must piece together the history of the romance between Joyce and Travis, and this mental activity works against an emotional investment in the love story. When closure does come, it takes the form not of the biracial, romantic coupling but of Joyce's reunion with her now-grown son. Even then, the story appears to start all over, as Joyce worries when he suddenly appears: "I knew I looked awful, but there wasn't any time to fret over appearances. Not now. I took a deep breath and turned to face him. I almost said make yourself at home, but I didn't. At least I avoided that. Sit down. Please, sit down."[125] In the novel as a whole, Joyce's story and the other three narratives are framed by two short pieces in which a nameless African father, speaking without being located in time or space, tells how he sold his children when his crops failed. His voice is woven seamlessly into at least two other voices: one of a white slave trader, the other belonging, at different moments, to different characters in the novel. Similar to Whitechapel's narrative in *The Longest Memory*, this framing encompasses the various tensions in the stories and recuperates all who have been lost or abandoned in their diasporic travels. Scanning the globe, this father figure finds his progeny in a variety of socioeconomic settings and circumstances in London, Paris, Brooklyn, São Paulo, Santo Domingo, Charleston, Oakland, the Caribbean, and Stockholm. But what does it mean for him specifically to reclaim not only Nash, Martha, and Travis, but Joyce as well? In fact, why should a story about the African diaspora privilege this white female character at all?

In an interview Phillips acknowledged that while writing the novel he was unable find a voice for Travis. But Joyce appeared and spoke to him in a Yorkshire dialect that he knew from his childhood.[126] Yet clearly Joyce has additional importance to the novel's themes, as becomes clear in its final words, spoken by the nameless African father:

> All. Hurt but determined. Only if they panic will they break their wrists and ankles against Captain Hamilton's instruments. A guilty father. Always listening. There are no paths in the water. No signposts. There is no return. A desperate foolishness. The crops failed. I sold my beloved children. *Bought 2 strong man-boys, and a proud girl.* But they arrived on the far bank of the river, loved.[127]

Thus, by loving Travis as a man—and not as someone marked by race—Joyce redeems both him and herself. Their romance thwarts a series of binaries—not only man/woman and black/white but also oppressor/victim. However, Phillips is neither sentimental nor necessarily sanguine about the nature of Joyce's love as transcendent gesture—we remember that she forbears telling her son to make himself at home, and it is unclear what the future holds for the reunited mother and son.

For Bénédicte Ledent, this ending offers the reader "not a blind escape into universality, which would signify the erasure of all differences into a supposedly neutral, yet Eurocentric, globality." Instead, Phillips offers "a genuinely cross-cultural dimension in which identities intertwine in ever-changing and unstable patterns."[128] Indeed, the untold story of Joyce and her grown-up, biracial son gestures toward painful interpersonal work that lies yet in the future, as the legacy of the African slave trade continues to shape human relations into the twenty-first century. Rather than having told *an* untold story of the African holocaust, Phillips has told several—including, most important of all, a "story" of how such a painful and conflicted narrative continually makes and remakes itself.

To summarize, then, the novels under discussion in this section have been less concerned with recovering *a* historical past and more interested in foregrounding the multiple narrative strategies that make it possible for us to know the past. Evincing a suspicion in the idea of totalizing narratives, and investing instead in the idea of pluralistic perspectives, these novels offer not the "whole picture" but pieces of stories that overlap, collide, and yet somehow cohere into meaningful statements. In these novels, the reader has the burden of making sense and doing the work of sifting through the various accounts. In the process, we learn to be wary of the idea of *the* truth and to attend to the role of language in conveying what purports to be truth. We learn as well to resist the binary impulses that prove fruitless in our attempt to come to terms with the legacy of the African slave trade. In the next section, we look at two novels that differ not only in their use of binary categories but also in their response to the demands of a popular audience.

Telling the Untold Story in *A Respectable Trade* and *A Harlot's Progress*

In the first chapter of this book, considering the statue of Colston in the city of Bristol led to a series of unsettling questions: What if the "untold story" of the African slave trade was to Colston not a story at all? Or, by extension, what if the "truth" is not simply the opposite of an "untruth"? What if speech is not simply the opposite of silence? In a world of such obfuscation, what would happen to the other oppositions that hang on the difference between a "told" and an "untold" story about a racial injustice? In this final section, my purpose is to critique the notion of telling the untold story, precisely because we stand to learn much more than some narratives have been willing to tell us. As we have seen in this chapter, the story of Britain's slave trade is best understood not as *a* story to be told but a series of messy, overlapping narratives of competing voices. Moreover, it may be the case that dangers lie in designating an untold story a told story when so much awaits discussion, however painful or confusing that discussion may turn out to be. A comparison of Philippa Gregory's *A Respectable Trade* (1995) and David Dabydeen's *A Harlot's Progress* (1999) takes us, then, to the question of the larger stakes of any popular attempt to "tell the untold."

Like the other novels we have discussed so far, both of these books are addressed to an audience ready to listen to a story they believe they have been denied. Set in 1787, *A Respectable Trade* tells the story of Frances Scott, the genteel wife of a Bristol trader, who falls in love with her Yoruba slave Mehuru and subsequently dies while giving birth to their child. As Dabydeen's title suggests, *A Harlot's Progress* retells Hogarth's story, this time from the point of view of the black slave who appears in the second plate of the eponymous series. But if both novels tell untold stories, they do so with a major difference. Whereas Gregory participates in the binary opposition that characterizes much contemporary popular thinking about the circum-Atlantic slave trade, Dabydeen's purpose is to shatter the binary, embedding untold in the told and silence in speech. Furthermore, whereas *A Respectable Trade* thematizes commodification and sensual fulfillment as opposites, Dabydeen demonstrates how a heightened craving for sensual experience inheres in a world of commodified human experience. In *A Respectable Trade*, suffering banishes the aesthetic; in *A Harlot's Progress*, beauty is coextensive with pain. Gregory's moral purpose deserves to be taken no less seriously than Dabydeen's, yet both the theme and the structure of a romance plot hamper that purpose. The transracial heterosexuality offered as the antidote to the commodification of race ultimately disappoints because it blurs what should be brought into sharpest relief: black and white—like male and female—are not clear "opposites" to be reconciled but messy categories that mutually constitute one another. In the end, reading *A Respectable Trade* against *A Harlot's Progress* not only illuminates the difference between a popular and postmodern approach to the eighteenth-century slave trade, but it also suggests how our fantasies of closure on this issue remain necessarily premature.

Gregory told *Radio Times* in 1998 that, as the child of parents who lived in Kenya until the early 1950s, she felt the need to communicate the truth about an African past: "With *A Respectable Trade*, I wanted to write something that celebrated the power of black survival and that confronted some of the myths about pre-slavery Africa. These people were not living in mud huts like savages; there were some very sophisticated cultures already in Africa." In statements such as the following, she announced the moral purpose of her fiction, a purpose that was taken seriously by her critics: "I would say that it's high time everybody in Britain was aware that slavery was not something that just happened in America and the West Indies. The principal beneficiaries of the slave trade were British individuals and companies, some of which are still trading. It is a 200-year-old injustice but it is still important in historical terms that there is a recognition of that injustice."[129] A well-respected author of contemporary fiction in Britain, Gregory was clearly a forerunner in the attempt to bring a difficult topic before a broad public audience. There were risks to the project, as also noted in *Radio Times*: "Anyone in search of quirky costume drama will be disappointed: what we have is something that puts our emotions through the wringer."[130]

In the novel, Gregory employs third-person omniscient narration, moving among several points of view, chiefly those of Mehuru; Frances; Frances's husband, Josiah; and her sister-in-law Sarah. The movement among the various points of view facilitates the reader's sense of contrasting perspectives. What looks like a perfectly respectable sitting room to Sarah, the daughter of a simple trader, is to Frances, former resident of Lord Scott's estate, an appallingly shabby and inhospitable little room. Both class and gender determine how the world appears to an individual, and the novel depicts the tragedy that occurs when individuals cannot bring their perspectives into alignment. But the story further suggests how cultural perspectives can similarly distort perception. Through the lens of her racist culture, Sarah simply fails to recognize the basic humanity of her brother's slaves. Choosing Mehuru as a central character and giving him a point of view allows Gregory to suggest how the Other looks back. Through Mehuru's eyes, we see not only the horrific conditions of the Middle Passage but also first impressions of white femininity. The view is not flattering: "[Frances's] looks were horrible. She was as smooth and as pale as polished ivory. But the worst thing about her was her hair, which was as long and as thick as weeds in the river and was piled upon her head with trails of it coming down around her shoulders and curling like water weed around her face . . . she moved . . . with small steps and a hunched body as if she hated herself, as if she were trying to hide her breasts and her belly."[131] Like Barbara Kingsolver in *The Poisonwood Bible*, Gregory seeks to decenter a Eurocentric viewpoint. She reminds her readers that the victims of the slave trade were not only objects but also subjects; black

Africans sold into slavery looked back, and what they saw were whites in their ugliest moments.

In contrast to Gregory's third-person omniscient narrator, Dabydeen alternates a first-person narrator with a third-person narrator who may occasionally be the protagonist himself. From the very beginning, Dabydeen's narration complicates the category of the told and untold, reminding the reader that what gets told depends very much not only on who asks for the story but also on what motivates the telling. Thus, like Phillips, he often employs a kind of pastiche in which fictional characters are barely fictional at all: Mr. Pringle, for instance, seems to both be and not be Thomas Pringle (1789–1834), an abolitionist who went to South Africa in 1820, where he edited two periodicals. Upon his return to London, he befriended Mary Price and edited her memoirs.[132] Similarly, the slaver Thistlewood is also only partly fictional.[133] In the novel, Pringle has come to record Mungo's story, hoping to capture with his pen a story that will galvanize his movement: "'Something must be said,' Mr. Pringle urges, 'there must be a story. . . . A beginning, Mungo.'"[134] Mungo is, from the start, acutely aware of a pressing need to tell, since his survival depends on the coins Pringle will give him if he is pleased with the story: "But a man has got to be grateful and feed Mr. Pringle's curiosity in return for all the pity he lavish on me, the shilling here, the new breeches there."[135]

At the same time, Mungo is equally aware that he must tell Pringle only what the abolitionist wants to hear—the story must have a shape and rhythm that Pringle can recognize, although the cacophony of Mungo's thoughts defies his efforts to narrate. The story must also leave out as much as it includes. It must not speak of what Pringle does not want to hear. For example, it must repress the slaver Thistlewood's pederasty, and it cannot speak of the Jew's essential humanity. Mungo exercises a powerful self-censorship in his dealings with Pringle, for which he is chastised by his ghosts:

> "Perhaps you should curse them outright as white devils, tell the story as it is and not bother with the consequences," Ellar says, sensing his anxiety.
> "What more can they do to you worse than slavery?"
> "They can refuse to buy my book, and I'll starve," [Mungo] says quietly to himself.[136]

The story Mungo hears in his head—the story he shares with the reader—defies logic, linearity, and reason. In that story, past and present, here and there, living and dead, and truth and lies, exist side by side. Even the protagonist's name is subject to revision—Mungo becomes Noah, who later answers to the name Perseus. The reader is privy to what Pringle is not: the chaos of Mungo's consciousness. Nonetheless, as a consumer of the text, the reader remains implicated in the commodification of Mungo's story. Like any story brought to market, this novel simply cannot and does not tell all. Dabydeen suggests that his story is inevitably "broken" even in the design of the first edition. The paperback cover of the first printing is unevenly laminated to imitate broken glass so convincingly that the book looks damaged. (I put back the first copy in the pile, thinking I could find a better copy.) Thus, Dabydeen's novel suggests the difficulty of telling the untold. At best, the told is a provisional category. Our knowledge of this will ultimately affect our ability to pass judgment on the characters of the novel.

In contrast, *A Respectable Trade* not only asks us to pass judgment but also makes clear at every turn what that judgment must be. Although we are encouraged to empathize with the antagonists as they err, and effort is made to retain the semblance of a complex, although flawed, human psychology, the novel is unequivocal about the roots of good and evil. Thus, "bad" characters consistently oppose "good," with the line drawn first between those who trade and those who do not. The novel opens by contrasting Mehuru in his precaptive days as a priest in the city of Oyo with Josiah Cole, the Bristol merchant in possession of only three ships who dreams of enhancing his business. Powerful sensual imagery situates Mehuru in his idyllic African world: "Mehuru woke at dawn with the air cool on his outstretched body. He opened his eyes in the half-darkness and sniffed the air as if the light wind might bring him some strange scent. His dream, an uneasy vision of a ship slipping her anchor in shadows and sailing quietly down a deep rocky gorge, was with him still."[137]

Meanwhile, Josiah is given an utterly bourgeois ambition: he wants to rise to the level of merchant-venturer. Gregory's trader is in every way a small man, driven by the wrong ambition into "social acceptance by the greater men of the city."[138] From his narrow point of view: "Without their friendship he could not make money, without money he could not buy friendship. It was a treadmill—no future for a man. The greater men ran the port and the city of Bristol. Without them Josiah would forever cling to the side of the dock, to the side of the Trade, like a rat on a hemp rope."[139] He offers marriage to Frances Scott, spinster niece to Lord Scott, as a business move—he plans to have Frances teach and train his slaves as house servants, thereby making them into even more profitable commodities. Besides, he hopes to exploit the name and connections Frances will bring. Everything Josiah touches is tainted by commodification.

Mehuru, in contrast, comes from a people who refuse to engage in commodifying practices. The first chapter of *A Respectable Trade* culminates ironically, with Mehuru's king prohibiting slave trading with white men of any nation. In the face of contested historical evidence of African complicity in the trade (in the writings of James Walvin and elsewhere), Gregory chooses this scene to establish a clear-cut opposition between the two men in her protagonist's life. This opposition is further drawn out—a trader who has spent all his life at the dockside, Josiah is also sensually inert. Most comfortable amid the stultifying odors and the noisy din of the waterside, he proves incapable of distinguishing true aesthetic value from mere ostentation, even as his genteel wife tries to teach him the difference. Needless to say, this lack of sensuality makes him the less-than-ideal sexual partner for Frances. In contrast, Mehuru is an extremely sensual individual who responds deeply to beauty and whose sensibilities, we are told, lie in a deep appreciation of the natural world. Having noticed Frances's fondness for flowers, he takes money from Josiah to buy Frances enough to entirely cover a bed.[140] In a scene that borrows its conventions from romance, he becomes Frances's dream lover on that very same bed. We are encouraged to trace this extraordinary sensuality not only to Mehuru's African origins but also to the fact that he does not commodify. Instead, like Frances, he is a commodity himself.

If it is disappointing to find a novel that purports to confront myths about Africa collapsing into clichés about the inordinate sensuality of African culture, it is equally troubling to recognize how commodifying practice—the "trade" referred to in the oxymoronic title—is here scapegoated as the cause of what goes wrong in the novel, from Josiah's callous indifference to his slave's obvious humanity to his inability to respond to sensual stimuli. Without defending commodification, it is nonetheless possible to criticize a position that aligns commodification with a dead sensuality and the absence of commodifying practice with sensual fulfillment.[141] The opposition between Mehuru and Josiah depends on the notion that a "deeper" or "more true" subjectivity can reside only where a commodifying mentality has not taken hold. However, it is equally possible, as has been argued elsewhere, that the illusion of a deep sensibility occurs in relation to the rise of practices of commodification[142] and that, far from deadening our receptivity to the sensual world, contact with commodification enhances it. The latter point is developed in *A Harlot's Progress*, where, as we will see, the slaver's inordinate craving for sensual experience is rooted precisely in his role as trader.

For Gregory, the distinction between those who commodify and those who do not is also signified as a class difference. Frances and Mehuru are both impoverished (albeit in relative terms, Frances bringing her meager dowry to her marriage), but lack of wealth ennobles them and paradoxically sets them apart as elite. In contrast, Josiah and his sister, as commercial people, are depicted as bodies without a single refined bone. This class difference was accentuated in the casting of the television version. The actors playing Mehuru and Frances, Ariyon Bakare and Emma Fielding, have delicate features—aquiline noses and thin lips—whereas the actor playing Josiah Cole, Warren Clarke, is a bulky man with a wide nose and large hands and feet. As black and white visual complements, Frances and Mehuru appear to be of the same "race," in the premodern sense of the term, before skin color was the determining factor; Josiah clearly issues from different stock.

Although in strictly formal terms, Frances is placed between the two men, with her necessary choice between them as a major force behind the plot, she is actually positioned on only one side of the binary opposition that divides the morally correct from the incorrect. Like Mehuru, she is a commodity to be traded. Also like Mehuru, she resists the commodifying practices that go on around her. Unlike either her husband or his sister, she recognizes rather quickly the inhumanity of trade and the human misery it causes: "She looked around the cellar at the thirteen black faces still as heartbroken statues in the shadows. The cruelty of the Trade suddenly opened before her, like a glimpse of hell beneath her feet. 'I did not know,' she said."[143] Again like Mehuru, she demonstrates a refined aesthetic sensibility, which is located in her refined upbringing. The daughter of a now-deceased clergyman who failed to provide adequately for her, Frances aimed too high in marriage. As a result, at thirty-four, she finds herself with two equally impossible options: to stay on as an unwanted "poor relation" in the house of her uncle Lord Scott or to work as a governess. Her marriage to Cole brings her not only far from the aristocratic comforts to which she is accustomed but also far from the salubrious English countryside that is her "natural" setting. Like Fanny Price exiled to Portsmouth, Frances in Bristol misses the clean air, the lush vegetation, the changing seasons. Moreover, Frances is given a "delicate constitution," a hereditary weakness of heart and lungs that symbolizes her vulnerability to her husband's harsh, commercial climate—whereas her mercantile sister-in-law thrives on the polluted urban air, Frances will be literally killed by it.

However, this association of Frances with the purity of the English country estate, like Jane Austen's alignment of Fanny Price with the salutary seasons of *Mansfield Park*, is arguably disingenuous; although neither female character engages in commercial enterprise, both would have been the indirect recipients of its proceeds. The Mansfield Park that Fanny comes to inhabit at the end of Austen's novel is an estate that has been enriched with West Indian sugar money, an idea that is directly taken up in Patricia Rozema's screenplay for the movie version of the novel. Similarly, the hospitality Frances enjoys at her uncle's estate is underwritten by a number of commercial enterprises, among them, we are told, a mine. Gregory's novel would have us fantasize about a class of individuals whose motives transcend profit making, whose subjectivity precedes the greedy pull of market. However, the distinction rings false in a world where "independent wealth" is in fact only an illusion.

Her sexual awakening and successful bearing of a half-African child precedes Frances's death. Mehuru is depicted as the source of her sexual fulfillment, as she gradually perceives that contact with him brings "fresh air" to her household: "She did not know why she suddenly felt as if joy were possible. She did not know why the air seemed a little cleaner and the house less oppressive."[144] A mythical "Africa" is evoked as the restorative alternative to the polluted air of Bristol. It is depicted as an idyllic place of sensual fulfillment, a place where sound, sight, hearing, taste, and touch are enhanced, and a place unspoiled by human contact, let alone cultural struggle. To soothe Frances to sleep, Mehuru describes his homeland: "You will like [Africa]. The trees on the plains are so broad and strong, their shade is sweet. When the wind is high in the palm trees they rattle and roar like a rainstorm. When it is calm you can hear a hundred, a thousand birds singing. The rivers are deep and very green, they carry the reflection of the forest so clearly that it is like two forests."[145] What he offers is a child's version of geography, a Disney-like landscape antithetical to Marlow's in *Heart of Darkness*. Where Marlow encounters a powerful white man "consumed" by primeval forces, Mehuru fantasizes about swimming in a place where "the little fish will swim around [Frances] and nibble at [her] white skin."[146] Consumption itself is rendered innocuous, untainted by any profit motive, as nature yields itself up for the white woman's taking: "I shall take you into the forest and you can eat all sorts of sweet fruits that are growing for free, Frances. No-one owns them, you can eat them all, you can eat all day if you want."[147]

As Frances moves closer to embracing Mehuru, Gregory's psychological realism is crowded out by a style that is clearly "romantic," as described by Janice Radway in her classic study, *Reading the Romance*. Radway hypothesizes that women readers' involvement with romance fiction entails a desire to be loved in a nurturant fashion.[148] Although *A Respectable Trade* is complicated by the fact that Frances owns the man she wants to own her, its recourse to conventional romance is readily apparent, as in the following passage:

> As [Frances] pushed her face into her pillow to weep without restraint for the first time in her life she acknowledged at last her vision of Mehuru as the only man in the world who could save her from the icy death-in-life of ladylike English behaviour, and she knew that for the first time in her life she had fallen, irretrievably and completely, in love.[149]

As Radway further explains, romantic fantasy is a fantasy about a "ritual wish to be cared for, loved, and validated in a particular way."[150] This "ritual wish" is expressed in a scene describing how Frances and Mehuru consummate their affair.

> He reached out his hand to her and put his finger against her cheek. Frances closed her eyes and leaned towards him. His desire for her rose up and he caught her to him and held her, feeling the warmth of her body against him, and the pleasure of her lips under his as she returned and sought his kisses. Mehuru lifted her easily in his arms, went into her bedroom, and tumbled her on to the bed as recklessly as he had thrown the flowers.[151]

At such a moment, many readers may be willing to suspend disbelief and find this unlikely coupling historically plausible. Walvin, for one, describes some "well-publicized cases" of women eloping with black servants in the 1790s.[152]

Thus, the problem is neither that the plot lapses into romance nor that it appears historically inappropriate. Rather, the problem is that romance conventions pull the reader in one direction while historical realism pulls in the other, bifurcating the story into its two genres. This scene of Frances's romantic sexual fulfillment contrasts with an earlier scene in Chapter Ten, where Frances overhears the brutal rape of a slave by a visiting Jamaican planter. In a vain attempt to stave off her rapist, the woman frantically cries out the one English word that Frances has taught her: "Table." Frances "was seated before her dressing table looking at her white face in the pier glass when she heard one scream of pure pain, quickly muffled by a heavy hand."[153] That she sees her own reflection at the moment of the rape may suggest that the victim is her double. Yet her privileged position on the other side of the door also protects her from harm. The slave, who calls herself Died of Shame, soon kills herself. Mehuru observes her death:

> He heard her moving softly in the darkness, lying down and wrapping her arms around herself. He heard her muffled lips name the people she loved, her little son, her husband, her mother, and the ancestors who might come to her, who might, despite all that was wrong in her life, forgive her. And then he heard the long silence of a woman waiting for death.[154]

Both Frances and the enslaved woman experience interracial sex, but Frances is given both the power to choose her partner and the freedom to desire. Through the third-person narrator, the reader becomes privy to Frances's pleasure and sense of fulfillment whereas the enslaved woman's torture is narrated only in terms of the effect it has on Frances. This has the effect of once more relegating Died of Shame to silence.

The conventions of romance demand that Frances find fulfillment only in her lover and he only in her: "'You are the first woman I have ever loved in my life, Frances, and I know now that it was a mistake for me. There is too much that separates us. Our color is less important than everything else.' His gesture took in their politics, their culture, their expectations, and their sense of what was important."[155] As we have already seen, despite their races, regardless of their cultural differences, Mehuru and Frances do belong together. They are a perfectly "matched pair." When she dies in childbirth, he reclaims her as his African bride: "'She is an African woman now. She is the wife of a Yoruba, she is the mother of my child.'"[156] However, memorializing Frances in this fashion has the inadvertent effect of effacing all the other black women in the novel, Died of Shame among them. Mehuru takes as his mission the curing of Frances's cultural malaise. But he is seen as powerless to help his African sisters. This is not the story of how he comes to "save" anyone but Frances.

The raped woman's tragedy is an event that ultimately serves to bring the romantic couple closer together, while the rape victim is consigned to her wordless suffering. Is Gregory thematizing, then, the silence of those who are powerless to protect themselves, or is she inadvertently exploiting it by having the one woman's pain become the necessary catalyst to another woman's fulfillment? The rape is only the first in a series of events leading to Frances's growing political consciousness. Her political and sexual awakening are depicted as simultaneous; the process of coming to terms first with the barbarity of the slave trade and then with Mehuru's full human dignity allows her to reach her sexual potential. Yet in this way, the novel repeats a trope found too often in popular culture. As Valerie Smith points out, too often "black women are employed, if not sacrificed, to humanize their white superordinates, to teach them something about the content of their own subject positions."[157]

Ultimately, *A Respectable Trade* founders on its dual purpose. Although it is serious in its attempt to tell an untold story and restore to African culture and heritage its rightful ascendancy, and it has important messages about decentering a Eurocentric perspective, it nonetheless cannot fulfill its promises to tell an African story. It is hampered by the conventions of romance, which reduce racial tensions to a binary to be reconciled through the deep attraction of a woman to a man. The heterosexual fantasy of male and female complements is also the fantasy of black and white meeting on a common ground, before an originary cause—commodification—estranged individuals from each other and from their own true natures. Gregory affords her heroine a tragic death, as if to concede the impractical nature of the black–white union. But she gives her reader a happy ending nonetheless—on her deathbed, Frances frees

Mehuru, leaving testimony that conveys hope for the future. Both thematically and structurally the novel moves toward closure.

In contrast to the privileging of the romance paradigm in *A Respectable Trade*, *A Harlot's Progress* resists both a romantic interpretation of sexuality and the closure it brings through a Blakean confounding of pain and love, violation and adoration. In Dabydeen's novel, the slaver Thomas Thistlewood is a pederast taking masochistic pleasure from the body of the boy slave whom, in his own way, he genuinely grows to love. In return, the young Mungo confuses pain with affection: "He pushed me to the ground in a reflex action, stamped his feet at my crotch, kicked me, and kicked me, until I fainted with the love."[158] Rather than hate his abuser, Mungo admires, even venerates him, taking to heart Thistlewood's message that the abuse—as well as the religious indoctrination that accompanies it—is for his own good. Yet this is not a simple case of a child's internalizing what his abuser tells him, for Mungo also has the power to see into the state of Thistlewood's soul:

> Still, I do not fear him, for his pain is great, more than my own, so I take his kick and blow and cease to moan and cry. I do not mind his strange ways from the time one night when he think I am in sleep, numb by wine, and he light his lamp and I peep as he goes to kneel to his blue God, and a huge sob break from his throat and his breast break in grief. He is mad in truth, mad, but I am sad for him, sad for the land he so loves but is far from, and for all the birds and beasts who are dead in the land.[159]

Dabydeen gives Thistlewood a complex, if perverted, psychology. In particular, Thistlewood reverently worships a mythical lost Albion, "a heaven of falcons and kingfishers and an earth roamed by hart and noble unicorn."[160]

The narrative underscores that Thistlewood's involvement with commodifying practice has not made him sensually inert. To the contrary, the deeper he is involved in the slave trade, the stronger grows his longing for powerful sensual experiences. His attachment to the magical power of beauty, for instance—symbolized in the paintings of myrtle, hyssop, cowslip, and pennyroyal he hangs on his cabin walls—intensifies as the brutal conditions of the slave ship take their devastating toll. Mungo perceives the violence done to the slaves as an aesthetic pain inflicted on Thistlewood as well: "He was deeply affected by the loss of his creatures, and could barely bring himself to countenance the bodies warped with fever; warped canvases slipped from their frames; fevers having melted their surfaces and depths so that the deck swam in the blue oil of a ruptured liver, the vermilion of a ruptured spleen."[161] Although he fails to see the humanity of his "creatures," Thistlewood is afforded a profound subjectivity. His brutality is not the opposite of his aesthetic sense but the surest sign that he feels deeply.

As witness to all this, Mungo absolves Thistlewood of his sins. He refuses to tell Pringle what he wants to hear about the slaver, knowing that "Mr. Pringle will of course dismiss [his] account as a subterfuge, as a desire on [his] part to conceal the abuses that [he] endured."[162] To the reader he says:

> So let me not give you a portrait of Captain Thistlewood as you think he is, but as I wish him to be. Let me paint him as a man who beat me as our Saviour was beaten, so that I would come to know the weight of the Cross of my sins. And he beat me to forget the very land of his imagining, the very land he taught me to name with reverence, for it had become the distant bank of death: you had enclosed it, maimed its spirit with your commercial plough, converted it into a plantation and city and emporium. You peopled it with urchins playing in gutters, or with clerks who tallied its worth. You made merchants and factories and ships of death and slaves and whores. You dug its belly for metals. You lusted. You sinned.[163]

Written in a fashion similar to Blake's *Songs of Innocence* and *Songs of Experience*, this passage is rich in irony and paradox, and the narrative manages to keep several complex truths in play simultaneously. As Mungo speaks, is he aware of the multiple possibilities he raises, for example, the way in which his absolution of Thistlewood is also a condemnation? An evangelical rationale for physical and sexual abuse may be morally unacceptable, but it is not necessarily insincere. The irony of a religious ideology deployed as an excuse for sadism appears to escape Mungo, but such irony has a lofty tradition behind it. And the fact of Mungo's abuse does not render him incapable of loving his abuser. Nor does it make him unappreciative of his role as Christ's surrogate. Moreover, the possibility that

Thistlewood uses a self-serving religious justification does not cancel out the weighty notion that Mungo becomes the sacrificial victim of England's commercial excess. Although we pinpoint with some difficulty the precise ironies of the passage, Mungo's perspicacity is astounding: the young slave recognizes that Thistlewood has projected onto him his profound distress over the consequences of commodifying practice. Mungo accepts the idea that he is to be the expiator for the damage done by mercantile capitalism. As a Christ figure he transcends his own status as commodity. In language that echoes Blake's "London," Mungo calls the reader to account. The sympathetic "you" who was privy to the truth about Thistlewood becomes the guilty "you" complicit in commodifying practice.

The effect of this kind of densely multilayered prose is to defy simplistic labeling. As Mungo writes, "Mr. Pringle's version of Captain Thomas Thistlewood is untroubled. Captain Thistlewood is a demon and I his catamite."[164] At a moment like this, oppositions between good and bad, right and wrong, love and hate, abuser and abused, and "them" and "us" deteriorate. Mungo leaves the task of passing judgment to the reader: "But you, my sympathetic reader, will judge whether I serve Captain Thistlewood faithfully by presenting him as a good and loving master; or whether my slavery to him is an act of self-mutilation, like the pauper's, or whore's or urchin's."[165] Dabydeen's account thus becomes the antidote to the poisonous effects of any moralizing narrative.

The powerful binding of Thistlewood and Mungo, slaver and slave, is only the first instance of a series of unlikely couples in the novel, each of which becomes a meditation on conventional heterosexuality. In both Africa and England, Mungo is paired with a series of women who function as mother substitutes, including Rima, who appears to have taken over for his biological mother; Betty, who prepares him for market in London; Lady Montagu, who sees him as a substitute for her dead pet monkey; and Moll, whom he nurses throughout her excruciating death. In each of these relationships, an infantile neediness is conflated with a more encompassing kind of erotic desire. Each of these relationships is rooted in a pull that seems "sexual" in nature, yet sex scarcely seems to be the point. Dabydeen's narration exposes the narcissism that lies at the heart of the child's powerful longing for the mother and that subsequently underlies so many erotic couplings. Now a teenaged boy, Mungo narrates his obsession with Lady Montagu:

But even though I am born in my father's sex I still want to know, so I study her Ladyface, but her smile mock me like a rip which she long ago mend with her needle to stop me now peeping. I can't seek in her eyes my mother's child, and so I feel lost in spite of her smile. I crave for her to look at me so I can see how I reflect in her eyes and can then talk out my true name.[166]

As another mother figure to Mungo, Betty finally does reflect back to him his own broken self-image. Once again, pain and love are inextricably linked—Betty tries to drown Mungo, only then to disburden her soul to him in a most urgent and intimate way. The roles reverse, so that Mungo becomes father to Betty the needy child, who tells him the fractured and contradictory story of Mary, now dead, who may have been in service with Betty, been her child, been hanged for petty larceny, or been framed by Betty herself. Dabydeen's prose is most lyrical when it describes the unlikely bond forged between Betty and Mungo: "I go into the smoke and disappear from her love of me."[167] What links Mungo and Betty is not their complementary status but their brokenness. As individuals who have been exiled from a "paradise lost"—Mungo when he first trespassed into the katran brush, Betty when she turned her back on her Yorkshire home in favor of the city—these two are powerfully linked by an initial act of transgression. Mungo uses the language of commerce to convey his utmost tenderness toward Betty. Like Tom Dacre in Blake's "Chimney Sweeper," he fantasizes about his power to protect the vulnerable, and he espouses a religious ideology designed to palliate the sufferings of the weak: "Heaven tempers the wind to the shorn lamb, and you therefore must withhold your disgust at Betty's stumblings. I bid for her with Christian coinage—which is Our Lord's Sermon on love—and having purchased her I free her into your care."[168]

A Respectable Trade gives us an African hero capable of redeeming one white woman, but *A Harlot's Progress* gives us an African protagonist who feels his burden is to make amends to all women for the abuses of all men. Rima's ghost taunts Mungo with the fact of his male prerogative and power:

"She bleeds," Rima tells him, "therefore she is doomed. Pity her."
In the sterility and hunger of the cellar, Rima returns to haunt him with remembrance of woman's plight, but Mungo dismisses her as an

irrelevant myth, belonging to the past. "It is a tale more ordinary than you know," he replies.

"You are the cause of her suffering. You hurt women in whatever you do. Are you not a man?"[169]

Mungo internalizes the message that, as a man, he bears the responsibility for patriarchy, which appears in the novel as a powerfully destructive force in the lives of women, regardless of where they live. In Africa patriarchy results in the cruel maiming and exile of widows past childbearing years. In England it results in a stultifying domesticity that imprisons women such as Lady Montagu and leads to their profound despair, even madness.

Patriarchal ideology tolerates, even promotes, unequal power relations, the tyranny of the strong, which in turn gives rise to the cruelty of the weak. It is difficult to say which is depicted as the more brutal place: Mungo's birthplace, where petty jealousies, rumors, and innuendoes lead to the horrific murder of an innocent man and his family, or Lord Montagu's apparently pacific estate, where servants nightly torture animals and slave boys behind thick, closed doors. Mungo knows that Pringle wants him to tell the tale of the slave ship's horrors, thereby allowing him a vicarious, sadistic pleasure in the scene of suffering. Mungo refuses, knowing that to give in to Pringle entails perpetuating a false distinction between the two cultures:

> You will reward me with laurels and fat purses for flagellating you thus, especially should I, with impoverished imagination, evoke for you the horror of the slaveship's hold, the chained Negroes, their slobbering, their suffocation, their sentimental condition. No, they laughed, they chattered, they gossiped, they cried, they desired, as they had always done in the villages in Africa. There were chains there too. They merely exchanged their distress for yours, when you packed them in your boat. And perhaps your distress will eventually prove to be more creative.[170]

Human motivation scarcely differs, whether in Africa or London. Mungo is equally stunned to find extraordinary acts of kindness in either setting, expecting most often to find the selfish impulse toward self-preservation. Thus, as the differences between love and hate, civilized and primitive, and England and Africa collapse in the novel, so too do the moral categories that distinguish the supposedly good from the bad. As is readily apparent by now, Dabydeen's abolitionist is given the narrowest and most self-interested of ambitions. So too is the artist Hogarth, who makes a cameo appearance at the end of the novel. Smelling of paint, he promises "to represent [Mungo and his company] in the best light, to immortalize [them] by his art . . . Yet for all the seeming realism of his art, he lied."[171] The "Jew," in contrast, is redeemed not once but twice: the first Jew, a humanitarian surgeon on board Thistlewood's slave ship, is barely distinguished from the second Jew, a quack physician who abandons his lucrative career as consultant to the rich in order to treat—ineffectually but with genuine solicitude—venereal disease–ridden prostitutes. As his assistant, Mungo describes the Jew's Christlike power to restore not the body but the soul:

> The truth is that he gave up all his worldly ambition so as to wait upon the most despised of women. . . . And the last meal he fed them was not his famed cordial . . . but a preparation of England's ancient verdure; ancient beyond the slum, marketplace, pawnshop, brothel and Bridewell that their lives had become in the city. . . . We could not save the women but we restored to them a taste of the innocence of their childhoods.[172]

At the same time, the Nazi holocaust conflates with the slave holocaust, as Mungo glimpses the future of anti-Semitism, by means of Ellar's ghostly prophecy.[173]

For Mungo, the ultimate proof that England and Africa exist on a continuous moral plain is the fact of his mysterious heritage, the result of "a battalion of Greek marauders of old who had wandered off path from North Africa and somehow ended up hundreds of miles away in an unfamiliar region."[174] Yet the result of this intercultural contact is ironic. Instead of the imprint of high culture in the form of philosophy, art, or music, it leaves a stamp of cruelty: "a peculiar sign called 'peia,' an "obvious corruption of the Greek pi, which we also signify as TT," that is branded on the palms of the women, who with heads shaved and wrists broken are exiled to death in the forest once their childbearing years are over.[175] For a reason he himself does not quite understand, Mungo bears the sign on his forehead: "Some germ of Greek civilization survived the suffocation of bush and blacks to flower on my forehead centuries later. I am certain that

I am an imprint of a lost tribe of Greeks, for how else can I explain the sign of Pi inscribed on my forehead?"[176] But Mungo confuses (intentionally, perhaps?) this marking with Thistlewood's brand, TT, put there, as Betty tells him, to indicate that he has been "breached and made accustomed to men."[177] Is Mungo marked, then, once, twice, or perhaps even three times? He seems to have been metaphorically marked at birth. Yet the advertisement for his sale refers to "some slight tribal scarring on his forehead,"[178] raising the possibility of a second, literal scarring, perhaps as a punishment for his trespass into the katran bush.[179] A third possibility is the scarring left by Thistlewood's iron brand. Or perhaps Mungo has been marked only once, and the multiple scarrings represent three versions of the same event. The images are embedded, one inside another, in a way that not only defies a rational accounting of Mungo's heritage but also suggests how he is the locus of complex intercultural markings. He is simultaneously the product of the Greek marauders, his African forebears, and white civilization.

What is marked on Mungo in a confusing and contradictory way is also what is written about Mungo for the reader. Dabydeen takes us full circle back to the theme of writing the unwritten, telling the untold; as was the case in *Cambridge*, *Crossing the River*, and *The Longest Memory*, the told is never simply the opposite of the untold. Rather, the told always consists of multiple possibilities or interpretations. Mungo's true, multiple stories defy linearity. Similarly, they thwart the reader's attempt to understand causal relations in the plot. For instance, when, at precisely the same moment that Jenkins's loss of an ear provokes an international incident, Mungo cuts off his own ear, does Mungo "cause" the war? Is his own gesture—staged (so he tells us) either to force the dismissal of the servants who have tortured him or as a sacrificial gesture directed at the salvation of Lady Montagu—an uncanny repetition?[180] Or is it a displacement of political disorder into the domestic scene of Lord Montagu's house? In a world where cause and effect can no longer be discerned, we are presented with another way of understanding history: not as a rational unfolding but as a swirling, chaotic vortex of events in which individuals randomly clutch at bits and pieces in a vain attempt to make sense of their world.

As Dabydeen refuses to allow us to experience closure through traditional heterosexual coupling, he similarly refuses to allow us moral complacency through a clear chain of casualty. Writing does not necessarily order experience. Nor does it "make meaning," and it cannot offer us hope. Even while it tells its tale, the novel betrays a lack of faith in narrative. Lady Montagu collects an archive on the horrors of the slave ship, in particular of an incident that fictionalizes the *Zong* incident, but her archive is full of contradictory and confusing evidence. Mungo/Perseus himself "is not foolish enough to believe that a single book will alter the course of history."[181] He recognizes instead that "Money, not ideas, is what holds the nation together, and as long as it is profitable to trade Negroes, slavery will thrive, and the state of England remain intact."[182] Whereas popular narratives repeatedly cite commodification as the originary cause of estrangement, Dabydeen's narrator identifies it as a force that brings people together, although in an especially brutal fashion. In this way, rather than bifurcating the world into those who commodify and those who are commodified, he implicates everyone equally in the horrors of the trade.

In the final pages of the novel, Mungo's narrative is increasingly deflated by the ghostly voice of Ellar, a spirit from his African past, who constantly chides Mungo/Perseus for his pretensions: "'Writing don't make you a god either,' Ellar says scornfully, mocking Perseus' achievement. 'Just because you are making a book of fancy words and the whiteman mark your forehead don't make you better than us.'"[183] Ellar's voice is the one Mungo fails to block out, and it is Ellar who "no matter how strong the poison, secure the grave, will break out, torch the katran bush, blow with disobedient angel breath, fan the flames, that not even God's Flood can drown them out, for when the waters ebb, there is smoke still, the first smouldering thing that arise is the spirit of Ellar."[184] The point is not simply that Dabydeen gives the last word to the black woman who—as if to counter a long tradition of silencing black women—"tells." Rather, Ellar confounds the binary between told and untold. She functions as an image of the irrepressible—she is what any narrator struggles to control in the process of telling. As a potential source of the told, she is also the untelling, as she threatens to seize control and undo whatever order the narrator, under the guise of the told, provides. Ellar is, then, an apt and precise image with which to close a novel that has resisted closure all along.

Published within five years of each other, *A Respectable Trade* and *A Harlot's Progress* offer two very different kinds of late-twentieth-century meditations on racial relations as they unfolded in the eighteenth century and as they continue to affect us now. Like many other popular narratives about Britain's slave trade, *A Respectable Trade* plays to an audience eager for closure. It locates the estrangement of black from white and woman from man in an originary cause—commodification—and it intimates that narrative itself is a restorative force capable of healing deep and painful rifts. In contrast, *A Harlot's Progress*, always self-conscious about its own status as a commodified object, refuses to locate an originary cause in commodification. Instead, it finds in human nature itself the best explanation for unspeakable acts of cruelty. Although it resists the notion that story telling is necessarily enlightening, it illuminates the complex investment of people in their stories. In the end, *A Harlot's Progress* has more to offer its readers. It encourages us not to simulate postmodern aimlessness but to call on a richly paradoxical, nontraditional tradition of ceaseless movement.[185] If it denies us the comfort of closure, it nonetheless offers us a vantage point from which to see the territory that still lies just beyond us.

In this chapter, I have asked: how can a novel successfully oppose racism? I have argued that an efficacious treatment of hybridity in the British novel at the end of the twentieth century resists binaristic treatments of themes and characters, and it experiments with generic conventions that decenter the solitary and overriding perspective of an omniscient narrator in favor of multiple and overlapping voices, a polyvalence that may not center on a particular assertion but that allows for more than one truth to exist simultaneously. Exposing the impossibility—and indeed the futility—of recovering one stabilizing and unifying historical narrative, a successful engagement with hybridity foregrounds the power of story telling and narrative. The emphasis thus shifts from the category of the "untold" to the process of the "telling": telling/narrating/making stories becomes a meaningful way to initiate conversation, to put conflicting ideas into play, and potentially to make meaningful transracial connections. If, as Kureishi writes, the aim is no less than to define a new way of being British, then the successful hybrid novel allows its readers to recognize a shared commonality as a crucial step in that direction.

Chapter Three

Seeing Slavery and the Slave Trade

In an often-cited scene in Jane Austen's novel *Mansfield Park* (1814), the heroine Fanny Price asks her uncle, Sir Thomas Bertram, the owner of a sugar plantation in Antigua, about the slave trade. Her query is cut short by a "dead silence" that literary critics have recently interpreted in a variety of ways. Perhaps the moment is highly freighted, the words "dead" and "silence" metonymically paralleling the theme of bondage, as Moira Ferguson suggests. Or, equally possible—as Marcus Wood asserts—perhaps silence relates to the characters' "boredom of overexposure" to the subject.[1] But in the 1999 film version of the novel, as adapted by Canadian director Patricia Rozema, a full conversation on the topic of slavery replaces the silence. More significantly, the audience observes the speaking Fanny boldly confronting her uncle Sir Thomas Bertram. As he casually mentions his intention to bring home a black slave as a house servant on his next voyage (a statement he does not make in the novel), she asks if "there would be some argument as to whether or not they should be freed here . . . if I'm not mistaken." She then confesses to having done some reading on the matter—"Thomas Clarkson to be specific," under her cousin Edmund's guidance.[2]

Thus, Rozema's Fanny is both heard and seen, not only here but also elsewhere, from the opening credits, during which she entertains her younger sister in bed with lurid, sentimental tales, to the closing frame, in which she listens avidly as Edmund (now her husband) tells her he has found a publisher for her works. Rozema's Fanny jumps down stairs two a time. She whoops and hollers, runs after Edmund, and wallops him with an article of clothing. Forsaking her sidesaddle, she gallops (in slow motion) across the rain-soaked fields.[3] She advances a literary career by penning—and then delivering directly into the camera—snippets from Austen's own juvenilia, evincing a decidedly feminist opinion on the subject of male history.[4] No one overlooks Rozema's Fanny and, unlike Austen's heroine, she no longer hides in the corner. It is unthinkable that her presence in a room could go unnoticed or that she would get a headache from cutting roses, as happens in the original text. But if Rozema's Fanny is the object of the filmgoer's gaze, she also does quite a bit of gazing herself. She sees lots of things, many of which a good girl should never see. On her way from her childhood home in Portsmouth to Mansfield Park, she observes—implausibly—a slave ship anchored off the coast. "Black cargo," the coachman explains, some captain's "gifts for the wife."[5,6] She stumbles across her cousin Maria's adulterous love affair in process, the lovers naked in each other's arms. And—as I discuss later—she discovers a series of pornographic drawings that indict her uncle as a colonial rapist.

In this way, Rozema's film reverses the binary oppositions that structure Austen's novel: where Austen privileges Fanny's indirection over her direct speech and her invisibility over visibility, making her discreet rather than confrontational, Rozema gives her audience the opposite. She privileges Fanny's speech over her indirection and her visibility over her invisibility, making her confrontational rather than discreet. It is not difficult to imagine that this reversal of the binary emerges in response to two kinds of contemporary pressure: feminism, which requires that women's centrality be recognized, and postcolonialism, which requires that the marginalized be similarly returned to a position of centrality.[7] Moreover, at this moment in contemporary history, it might seem morally reprehensible *not* to portray the evils of a colonial society that depended on slavery. Who in due conscience, at the turn of the twentieth century, could choose to forgo an opportunity to visualize and make explicit the terrible costs of the eighteenth-century slave trade?

Yet I ask what it means for Rozema to reverse Austen's values. In particular, what does it mean to invest ourselves in what we might call a politics of the visible? Simply put, if social justice is an acknowledged goal, is visibility necessarily more efficacious than invisibility? Can rendering seen that which has been unseen thereby right a historical wrong? What are the politics of confronting the visible and the seen? These are questions I ask not only about Rozema's controversial film but also about other film and television representations of slavery and the slave trade appearing in Britain at the end of the twentieth century. Thus, in addition to Rozema's *Mansfield Park*, this chapter examines a biographical documentary, or biopic, a televised version of a novel, and a four-part television documentary. Although each of these film representations has a strong narrative element, ranging from the voiceover of the documentary to the screenplay of a costume drama, each also works on the level of its images. Each *tells* us something, but each also *shows* us something. Yet, how does what is told correspond to that which is seen? A quick survey of these film projects suggests a range of artistic intentions, with different points of focus, as well as an array of political goals.

To begin, 1995 saw the release of a twenty-eight-minute biopic on the life of Olaudah Equiano entitled *A Son of Africa*.[8] From the opening frame, depicting Equiano, in black wig, silk knee breeches and embroidered waistcoat, emerging from a church with his white bride on his arm, to the closing scene, in which Equiano resplendent as before in his late-eighteenth-century attire, speaks against the evil of slavery to an admiring circle of white gentlemen, the film places Equiano as a writer, abolitionist, and statesman at the center of British eighteenth-century culture and society. Making a different kind of statement, yet also featuring a handsome and elegantly costumed black actor, the BBC production of *A Respectable Trade*, with a screenplay by Philippa Gregory, originally broadcast on April 19, 1998, told a story about everyday black and white contact in eighteenth-century England.[9] The miniseries was filmed on location in the Pinney House in Bristol and in Bath, with great attention to recreation of historical detail. Using the costume drama, the series provided its audience with a crash course in the realities of the slave trade.

For those who missed the history lessons in Gregory's screenplay, another opportunity to learn the social, political, and economic history of the trade arose. In 1999 Channel 4 broadcast over four consecutive Sunday nights in October (Black History Month in the United Kingdom) a series entitled *Britain's Slave Trade: Telling the Untold*.[10] Produced by noted U.K. journalist Trevor Phillips and Philip Whitehead, the series was handsomely presented, and it was accompanied by an extensive Web site and a bound volume. *Britain's Slave Trade* took as its topic the dark side of Britain's glorious imperial past. To an audience accustomed to gazing on the monuments of empire—whether as tourists in Georgian cities such as Bath, as visitors to great houses such as Blaise Castle, or as consumers of yet another film about Jane Austen's England—the series had a simple message: the money for all this splendor came from somewhere. And in eighteenth-century England, far too often the origins of such wealth lay in the traffic in black slaves. Roughly coinciding with the release of the Rozema film, the television series secured prime-time coverage for the eighteenth-century transatlantic slave trade.

Thus, all four of these film projects trace existing race relations in the United Kingdom to a specific set of eighteenth-century circumstances. This chapter explores their work as artistic renderings that privilege and commit to the idea of a visually accessible history of the transatlantic slave trade. The first section, "Slaves in Silk Knee Breeches," discusses how *A Son Of Africa* and *A Respectable Trade* populate eighteenth-century English cities with black faces to tell stories about eighteenth-century interracial relationships. As a historical film, *A Son of Africa* depicts actual figures from history in the historical context, whereas *A Respectable Trade*, a costume drama, presents fictional characters in historical settings.[11] I read both representations against Pam Cook's assertion that the historical costume film is a key site for the negotiation of national identity.[12] By figuring an alternative version of an "authentic" England, where otherness was already a part of the fabric of English daily life, these representations attempt to redefine contemporary British society as well. Yet, as we will see, implicit tensions between the "seen" and "told" in each of these representations suggests that the project of visualizing the legacy of the British slave trade has not yet fully accomplished its purpose.

The second section, "Filming Britain's Untold Story: Secrets and Lies?" explores how the trope of the family permeates the four-part documentary on the slave trade. As white Britons discover their black "roots," English hybridity is visualized as existing in the heart of the English family itself. However, I argue that an insistence on the idea of "family connections" does not necessarily ensure a commitment to politics of antiracism, as a brief discussion of the treatment of racial otherness in Mike Leigh's 1996 film *Secrets & Lies* reveals.

In the last part of this chapter, "Filming the Invisible in Mansfield Park," after situating Jane Austen's *Mansfield Park* in the context of current critical debate, I explore Patricia Rozema's decision to foreground a proactive heroine, one who becomes an articulate critic of the slave trade.

This section further examines the director's decision to put a range of sexual behaviors and attitudes at the center of her representation, thereby alerting her audience to the "corruption" that lies at the center of the British estate that gathers its income from the Caribbean. By focusing our attention on the film's depiction of Tom Bertram and considering how Rozema deploys metaphors of illness and corruption, we come to the heart of the matter: in reversing Austen's binaries, Rozema aims to tell and show her audience more. Yet ultimately her film fails to allow the viewer an important moment of enlightenment—paradoxically, the more the film shows us about the evils of slavery, the less her audience stands to learn. As I will argue, at stake here is a comparison of not only two very different approaches to visualizing the slave trade but also two very different understandings of how an audience comes to reflect in a meaningful way on a historical wrong.

Slaves in Silk Knee Breeches: *A Son of Africa* and *A Respectable Trade*

Until very recently, the biography of Olaudah Equiano (1745–1797)—enslaved African, sailor in the British navy, witness to colonial wars, adventurer and explorer, free man and petty capitalist, spokesman for abolition, and Christian missionary—would have been relatively unfamiliar to most people. Although nine editions of his autobiography appeared during his lifetime, followed by four early-nineteenth-century editions, interest in Equiano's life waned for a time, until Paul Edwards published an abridged and edited version in 1967. Edwards followed with a reprint of a facsimile of the 1789 edition in 1969, the same year in which the Negro Universities Press reprinted the 1837 Boston edition. Then, in 1987, Henry Louis Gates included the Equiano autobiography in his edition of *The Classic Slave Narratives* and initiated what is now a virtual Equiano industry—versions of Equiano's text, mostly designed for classroom use, were published in 1988, 1989, 1995 (two versions), 1996, 1998, and 1999. The Norton Critical Edition of *The interesting narrative of the life of Olaudah Equiano, or Gustavus Vassa, the African, written by himself*, edited by Werner Sollors, appeared in 2001, as did another edition by Broadview Press. These were followed by Vincent Carretta's 2003 second edition for Penguin, with its controversial claim about the origins of Equiano's birthplace, a claim that promises to ensure a lively discussion about Equiano's identity well into the twenty-first century.[13]

It is somewhat surprising, then, that this interest in publishing the Equiano story should have yielded only one film version so far: a brief (twenty-eight-minute) documentary for the BBC. Perhaps this absence of film representation can be explained by the far-reaching scope and geographical sweep of Equiano's life and travels. A diagram in Werner Sollors's edition for Norton illustrates how difficult it is to track Equiano's lifelong peregrinations—lines on a map of the Americas, the coast of Africa, and Western Europe track Equiano's many destinations. The lines are disorienting in their sheer number; a legend identifies eighty-one places to which Equiano traveled, including such far-flung places as Cape Breton, the Archipelago Islands, and Latitude 58–59.[14] What kind of screenplay could possibly situate Equiano's wanderlust and do justice to the experience he garnered in so many different settings? What kind of film narrative could tell us the story of Equiano as world traveler?

The movie produced by Aimimage Productions for the BBC refers to several of Equiano's travels, putting them in the context of his experiences as a slave, sailor, and adventurer. Nonetheless, working within the obvious limits of the short documentary format, it portrays one "journey" in particular: that of Equiano from enslaved Africa to free man and spokesman for abolition. The title of the documentary is "A Son of Africa: The Slave Narrative of Olaudah Equiano." Tellingly, Equiano's Christian name, Gustavus Vassa, is left out of this title, even though Equiano used it throughout his lifetime—on his wedding day, for example. (The script does explain the ironies arising from this name, borrowed from a Swedish king: "The king is powerful, honored respected, the slave is disempowered, not honored, not respected.") Also omitted from this title are the other two continents that might claim Equiano as their son: Europe (more specifically England, where Equiano chose to spend much of his adult life) and America (where he also spent considerable periods of time—possibly more than he admits, especially if Carretta is correct). But who exactly was Equiano? What are some ways of telling his story? Which version does the film tell?

By designating Equiano a "Son of Africa," the film alerts viewers to his diasporic identity. An important term in postcolonial and transnational studies, diaspora signals the violent removal of a population from its homeland, under circumstances not of its own choosing, and it implies as well an ongoing sense of cultural and linguistic alienation. A diasporic population, by definition, then, seeks to return to its homeland. It remains invested in the myths of its original society, often offering continual support for the homeland from abroad. Finally, a diasporic community gains a collective identity arising from its shared relationship to a homeland.[15]

Turing back to the narrative for a moment, we see that evidence of Equiano's diasporic identity is especially strong in the early pages, where he tells the story of his African origins and youth, writing with great clarity about tribal customs, beliefs, and practices. Equiano often uses the pronoun *we* to denote an ongoing identification with a people among whom he would not have lived for nearly forty years at the time he wrote his autobiography: "We are almost a nation of dancers, musicians, and poets.... We have many musical instruments, particularly drums of different kinds, a piece of music which resembles a guitar, and another like a stickado [xylophone]."[16] Or: "Before we taste food, we always wash our hands: indeed our cleanliness on all occasions is extreme."[17] With its apparent fidelity to an African point of view, this early section has invited the scrutiny of African scholars such as Catherine Obianju Acholonu, who discovers discernible resemblances between Equiano and contemporary inhabitants of Isseke, Nigeria.[18] Equiano's diasporic identity—his sense of alienation and estrangement—is seen as well in his painful description of his capture, his descriptions of his first encounter with white culture, and his account of the Middle Passage, which, until recently, served as a rare and therefore invaluable firsthand account of that experience. As mentioned earlier, for instance, the Liverpool transatlantic slavery exhibit uses a tape of Equiano's words as documentary evidence.

However, the idea of Equiano as an "authentic" African who speaks for a diasporic population has recently been challenged: Vincent Carretta's research into naval records suggests that Equiano may have been born in South Carolina, not Africa.[19] Much is at stake in this research, and scholars currently debate the accuracy, interpretation, and consequences of Equiano's claim to have been born in what is now Nigeria. Whatever the outcome of this discussion, we are left with an interesting question, raised by Carretta himself: is it possible that Equiano, regardless of the location of his birth, regardless of his own personal experience, can nonetheless provide an "authentic" account of a collective event that may well have been conveyed to him by a community of enslaved Africans in South Carolina? Does Equiano have to have personally experienced both life in Africa and the Middle Passage for his record to be a true and accurate account?[20]

In many ways, Equiano's extraordinarily complicated narrative expresses not one but two conflicting voices. In contrast to a diasporic voice, or a *we* voice, his narrative also contains a powerfully cosmopolitan voice, an *I* voice, that is just as inclined to refer to Africans as *they*, as in the following: "The natives believe that there is one Creator of all things . . . They believe he governs events, especially our deaths or captivity."[21] This cosmopolitan voice differs from the first voice in several ways. First, although it neither forgets nor downplays the traumatic conditions of enslavement, it tends to seek within slavery possibilities for enhancement and self-development. In Equiano's case, he raises the money through petty trade to buy his own freedom, seizing on the promise of a Quaker, a man who Equiano knew could not go back on his word. Second, the cosmopolitan voice tends to forgo nostalgia for the homeland in favor of an avid interest in multiple cultural experiences, all of which can be compared to one another.

Although Equiano the cosmopolitan does not forget his original culture or language, he remains open and animated about intercultural contact and practices. Instead of alienation from the new worlds he encounters, he experiences a sense of continuity between and among different peoples. He finds, for instance, frequent comparisons between his indigenous culture and that of the Jews. Moreover, he is excited by all his travels. He writes, for example, of his enthusiasm for Villa Franca, Nice, and Leghorn, finding himself "charmed with the richness and the beauty of the countries, and struck with the elegant buildings with which they abound."[22] Equiano the cosmopolitan does want to return as a missionary to Africa but is also passionate about the idea of Africa as a market for British goods: "A commercial intercourse with Africa opens an inexhaustible source of wealth to the manufacturing interests of Great Britain, and to all which the slave trade is an objection."[23] Although he may be writing strategically to appeal to a British public more responsive to economic than moral arguments, his own faith in capitalism seems genuine.

And here is another crucial difference between the diasporic and cosmopolitan Equiano: the latter is an entrepreneur, an individual, a capitalist, and a Christian who interprets his financial success as a sign of God's special interest in him. For example, on a trip to the West Indies the captain denies Equiano the opportunity to bring bullocks—"a very profitable article" to trade—on board ship. He is given permission to carry turkeys instead. The Captain's bullocks die, but Equiano's turkeys live to be sold, yielding him three hundred per cent profit. He comments: "I could not help looking on this, otherwise trifling circumstances, as a particular providence of God, and I was thankful accordingly."[24] In addition to being a trader, Equiano becomes skilled as a hairdresser (a lucrative skill in the era of the wig). He also becomes proficient at playing the French horn. He hires himself to Dr. Charles Irving, a scientist who had experimented with the making of fresh water from salt water. On a journey to the Musquito Shore, he boards a "Guineaman," or slave ship, to "purchase some slaves to carry with us, and cultivate a plantation." If he sees any irony in the fact that he "chose them all from my own countrymen," he fails to mention it.[25]

One way to see Equiano's cosmopolitan identity is to begin at Chapter Ten, at the point when Equiano is now a free man who has just returned from his trip to the North Pole. He writes, "I was again determined to go to Turkey, and resolved, at that time, never more to return to England."[26] Equiano had previously been in Turkey, in 1769, when he had had very favorable impressions of the people and the culture:

> [Smyrna] is a very ancient city; the house is built of stone, and most of them have graves adjoining to them; so that they sometimes present the appearance of church-yards. Provisions are plentiful in this city, and good wine less than a penny a pint. The grapes, pomegranates, and many other fruits, were also the largest I ever tasted. The natives are well looking and strong made, and treated me always with great civility. In general I believe they are fond of black people; and several of them gave me pressing invitations to stay amongst them, although they keep the franks, or Christians, separate, and do not suffer them to dwell immediately amongst them.[27]

Evidently Equiano felt very comfortable in Turkey. Although some of its customs surprised him, he characteristically noticed cross-cultural similarities:

> I was astonished in not seeing women in any of their shops, and rarely any in the streets; and whenever I did they were covered with a veil

from head to foot, so that I did not see their faces, except when any of them uncovered them out of curiosity to look at me, which they sometimes did. I was surprised to see how the Greeks are, in some measure, kept under by the Turks, as the Negroes are in the West Indies by the white people. The less refined Greeks, as I have already hinted, dance in the same manner as we do in my nation. On the whole, during our stay here, which was about five months, I liked the place and the Turks very well.[28]

In a later passage, he writes that a "seraskier or officer took a liking to me here, and wanted me to stay, and offered me two wives; however I refused the temptation."[29]

What Equiano mentions only obliquely is that Turkey was then—as it remains today—a predominantly Muslim country. To emigrate there would not necessarily involve converting to Islam (indeed, he comments on the segregation of Christians as if it would apply to him), but in moving to Turkey Equiano would have resituated himself in a Muslim cultural context. But he did not emigrate to Turkey. As he puts it, he "was prevented by means of his late captain"[30] as well as a series of circumstances beyond his control. The chapter concludes with a protracted account of his conversion to Christianity. This chapter, then, paints a portrait of a man who once saw himself as having options, not only between nationalities and cultures but also between religious identifications. Not as victim but as someone who was "saved," he sees Christianity choosing him. We must take seriously the idea that Equiano found what he needed in Christianity and his British identity. He could have chosen to emigrate to Turkey and situate himself among what remained of the former Ottoman empire at the end of the eighteenth century. Instead, he forges for himself an identity in a nascent empire, one in whose colonial battles he had already participated and whose future he most likely intuited. In short, as a cosmopolitan, Equiano makes a decision that his future lies with the spiritual and economic possibilities offered by Britain. It is important to stipulate that a reading valorizing Equiano's cosmopolitanism does not justify his slavery. Rather, such a reading grants him agency by recognizing the extent to which he was able to turn a calamitous situation to his own advantage.

A Son of Africa privileges Equiano's connection to the abolition movement over questions of his nationality or residence. Stuart Hall, one of three academic commentators appearing on screen, articulates the "thesis" of the biopic and suggests how the theme of Equiano-as-cosmopolitan yields to the theme of Equiano as African statesman. After speaking of the "historical amnesia" that led to Equiano's falling into oblivion, Hall continues: "We forget that slavery is what lies at the root of and shapes predominantly relations between black and whites in the west. Abolition has written out the agency of blacks. It's as if abolition were really a gift by liberal and reforming whites to the enslaved peoples and not one in which slaves themselves played an active part."

In the biopic, South African actor Hakeem Kae-Kazim portrays the adult Equiano, in short black wig and ruffled white shirt, scratching out his memoir with a quill pen. We hear his voice narrating direct quotations from the text. Selected scenes from the memoir are then represented on screen, skillfully presented by actors in a range of settings. Historically precise costumes, as well as expert direction, make the scenes visually compelling. The scenes portray Equiano as a young child captured in Africa; as a house servant in Virginia; as a young boy aboard a British naval ship, where he gains literacy and mathematical expertise; as a young man buying birds at a market; as a stately presence confronting Robert King over the promise that he can buy his own freedom; as dignified advocate for another slave, John Annis; as a statesman for abolition, garnering the attention and assent of a group of white abolitionists; and finally as a subject for a portrait, the painting now familiar to students of Equiano's life and works. (A color reprint of the portrait is on the cover of the 2003 Penguin edition.[31]) These scenes are intercut with appearances by three commentators—in addition to Stuart Hall, Ian Duffield, and Hakim Ali—who appear in what seem to be academic settings. An invisible woman provides a voiceover that weaves together the four male voices.

But the narrative voiceover also occasionally departs from the text to impose its own interpretation on the original story. For example, during a scene depicting Equiano's baptism the narrator announces: "As a condition of his reception into this new world, Equiano is forcibly baptized Gustavus Vassa after the Swedish King." This significantly differs from the original text, in which Equiano writes that he "pressed" his benefactress, Miss Guerin, to be baptized until "to my great joy" she made it possible.[32] There is, no doubt, a world of difference between the two statements. Although there are several possible reasons for Equiano's eagerness to be baptized (including the one he mentions—the fear of not

FIGURE 4   Hakeem Kae-Kazim as Equiano from *A Son of Africa*.
Source: Courtesy of California Newsreel. http://www.newsreel.org.

getting into heaven), the voiceover text denies the idea that Equiano chose Christianity and instead intimates that Christianity was a kind of false consciousness that was imposed on him. Yet this distortion is consistent with—and perhaps even necessary for—the diasporic subtext to the film, one that can be seen in early scenes in the documentary. In woods meant to represent Africa (although looking a lot like England), a tribal elder tells Equiano the meaning of his name. He also explains the circumstances that have led Africans to participate in the slave trade. This opening scene is followed by one in which the young Equiano, at play with his sister, is seized and taken into slavery: "tragically Equiano was never to see his family or Africa again." Thus, his fate as diasporic subject is sealed; he is destined to be forever alienated and rootless.

However, one result of this diasporic interpretation is that the film pays less attention to the many questions that arise from Equiano's dual status as a diasporic *and* a cosmopolitan individual. Equiano's conversion, for example, may have entailed strongly conflicting impulses that contemporary readers might want to query: to what extent was Christianity a necessary and expedient move for him, given the political climate in which he found himself? Does his narrative in fact tell the whole story? Is it possible that he writes about his conversion under compulsion to satisfy a particular audience, perhaps a group of powerful Christian subscribers? Are we compelled to take Equiano at his word on the subject of his conversion? Conversely, what does it mean not to? Do we deny Equiano agency by assuming that he could not have freely chosen Christianity? (Would we have the same doubts if he had chosen to become a Muslim?) By imposing a single interpretation on this issue of Equiano's faith, the film not only avoids this line of inquiry but also loses the opportunity for a rich discussion of the complicated and conflicted nature of human identity. Similarly, this particular spin given to his character forecloses the complicated topic of Equiano's capitalist activity. We learn the fact that Equiano, as an enslaved African, was cheated of his prize money. However, except for one scene showing the adult Equiano buying birds at a market, the viewer receives little indication of his lifelong interest—and success—in commerce and commercial enterprise. For brevity's sake in the film, Ian Duffield efficiently explains Equiano's interest in capitalism: "Equiano was a sharp cookie." But the film makes no mention of Equiano's plea for abolishing the slave trade as commercial opportunity, thereby sidestepping questions about the relationship between capitalistic self-interest and abolition.

Both the strengths and weaknesses of the film's portrayal of Equiano can be seen in one scene in particular, in which Equiano encounters William Kirkpatrick, a man who took John Annis, Equiano's close friend, forcibly—and illegally—from England back into slavery in Jamaica. In this scene, Kirkpatrick's thugs accost Equiano and Annis as they walk through a field. Annis is dragged away, while Equiano is knocked down, his nose bloodied. (This is the worst violence done to Equiano in the film, although the narrative describes other, more brutal racist encounters.) In the following scene, Equiano confronts Kirkpatrick on the grounds of his estate. He presents him with a legal document demanding that Annis be freed. But Kirkpatrick responds with racist slurs: "You come here, attires yourselves, put on a fancy waistcoat, and assume an even fancier name then delude yourself into thinking that you're free the equal of any white man . . . behind all that frippery you're just a nigger not long down from the trees and no amount of holy water can wash away the fact." Equiano maintains a stony silence during the outburst and replies, "See you in court, Kirkpatrick." The dramatic tension in the scene is visually powerful—the actor playing Equiano towers over the actor playing Kirkpatrick, and the former is also better attired (Kirkpatrick's hair is badly dressed), adding to the sense that Equiano is the more dignified, educated, and rational of the two.

However, the encounter never took place as represented. Equiano did, in fact, obtain habeas corpus for Annis, but he got a constable to deliver the document while he watched Annis's house, disguised in a "whitened face" so that Annis would not recognize him.[33] After a visit to Granville Sharp, Equiano enlisted the aid of another lawyer, who "took [his] money, lost [him] many months employ; and did not do the least good in the cause."[34] If the actual sequence of events lacks the dramatic intensity of the scene as visualized, it is nonetheless equally powerful for its ironies: the image of Equiano casing Kirkpatrick's house "in whitened face" may be less heroic, but it is still proactive. Equiano's agency was ultimately ineffective, not because he lacked the resolve or commitment or the power of articulation but because of the slowness and inefficiency of an English court system that was unmotivated to right a racial injustice. My point is not to criticize the film for its lack of verisimilitude; I readily concede that all documentary films make "truth" in their own complicated and intricate manner.[35] Yet I have been arguing that Equiano's life consists of a series of coexisting truths that testify powerfully to human resourcefulness under conditions of extraordinary duress, and that the film works best when it contributes to this sense that Equiano's motivations were complex and even, at times, conflicted. If, as Paul Gilroy writes, "racism rests on the ability to contain blacks in the present, to repress and to deny the past,"[36] then the film accomplishes a very important goal by working against the denial of black historicity. In addition, by bringing the portrait of an elegant, articulate, and activist eighteenth-century Equiano to the screen, it provides an image with the potential to unseat powerful visual stereotypes of enslaved Africans as dependent victims, as mute, kneeling "slaves" dressed in loincloths, arms raised in supplication.

In conclusion, it is somewhat ironic that in school curricula in both the United Kingdom and the United States the American film *Amistad* (1997) has overshadowed *A Son of Africa*.[37] The film, directed by Steven Spielberg, tells the story of an enslaved African called Cinque, who freed himself while aboard a Spanish slave ship. Cinque was subsequently imprisoned and tried in New Haven, Connecticut, after the ship's crew tricked him by sailing the ship east and northwest rather than back toward Africa. The story of Cinque's capture is told in flashbacks; the main action is set in a Connecticut courtroom, as it unfolds around the efforts of the white abolitionist lawyers to free the enslaved men. As Sally Hadden explains, DreamWorks Studio heavily marketed the film to college and high school teachers, claiming (in the words of the press release) that it would "encourage critical thinking about the value of history in light of the long-faded chapter restored to American history in the film."[38] We do not have documented proof of the number of teachers in the United States or Britain who adopted this film as a pedagogical device, but in the United States it was popular enough to generate several online discussion groups and a special section in the journal *The History Teacher*. In Bristol, the curators of the exhibit "A Respectable Trade? Bristol and Transatlantic Slavery" included a video selection from the movie depicting the brutal treatment of the enslaved Africans to represent the Middle Passage.

For historian Steven Mintz, a key question raised by the pedagogic use of Spielberg's film is "whether Hollywood films like *Amistad*, with their romantic aesthetic and their relentless desire to 'humanize' characters, can adequately address the complexities of motivation and causation or . . . impersonal historical process."[39] Other contributors to the special section of *The History Teacher* discussed the film's accuracy, its commitment to black history, its visual style, and its representation of agency and the film's hero. Despite the reservations of the historians, the *Amistad* continues to serve as a powerful teaching device, in the United States at least; a replica of the ship travels along the East Coast, docking at cities and towns, as a way of educating people not only about the ship's special history but also about slavery in American history in general. In this way, an image of African empowerment launched by Hollywood has been appropriated as a popular symbol for an antiracist platform.[40] Yet there ought to be room in school curricula in the United States and the United Kingdom for both the *Amistad* and the Equiano stories, as the stakes involved in the classroom use of these two representations are quite different. Whereas the *Amistad* story inevitably focuses attention on white liberal intervention, Equiano's life provides vitally important lessons in black subjectivity.

Like *A Son of Africa*, the BBC production of *A Respectable Trade* also gives its audience access to an eighteenth-century, multiracial world—in this case, Bristol at the time of the defeat of the first abolition bill in 1787. We have already seen in the previous chapter how a powerful binaristic logic limits the message of the novel. At first glance, the film version of *A Respectable Trade* seems an improvement. To begin, Philippa Gregory's screenplay, which makes some changes in the narrative, comes across as more nuanced, owing in part to expert casting with accomplished actors who give added depth and complexity to the characters from the novel. To take just one example, Sarah Cole, as played by Anna Massey, — although no more sympathetic on screen than she is in the novel—comes across as understandably desperate to hold onto what she can in a patriarchal world of business relations that has pushed her to the margins. The actor portrays well both the fundamental unlikability of her character and the various ways in which her unpleasantness results from being locked up in a world of limited understanding. Massey's face, made up to accentuate its paleness and pinched features, convincingly conveys a stubborn provincialism that resists greater tolerance and compassion. The film's principals—Warren Clarke as Josiah Cole, Emma Fielding as Frances Scott, and Ariyon Bakare as Mehuru—are similarly skilled at teasing out the fullest range of human emotions from their characters.

The film is visually compelling and largely satisfying, in large part because of the historically convincing sets and the lavish, attractive costumes. No doubt it is geared largely toward women of a certain age, women who also possess a passion for English history—a description that fits me. Yet having recognized the deep emotional appeal of the miniseries, I am left with certain questions. How can a film that represents the horrific nature of eighteenth-century slavery—in this case locating it squarely in the middle of English domestic life—also be so engrossing, so pleasurable to watch? Given its topic, how does *A Respectable Trade* work as a costume drama and a "woman's film"? In addition, how do the very pleasures of watching this costume drama correspond to its narrative inclination to make viewers uncomfortable with the historical facts of this "hidden" chapter in British history?

In *English Heritage, English Cinema: Costume Drama Since 1980*, Andrew Higson provides a useful argument that allows us to see the double nature of this film. Higson begins by linking costume dramas to the idea of English heritage, rehearsing in the process the existing debate over whether, as a concept, English heritage is conservative or radical. Among those arguing that heritage is an essentially conservative concept is Robert Hewison in *The Heritage Industry*, for whom the marketing of an "English" past is a suspect form of corporate consumerism. From another perspective, which Higson locates in the work of Raphael Samuel—but that belongs equally to film theorist Pam Cook—there is much more to say on the subject of investment by a popular audience in the idea of English heritage. Arguing for the necessity of understanding the concept from a more democratic perspective, writers such as Samuel and Cook, who are suspicious of an apparent antipopulism in the argument of critics such as Hewison, explore the complex meanings of cultural representations of an English past.[41] Higson's own contribution to the debate is to argue that, in fact, cultural representations of heritage are both conservative and liberal, and he demonstrates this point by looking more closely at the English costume drama. As an expression of a heritage industry, the costume drama is structured to invite two competing readings with opposite political effects: one appropriate to what he calls the "image tract," the other appropriate to the narrative lines. Through a close examination of several English costume films from the 1980s and 1990s, Higson demonstrates how this genre is conservative in its visual display of heritage property and its celebration of "the culture of privilege and the architecture and landscapes of wealth" *and* liberal in the intent of its plot.[42]

Higson's elucidation of the double message of the costume drama is directly relevant to *A Respectable Trade*. The screenplay carries over the liberal message from the novel. Josiah Cole is an immoral man, driven by ambition and greed to extract as much money as possible from the lucrative slave trade in order to be accepted into a newly wealthy mercantile class that is depicted as self-serving and dishonest—in other words, scarcely worth the sacrifice of principle. Josiah's wife, Frances, is both more socially acute and morally aware. Her love affair with Mehuru carries the message of her greater humanity and tolerance, and her death as a result of giving birth to Mehuru's child renders her the sacrificial victim to a corrupt and depraved system.

Yet all this happens on the level of the narrative. What unfolds on the "image tract" is something quite different, as we are asked to appreciate visually the bucolic and pacific qualities of Whiteleaze, home to Sir Francis Scott, Frances's uncle; to gaze at the stately exterior of the Coles' new home in Queen's Square (in point of fact, the Circus in Bath); to linger over the graceful furniture and lovely utensils that appear in every interior shot (filmed in the Pinney House in Bristol); and to revel in the luxurious finery of France's eighteenth-century dress, her gowns and large, picturesque hats. In other words, in its loving and faithful recreation of English heritage, the "image tract" of the film elicits our affection for the very world that created the slave trade. On an intellectual level, *A Respectable Trade* asks us to engage in a historical critique and to hold English ancestors to a high standard of accountability. But on a visual level, it gives us tremendous pleasure and satisfaction at the sight of those same ancestors, as we take in the material texture of their lives.

Even when the camera takes up the less seemly side of eighteenth-century life—the teeming quays and the bustling taverns—the viewer experiences the vicarious thrill that arises from being given a "peep into the past." Admittedly, this film also gives us images likely to make the viewer turn away; an early scene in which emaciated and filthy slaves are brutally unloaded from beneath the decks of a ship is especially harrowing to watch, as is the scene in which Frances places a iron mask on a female African, who, after being raped by a Caribbean planter, a houseguest of the Coles, has begun to eat dirt in an attempt to kill herself. In this scene in particular, the black actors make the humiliation and terror of the enchained Africans viscerally immediate. But the "slaves" are soon cleaned up and brought into the upstairs world of domestic servitude. The women's dress becomes vaguely "Caribbean" in style, as denoted by colorful, towering turbans. These picturesque costumes show the exotic difference of the enslaved Africans to an advantage, and the viewer is given access to their cultural heritage through scenes in which they either dance or sing an "African" song (despite the point, made explicit in the narrative, that they come from very different linguistic and cultural communities).

Here we might ask whether the choice to represent the lives of enchained Africans makes this film unusual. Higson's survey suggests not, since, as he points out, costume films from the 1980s and 1990s

> frequently focus on poignant problems in the English past, on narratives of dissolution, or on the marginal and displaced as much as the apparently privileged—and . . . they often do so from an un-English perspective. Such films, it seems, are capable of producing a sharp critique of the limits of past and present social and moral formations. On the other hand, and somewhat paradoxically, they also seem to offer decidedly conservative, nostalgic, and celebratory visions of the English past.[43]

He further explains that, visually, "the impression is that England is a wonderful, desirable place of tradition and privilege. At the level of *narrative* . . . that heritage is unstable, at risk, in disarray; social and cultural traditions are exposed as repressive; privilege is revealed as exploitation."[44] Hence, as is characteristic of the costume film, *A Respectable Trade* manages to include its political critique within its loving recreation of an English past. It foregrounds—sometimes in graphic and shocking manner—the master's treatment of his slaves, while at the same time offering its viewers the chance to appreciate the aesthetic pleasures of the period. But those aesthetic pleasures are made possible by the very system of political exploitation that the narrative asks us to censure.

The tension between the liberal narrative and the conservative mise-en-scène is most intense in its treatment of Mehuru, who is split between his position as a potential subject with depth and as the object of Frances's erotic desire. Initially, the director, Suri Krishnama, appears self-conscious and even self-referential about this tension. An early shot, set on the Whiteleaze estate, puts Frances in the foreground while her aunt appears in the distant background with a costumed black slave. This first appearance of an enslaved African forecasts the main project of the film: to move black subjectivity to the foreground, where its full humanity can be presented and comprehended. In keeping with this narrative objective, the screenplay gives Mehuru a backstory in which he learned to speak English before coming to Bristol, a fact that allows him to converse freely with Frances and to become an spokesman for African civilization and culture. For example, in one scene he explains to the incredulous Frances that Africans have sophisticated cities and trade routes. The film also show Mehuru in the company of abolitionists who meet in a Bristol pub. There he encounters a freed black from Virginia, a man who supports himself by running a printing press in London. This character also appears in the novel (although with roots in Jamaica, not Virginia), but here the work of the actors is to provide an important visual reference for a historical reality, namely, the presence of blacks themselves in the abolition movement.

However, these liberal attempts to narrativize Mehuru's life and to give him a backstory and a credible psychology are not strong enough to counteract a scopophilic impulse that repeatedly keeps him the object of the viewer's gaze. Ariyon Bakare, as Mehuru, is charismatic and visually alluring—both to the other characters in the film and to the audience. He is often filmed to good advantage, in a manner than shows off his fine physique. Small details in Bakare's performance—his crisp accent, his demeanor and quiet self-control—enhance our investment in him. Throughout the latter part of the film, he is costumed in elegant gold livery, parts of which are removed in key scenes to expose his manly chest. Yet livery has profound historical significance, as Ann Jones and Peter Stallybrass point out. During the Renaissance, livery, or clothing given to servants as part of their wages, "came to mean not just clothing but *marked* clothing, which encorporated retainers and servants into the social body of their master or mistress." Later, "livery was a form of incorporation, a material mnemonic that inscribed obligations and indebtedness upon the body."[45] Although that signification had diminished considerably by the eighteenth century, in the film Mehuru's gold coat and knee breeches continue to symbolize how Frances possesses Mehuru. At the same time, the cut of the dress, the breeches in particular, is extremely flattering to the actor. For the modern viewer, on whom the original meaning of livery may well be lost, Mehuru's costume simply adds to his physical appeal, and Mehuru, especially when he is in livery, remains something to be visually savored. In other words, the effect of this costume, with its "fetishistic attitude toward surface impressions"[46] is to keep Mehuru close to the idea of a "prop." As Higson writes, in the costume drama an emphasis on "pleasures of costume and interior design ensures that political context is often reduced to decorative specta-

FIGURE 5   Cover, paperback edition of *A Respectable Trade*.
Source: Copyright 1995 by Philippa Gregory. Reprinted with the permission of HarperCollins Publishers.

cle."[47] As long as the viewer is attracted to the sight of Mehuru, looking charming in his precisely reproduced historic setting, his story becomes subjugated to our pleasure of looking.

This problem is exacerbated by the fact that Gregory's screenplay—unlike her novel—has no space or medium for the expression of Mehuru's interiority. We are never given direct access to his consciousness, and his character can be exposed only through conversation with white characters, in which he is unlikely, for example, to express negative comments on the subject of Frances's appearance.[48] Instead, the screenplay allows the viewer to see and know Mehuru only as Frances sees and knows him: first as a smoldering, silent, and potentially resistant slave and later as a noble, articulate, and very sexy African. Throughout the film, the "image tract" offers viewers the pleasure of watching Frances and Mehuru come together. It is aesthetically and emotionally satisfying to see Frances dancing alongside Mehuru, as she does in a scene where she has sought him out in the kitchen with that purpose in mind. The two actors, graceful and equally attractive, invite our sympathetic identification. It appears that the objective of the film is to make the viewer fall as much in love with Mehuru's noble otherness as does Frances. Yet here that purpose cannot be accomplished without constantly returning to and centering on Frances's point of view, an effect emphasized by the award-winning score for the film. As Frances gradually begins to master the intricate steps of Mehuru's dance, for instance, the viewer hears the "African" theme of his music slowly yielding to the swelling, lyrical theme of her music, just as Frances's story continually crowds out that of her African partner.

In the end, the story stays very close to Frances's point of view, beginning with her failed attempt as a governess and ending with her picturesque death under a tree. The screenplay leaves little room for Mehuru's development. He is left as erotic object for Frances's/the viewer's gaze; the viewer yearns to "possess" Mehuru just as insistently as does Frances. The film panders to this scopophilic desire with a melodramatic scene of the pair making love on a bed of flowers—not in Frances's bedroom this time but outdoors. Putting Mehuru (literally) on top for once, the camera lingers over the spectacle of black skin on white. Yet the screenplay gives little motive to Mehuru or provides little explanation for why he might find Frances attractive or why he might be willing to take such risks for her.

In the screenplay, Mehuru returns to Frances from London, after having led the other Cole slaves to their freedom in London. After their child is born, Frances sends Mehuru to her uncle's estate to take a position as a house slave until she, he, and their child can escape to London. But Frances begins to hemorrhage while on her way to join him. Her death scene is played under a tree, set on her uncle's estate. Mehuru runs to her, just in time, and Gregory moves Mehuru's description of Africa, which in the novel accompanies their earlier lovemaking, to this moment, where it plays out like an elegy: "I will take you to swim in the river where the sand is white and clear and when you lie in the water the little fish will swim around you and nibble at your white skin." Viewed on screen, Frances's death scene—her very white, still profile filling the lower right foreground of the screen, with Mehuru behind her, slightly eclipsed—evokes the memory of other tragic black–white romances—*Othello*, or perhaps certain eighteenth-century versions of *Oroonoko*.

But if all along this has really been Frances's story, then whatever happens to Mehuru and the biracial son unfolds only as a footnote to her tragedy. When Mehuru, after Frances's death, asks the kindly Dr. Hale whether there is a future for him and his son, the doctor is unable to answer. As Russell Baker pointed out in his comments after the screening of the film on public-television station WGBH, slavery would not be abolished until 1807 in England, "twenty years after we saw Mehuru riding away with his son." And, by the time slavery was abolished, "Mehuru would have been an old man and his son middle-aged." In other words, there are at least two more lifetimes to play out after Gregory has killed off her heroine. We would need a very different kind of film—with a very different kind of historical vision—to hear the story of those lives.

In conclusion, as a costume drama, *A Respectable Trade* offers its viewers a mixed experience. On the one hand, its narrative encourages reflection on eighteenth-century trade, and it elicits moral outrage that human beings should ever have been taken in slavery. But on the other hand, its image tract plays to a scopophilic impulse, in which we are encouraged to love visually the very world we have been asked to judge intellectually. In addition, by aligning the narrative with Frances's point of view, the mise-en-scène encourages the viewer's identification with her erotic attachment to Mehuru. Although the narrative struggles to complete Mehuru's story and to represent him as an individual with agency, the film's image tract relegates him to the object of Frances's—and the viewer's—gaze. Thus, while the narrative line gives us a Mehuru who is set free, the image tract gives us a Mehuru whom we can possess with a look.

Filming Britain's Untold Story: Secrets and Lies?

On four consecutive Sunday evenings beginning October 3, 1999, Channel 4 broadcast its series *Britain's Slave Trade: Telling the Untold*. The first episode opened with the dedication of the Pero Footbridge in Bristol, an event that had taken place in March of that year. "This moment is a sign that Bristol is waking up to its slave trading history," announces the narrator. As we have already seen, the footbridge, a graceful walkway spanning the city's floating harbor, signifies a municipal commitment to the public commemoration of the legacy of the slave trade in Bristol. The four-hour television series aims to repeat the gesture of the bridge. It too is designed to make a connection between an eighteenth-century past and the present by creating a visual and narrative pathway for its viewers. The narrative moves back and forth in time, but also with broad geographic sweeps, as the film crew skirts the circum-Atlantic, traveling to the former Gold Coast of Africa, the Caribbean islands of Jamaica and Barbados, Welsh estates, and the cities of Bristol and Liverpool, gathering both personal and academic testimony. Unfolding in generally chronological order, the four-part series is organized around topics: the slave trade as the exportation of human cargo, the far-reaching effects of the trade on the British economy, and movement toward abolition and emancipation in the nineteenth century, as the "Victorians replaced shackles of iron with racial prejudice."

As a documentary film, *Britain's Slave Trade* possesses three characteristics: it posits an organizing agency that possesses information and knowledge; it offers a text conveying this information; and it creates a subject who will gain knowledge—that is, someone who can take the place of a subject-who-knows.[49] In this series the organizing agency, or the he-who-knows, is represented on screen by historians and other academics, among them David Richardson, Madge Dresser, Robin Blackburn, and David Dabydeen, who in their cameo appearances give weight and authority to the claims made by the text. The text itself is construed as an untold story, or a secret to be revealed—namely, Britain's extensive involvement with the eighteenth-century transatlantic slave trade. As Trevor Phillips explains in his introduction to the companion volume to the series: "Looked at dispassionately, it is almost impossible to imagine how the glories of the Elizabethan and Georgian eras could have been achieved without the slave trade. Yet today Britain's contribution to slavery and the slave trade is primarily seen as the moral task of leading to its abolition."[50] Phillips further maintains:

> There is nothing wrong in this, but, set by itself, the perception robs us of two vital aspects of British history. One is the deep integration of the slavery story into the mainstream of history. The other is the continuing impact of the plantation economy on Britain and its way of life over the past four centuries. Put baldly, but for slavery none of us would probably be where we are now.[51]

Thus, the narration is geared toward a broad, popular audience, presumably one unfamiliar with otherwise predictable images and ideas used to teach the history of slavery: the famous diagram of a slave ship, with its rows of mute, static, enchained Africans; the more sensational aspects of the Middle Passage and the harrowing conditions of slave labor; the *Zong* incident; and the story of William Wilberforce.

As Michael Renov explains, any documentary text contains fictive elements, not "fictions," per se but "moments at which a presumably objective representation of the world encounters the necessity of creative intervention." These include the construction of a character who emerges "through recourse to ideal and imagined categories of hero or genius, the use of poetic language, narration, or musical accompaniment to heighten emotional impact or the creation of suspense via the agency of embedded narratives . . . or various dramatic arcs."[52] In *Britain's Slave Trade*, creative intervention is apparent in fast-paced editing and montage, which are employed to bring together disparate times, peoples, and places quickly and in surprising and memorable ways, juxtaposing this place against that time, this human experience against that historical past. For example, shots of empty Caribbean manor houses, desolate and left open to the weather, testify to the legacy of former British occupation of the sugar islands. However, rather than catalog all the series' features as a documentary, I am interested in one of its most prominent "fictive" elements, or one dramatic arc that reappears in the series through embedded narrative: its use of ordinary Britons, people whose stories are embedded to disclose a surprising discovery or family "secret," namely, that research of one kind or another reveals that they have a black ancestor. Or, as Trevor Phillips puts it elsewhere, "There is a slave past in many who would not have dreamed that they have anything other than a common-or-garden

'English' background."[53] This idea is certainly not original to the series; we have seen the interest in "black blood" in novels from the 1990s. In other words, one version of Britain's untold story emerges as the narrative of its hybrid roots. In this section, I explore the decision to foreground this trope of black ancestry, or of a hidden racial past that is revealed to assert a hybrid identity, in order to ask about its cultural work. How does this familial trope ask ordinary viewers to connect to the legacy of the slave trade? What kinds of ideas are facilitated in the moment when Britain looks in the mirror and discovers its own black ancestors? What are the potential limits of telling the story of the slave trade by making this trope of blood and family connection visually immediate?

The text of *Britain's Slave Trade* begins with a central assertion concerning the role of slavery in England's imperial strength: "The legacy of our slaving past is all around us." Although African slaves were never present in large numbers in England itself, viewers are asked to consider how thoroughly Britain's rapid economic expansion during the eighteenth century was dependent on trade with the West African coast. In other words, "Our industrial might sprung from the labor of millions of slaves." This claim is supported by connecting various activities of eighteenth- and nineteenth-century British businesses to the markets they served and the clienteles they developed. Near Bristol, a man named Gouldney plows his profits into the factory of a local man named Dardy, who makes the iron bars that are traded on the African coast. In Manchester, the slave trade is said to have kick-started the industrial revolution by creating a market for goods made in local factories. In the nineteenth century, the Pennant family (more on them later), whose earlier wealth depended on owning slaves, makes a fortune on steam engines sent to the Caribbean, smoothing Pennant's political rise to Member of Parliament for Liverpool. Prominent British banks that are still household names today, including Barclays, HSBC, and the Royal Bank of Scotland, are all shown to have been founded on lucrative slave trade of the 1770s. Later, British mills were financed by the same banks, as was the importation of cotton from American slave plantations. British insurance is also an industry that owes much to the slave trade, as it first saw profitability from insuring slave ships.

With its interest in awakening the British public from its "amnesia," the series reveals little-known secrets about notable British citizens, who are presented as family members with ghosts in their closets. John Pinney, former occupant of the Georgian House, a Bristol landmark, features prominently as a troubling ancestor, whose memory sits uneasily with his family members. One modern-day descendant reads from Pinney's letters, finding condemning evidence of the family's slave-owning legacy. When Pinney sold the slaves on his sugar plantation on the island of Nevis, he left their fate in the hands of a brutal man named Huggins. After the slaves tried to escape, Huggins publicly flogged them. One woman died of the 291 lashes she received. Pinney rued the whippings, feeling some responsibility for having sold the slaves, but Huggins was acquitted of murder. Pinney's descendants are left to consider their own connection to the tragic series of events.

Meanwhile, a black woman by the name of Diane Pennant travels to North Wales to meet the family who owned her ancestors as slaves. She is graciously, even warmly, received by descendant Edmund Pennant, who shows her around the estate, explaining to her the Welsh origins of her name. The voiceover adds, "Diane's family name is Pennant because his ancestors took her family name away." Edmund reads Diane excerpts from a racist letter by one of his ancestors. Later she finds the record of her ancestor, Edward Pennant, a waiting boy. Throughout the visit, Edmund is apologetic, eager for bridge building. Diane is understanding of the historical circumstances but feels her story will never be complete.

In another sequence, scholar and writer Marina Warner considers the slave owners in her own ancestry. Recalling a family photograph of her grandfather playing cricket with a black boy, she recounts her surprise when she discovered her grandfather's past life as part of a slave-owning family in the Caribbean; according to the narrator, the Warners are "one of many families who rose on the back of slaves." In another scene, shot in the archives of a Liverpool library, Lawrence Westgraph, descended from Robert Cox, a slave trader, discusses how "slave traders and merchants' money built 19th century Liverpool." Did families, then, hide the dependence of family coffers on the slave trade and slave labor? The palm oil necessary for nineteenth-century factories, for instance, would have been produced by enslaved Africans. After the British abolition of the slave trade, enslaved Africans in the United States continued to labor to produce cotton for English mills. Although most of the featured contemporary descendants come across as reflective or sympathetic, a few appear entrenched and unapologetic. Julia Elton is a descendant of Abraham Elton, a manufacturer of copper who made a fortune when he found a market in Africa for his British-made brass products. Julia Elton, poised on the sofa in a grand drawing room of a large house on her family's estate, defends her grandfather's commerce, reasoning that "the slaving past was just part of the culture of trade." But the invisible narrator contests Elton's assertion, suggesting that the origins of English wealth have been "obscured."

Thus, the very purpose of the series is to illuminate the "obscure" and to bring into the light the inextricably intertwined histories of Britain and Africa. This goal is accomplished through a political narrative that introduces the theme of African complicity: the "African role mustn't be swept under the carpet." Africans are shown to have been collaborators who became trapped in the selling of people. Once an indigenous practice, the kidnapping of Africans expands as traders go farther inland for slaves, until "Africa was decapitated and slave trade left an indelible mark. African underdevelopment can be traced to this period." The history of the trade is a story of coconspiracy between greedy African traders and greedy Europeans, yet Africa was irreparably damaged by the arrangement.

But the interconnection of Africa and England is made visually immediate in *Britain's Slave Trade* through the stories of Britons whose identities are revealed to be hybrid. These stories—four in all—represent a "secret" about a supposedly "pure" English blood: that it includes the legacy of earlier intermarriage between blacks and whites. One example emerges in the story of Dennis Barber, the descendant of Francis Barber, the black servant of Dr. Samuel Johnson. Born on a Jamaican slave plantation in 1735, Francis Barber was brought to England in 1750. He received some schooling in Yorkshire before going into service. He went to work for Johnson in 1752, ran away to sea for two years, and returned to Johnson's employ as his butler. He continued his education at a grammar school and married a white woman. After Johnson's death, Barber became a schoolteacher and died in 1801. Barber's story, then, is important because it testifies to a time when intermarriage for black men was not only acceptable but even the norm. Like Equiano, Gronniosaw, and other men of African descent in late-eighteenth-century England, Barber would not have done anything unusual by marrying a white Englishwoman, especially given the relatively few eligible women of African descent. Dennis Barber's appearance in the series thus introduces an eighteenth-century story of interracial contact, one in which miscegenation does not seem to have been an issue. It also suggests how an African heritage has been thoroughly integrated and made invisible over time.

In the case of Jayne Prior, another white Briton, the hybrid nature of her identity was so inaccessible that it became apparent only when she discovered she has the gene for sickle-cell anemia. This condition can be explained only by the presence of black forebears in her bloodline. Her mother appears unfazed by this startling news: "If there hadn't been a slave trade we wouldn't be here." Meanwhile, in Dumfries, Scotland, a man named David Jolly suspects that he has a black ancestor. "David feels haunted by a past he cannot understand," according to the narrator. "He believes he can see evidence of African ancestry even in his grandchildren." Ten miles away, Jolly discovers a portrait of a local family named Maxwell with its black pageboy, dating from 1765, seven generations ago. Michael Maxwell suspects that Jolly is descended from a family incorporating Irish immigrants and the black pageboy. The camera cuts between the eighteenth-century portrait and David, who believes he sees a resemblance between himself and the servant. "David believes he has finally found his black ancestor," declares the narrator. The discovery of David's black roots is taken as proof that "the legacy of our slaving past is all around us."

The stories of Barber, Prior, and Jolly are integrated into the overall narrative as brief episodes that punctuate a larger story about the legacy of intercultural contact between Britain and Africa. They serve to unsettle a myth of racial purity but also to suggest that history leaves a physical imprint. In particular, the history of the British slave trade leaves its mark on English families, English bodies, and English identities. The hybridity of Barber, Prior, and Jolly is an invisibility that is made visible. The immediacy of their hybridity, accessed through the close-up on screen, has the potential to shock and disorient. On the one hand, the truth about their genetic makeup subverts national categories, and it opposes an essentialist understanding of English character. In addition, it potentially counteracts a xenophobic impulse to define a purebred Englishness. On the other hand, privileging the idea of an English hybrid identity has the power to normalize the very idea of hybridity. If black blood runs so freely in English veins, what happens to the category of blackness? Does visualizing hybridity in this way threaten to subsume racial difference, making blackness merely another feature of white identity? To put this another way, do black roots that reveal themselves in the physiognomies of these white faces retain anything of their traumatic originary circumstances?

Unlike Prior or Jolly, Janet Randall, the fourth featured individual of mixed heritage, grew up with an awareness of her black ancestry through her black grandfather. Randall is filmed living her ordinary English life. Nothing in her appearance or manner, nothing in the very typical English style of her home or garden, suggests that she is anything less than a true Briton. Randall herself insists that because of her English way of life she has never felt "coloured": "I've never felt anything but British." The narration does not directly challenge the specious distinction between being British and being black. Instead, it follows Randall as she travels to Barbados in search of the story of her black grandfather, a man named Ward. When she shares photographs of her grandfather with black Barbadians, she believes she discovers a family resemblance as well as the missing pieces of her family tree. A trip to the local records office reveals that both her great-grandparents were slaves: "How can I feel what they felt?" wonders Randall. The camera follows her as she walks, in deep reflection, through a modern sugar plantation.

Yet here Janet's connection to England's secret involvement in the slave trade follows from her recognizing the slave within her. If Janet, as a "typical" English person, stands in for all of Britain, then the message appears to be that a full reckoning for the past traumas of slavery results most powerfully when the viewer, like Randall, makes a *biological* connection between her own family and slavery. However, what would it take for Janet Randall to care about Caribbean slavery as a category of human experience that was not part of her family's legacy? How might she have accomplished the more difficult moral task of making the connection between her "British" way of life and the historical legacy of slavery? Here hybridity grounds Janet Randall's growing awareness, reflection, and response to the slave trade. It allows her to bridge the gap between her experience as a white, contemporary Briton and the horrors of eighteenth-century slavery. But here too hybridity paradoxically requires another kind of essentialist understanding; her personal reckoning with slavery depends on her acknowledging her black blood.

This critique leads to a broader question concerning the power of hybridity as an antiracist tool: how useful is hybridity to the project of deconstructing narrow and racist definitions of a national identity? In an essay on the dialectics of cultural hybridity, Pnina Werbner provides an answer to this question: "Hybridity is not the only mode of resistance to homogenizing ideologies" such as the myth of an all-white Britain. She continues:

> Whether nationalism or ethnicity are "good" or "evil" depends on the ability (and right) of members of ethnic or national collectivities to engage in reflexive self-critical distancing from their own cultural discourses, and hence also to recognize the potential validity of other discourses/communities of language.[54]

Thus, following Werbner's point, we see that Janet Randall's story might have been more powerful if it had gone beyond exposing her hybrid roots. For instance, it might have shown her engaging reflexively and self-critically in a white racist discourse that insists on distinguishing "British" from "coloured." The difficulty is not to get Janet Randall—or the audience—to see the slave within but to elicit an acknowledgment of the legitimate and valid claims of Britain's black community for social justice, regardless of whether a family connection exists.

While *Britain's Slave Trade* gives us three stories of individuals who reckon with—or even embrace—their hybridity—it also gives us one story in which the search for hybrid roots is associated with pain, not pleasure. Throughout Parts II and III of the series, Janet Randall's story is intertwined with the story of Robert Beckford, a black Briton of Jamaican ancestry who believes that he has white blood, most likely as the result of the rape of one of his black foremothers. Like Randall, Beckford travels in search of his Caribbean roots, in his case to Jamaica. There, however, he discovers that his black relatives remain proud of their white name because of the powerful history it signifies. When Beckford tells them of his alienation from that history—and of his desire to rename himself—they counsel him to keep the name because the Beckfords "taught us to respect the family." But Beckord's disaffection—and his radicalism—increase first as he discovers white racist ancestors, whose interpretation of Christianity he deems especially hypocritical, buried in the local churchyard and again when, back in Bath, he visits William Beckford's extravagant home built with the profits from the sugar plantation.

Unlike Randall, Beckford never finds any evidence of his white heritage. Instead, he eventually discovers a Robert Beckford among the list of those punished after Sam Sharp's revolt. Sharp was a black Baptist preacher who organized slave resistance in the form of a work stoppage on Christmas Day 1831. The action quickly escalated as armed slaves banded together, but in the end 580 rebels were executed.[55] Beckford feels that the discovery of this rebel ancestor makes the Beckford name noteworthy and affirms his identity. Thus, Beckford's story resolves with his identification with his rebellious black ancestor. If he fails to prove that he has white blood, neither can he prove that he does not. For him, the possibility of hybridity begins with a sense of violation and rupture, not connection. Yet ultimately he finds agency, despite his initial sense of a compromised identity.

Throughout the viewing experience of *Britain's Slave Trade*, the text has moved the audience, the "subject who will gain knowledge," closer to the position of the subject-who-knows. By the end, the viewer also carries information concerning Britain's secret past, its deep involvement and continuing engagement with the repercussions of the slave trade. The viewer also has access to a secret she is meant to locate in the bosom of her British family. But here Bill Nichols is useful in helping us to think about the purpose of this documentary. In particular, Nichols explains how the knowledge produced by a documentary,

> as much or more than the imaginary identification between viewer and fictional character, promises the viewer a sense of plenitude or self-sufficiency. Knowledge, like ideal-ego figures or objects of desire suggested by the characters of narrative fiction, becomes a source of pleasure that is far from innocent. Who are we that we may know something? Of what does knowledge consist? What we know, and how we use the knowledge we have, are matters of social and ideological significance.[56]

In partial answer to Nichols's questions, I have been suggesting that what we come to know throughout *Britain's Slave Trade* is that the legacy of slavery touches all Britain's citizens. As we come to this knowledge, a pleasure arises from the stories of individuals who connect with their hybrid "roots." The satisfaction that they gain from knowing the truth about their family connections, the fact of their genetic legacy, is the viewer's satisfaction as well. At the same time, a sense of plenitude arises from the expanded, now "complete" family circles represented on screen. However, when the documentary text literalizes and makes visually immediate the idea of England's hybridity, showing us white Britons who have black blood, it defaults in favor of biology. Privileging family connections over more abstract universal human rights, genetic connection over looser affiliation, it misses an important opportunity to appeal to a broader humanitarianism. In such a humanitarianism what matters is not how we respond to those we can locate physically in our family circle but how we respond, with due conscience and with a sense of responsibility, to those who are not directly related to us.

As a coda to this discussion, I note that some of the work of this series had already been anticipated in the form of Mike Leigh's 1996 film *Secrets & Lies*, the story of a contemporary black Londoner who goes in search of her true parents, only to discover that her mother is white.[57] In several ways, Leigh's film lies beyond the parameters of my discussion. Set in London in the 1990s, it neither visualizes the lives of eighteenth-century slaves nor takes up the legacy of the slave trade. Yet this film is central to my argument because it takes a profoundly antiracist position by going beyond the idea of biological connection. Although the film also shows its audience the black blood that circulates within a white family, unlike the television documentary it does not make an antiracist statement that is contingent on finding the slave within.

In a sense, then, the film is important for what it does not do and for what it does not need to say—it does not develop the idea of "roots" and it does not need to say that blackness creates a specific kind of British identity. Hortense Cumberbatch (Marianne Jean-Baptiste) is an educated and sophisticated professional black woman, an optometrist living in a tastefully decorated flat in a fashionable neighborhood in London. As the film begins, her mother has just died, and the camera pans to cover the black West Indian mourners at her funeral. The death of her adopted mother sets into motion Hortense's desire to find her birth mother, who turns out to be Cynthia Purley, a working-class white woman, a factory worker who, never having been married, lives in a ramshackle flat with her foul-mouthed, hostile, twenty-one-year-old daughter, Roxanne. The film follows Hortense's efforts to track down Cynthia, to convince her to meet with her, and to develop a bond with her. The action culminates at a family birthday party for Roxanne to which Cynthia has brought Hortense, where she reveals the shameful secret of Hortense's illegitimate birth and her subsequent placement of the baby for adoption.

FIGURE 6 Brenda Blethyn as Cynthia and Marianne Jean-Baptiste as Hortense in *Secrets & Lies*, directed by Mike Leigh.
Source: Courtesy of FilmFour.

Curiously, throughout the film, although the mise-en-scène repeatedly focuses on racial difference, the characters pay little attention to Hortense's race. Cynthia is, of course, taken aback when her black daughter presents herself, and she initially insists that the birth record must be mistaken. But, remembering the circumstances of her conception, she quickly accepts Hortense, finding in her a striking resemblance to herself. She tells Hortense: "You look more like me than [Roxanne] does. Same build."[58] Hortense's adopted family is significantly different from her biological family not because of its race but because of its social class and professional accomplishment; whereas Cynthia and Roxanne, who collects trash for the Council and resists "using her brain," are barely surviving financially and belong to a marginal working class, Hortense's mother was a midwife, a profession Cynthia admires. Apparently Hortense's mother owned a house. Hortense's brothers also have good jobs. A quick allusion to a family trip by plane to Barbados (to see family?) rounds out the portrait of Hortense's comfortable middle-class upbringing.

The estrangement and alienation in the film are intrafamilial, not interracial; Cynthia fails to connect with the angry, spoiled Roxanne. She is lonely and isolated as well from her younger brother, Maurice, a successful photographer living in a posh neighborhood, who in turn craves affection from his deeply unhappy wife, Monica, who, it is revealed at the end, has struggled with her infertility for fifteen years. Monica and Cynthia can barely speak to each other, and the tension between them is palpable. The film depicts a profound failure of human connection, and it depicts the family as the place where that failure is felt most immediately and most deeply. Yet in the end Hortense's role is to create bonds and facilitate connection. Her surprise appearance at Roxanne's birthday party leads to the disclosure of a series of family secrets, best summarized by Maurice:

> Secrets and lies! We're all in pain. Why can't we share our pain? I've spent my entire life trying to make people 'appy, and the three people I love most in the world 'ate each other's guts, I'm in the middle AND I CAN'T TAKE IT ANY MORE.[59]

Turing to Hortense, he apologizes and tells her, "But you are a very brave person." "A very stupid person," responds Hortense. Maurice responds: "No, you're not. You wanted to find the truth, and you were prepared to suffer the consequences. And I admire you for that. I mean it." Maurice's outburst leads his family not to a happy ending but to small conciliatory steps, and the film leaves us with a series of scenarios in which the characters move toward reconnection.

By declaring Hortense "brave" and giving her the role of a facilitator who sets into motion the airing of painful secrets, the film assigns her an admirable role. It depicts her as possessing rare and quiet strengths. Eliding discussion of her origins, ancestry, or "roots," the film makes Hortense's "difference" a sign not of her racial heritage but of her human gifts, her moral superiority, her integrity, and her courage. By elevating itself above the specific discussion of Hortense's race, the film becomes a profoundly antiracist statement. Among the many secrets revealed by this film, the biggest may be the nature of the family as an overburdened and inadequate structure for ensuring human connection. Hortense's role in the film is to both air the lie and to provide some hope that, by taking in those we are least likely to recognize as our own, we can shape the family into a sustainable human experience.

Filming the Invisible in *Mansfield Park*

Like *A Respectable Trade*, Patricia Rozema's *Mansfield Park* is a costume drama. Unlike *A Respectable Trade*, however, it is also a pastiche—a film that self-consciously plays with the representation of history in both its narrative and its mise-en-scène.[60] Some characters wear historically accurate costumes; others wear clothes designed to denote their personalities—Mary Crawford's "spider dress," which she wears twice in the film, is clearly meant to say more about her predatory behavior than about late-eighteenth-century fashion. In addition, Rozema's recourse to events that never took place—for example, the slave ship anchored off Portsmouth—signals her willingness to play with the idea of history as mimesis. Her intent appears to have been to compress historical events in a way that ignores historical accuracy, but that leaves the viewer somewhat conscious of historical narrative. Her Fanny not only represents the youthful Jane Austen but also self-consciously references the art of telling stories. Thus, to her credit, Rozema avoids the ambivalent statement of a costume drama such as *A Respectable Trade*; here her self-aware image tract, together with her wry narration, works to create a consistently ironic film. Yet, we are left to consider what the movie conveys. To the extent that Rozema's film contributes to an existing conversation about British participation in the eighteenth-century slave trade, what is her message and how is it structured? To answer these questions, this section first takes a detour through the academic debate that preceded the film. It then explores Rozema's decision to make visible, immediate, and accessible a series of ideas that apparently remain hidden in the original novel.

Rozema's adaptation takes up Austen's most contested novel, one that had already been at the center of an extended academic debate before the film appeared in 1999. This debate was initiated by Edward Said's controversial assertion in 1993 that readers are compelled to see Austen's novel as "resisting or avoiding" the fact that the Bertram family money derives from a sugar plantation in the West Indies. Yet, according to Said, the novel's "formal inclusiveness, historical honesty, and prophetic suggestiveness cannot completely hide" its colonial politics.[61] Over the next few years, Said's suggestive comments led to a wide-ranging forum, with critics weighing in both to extend his critique and to defend Austen against more serious political charges that the novel is complicit with a politics of imperialism. It is helpful to see the issues of that forum as a series of questions, beginning with biographical queries that seek to clarify Austen's knowledge about and relationship to slavery, the slave trade, and abolition. The critical consensus is now that "Austen knew a great deal about both the 'manners' of the West Indies, and the various 'representations' of them current, not merely from her reading but from [her father] George Austen's trusteeship of an Antigua estate, her brothers' naval stations in the West Indies, and through [her sister] Cassandra's fiancé and other friends of the family."[62] Detailed accounts of what Austen read—from Thomas Clarkson's *The History of the Rise, Progress, and Accomplishment of the Abolition of the African Slave Trade* (which, as we have already seen, is also on a reading list for Rozema's Fanny Price) to Captain Pasley's *Essay on the Military Policy of the British Empire*—help to establish the cultural and intellectual milieu in which Austen's politics apparently would have developed.[63]

Biographer Claire Tomalin argues that a short story entitled "An African Story," written in 1809 by Austen's niece Fanny, points to a proabolitionist sentiment in the Austen family.[64] Further clues in Austen's novel to the scope of her knowledge about the political issues of her day are found in her choice of highly evocative names in her novel: "Mansfield" itself suggests the Lord Chief Justice who decided the famous Somerset case, and Fanny's Aunt Norris bears the name of a notorious real-life slave captain.[65] Thus, many biographical critics assume that Austen had a degree of interest in and sympathy for the cause. Ruth Perry provides an apt summary of the complicated nature of Austen's political position:

> Neither "unreflective" nor "uninflected," Austen's references to British colonialism are complicated and refracted through the controversies of her day. . . . Living in an expanding imperialist society, Austen represented its ideological pressures even as she was susceptible to them. Rather than demonstrating her obliviousness to the privileges of class and global location, Austen's colonial references reverse. . . . the deep contradictions of Enlightenment thought, the problems implicit in exporting humanism, capitalism, and technology to the rest of the world."[66]

Similar to questions about Austen's biography and intellectual development are those concerning her readership. For whom did Austen write her novels, and what might she have expected her readers to know or think beforehand about the transatlantic slave trade or the recent abolition movement? It would be convenient to assume that "many of Austen's early readers would have found the Bertrams' West Indian income [from their sugar plantation] morally dubious" and that "all would have been aware of some voices condemning it," but historical sources cannot demonstrate this readerly consensus with any certainty.[67] Moreover, readers of the novel, regardless of their era, must bring a keen historical awareness to the moment in which Austen sets her novel. As Brian Southam argues, it matters less what the reader thinks of Fanny's question to Sir Thomas than whether, within the setting of the novel, the question is meant to have been asked before or after abolition in 1807.[68]

In fact, when we ask about the politics of Austen or her readers, we do not necessarily resolve the question of what the text itself says on the subject of the slave trade—whatever Austen or her readers "knew," whatever the political climate in which she wrote, a second group of critics is inclined to argue that the novel makes its own statement. Two major quandaries preoccupy this group of largely formalist critics. First, what is the nature of the relationship between the novel's narrator and the main character Fanny Price? Does Fanny merely "ventriloquize Austen's spiritual beliefs," perhaps becoming a "eurocentrically conceived 'grateful Negro'" in the process, or do we find a skeptical distance between the narrator and the character?[69] Thus, further questions arise concerning the tone of the novel in general and the role of irony in particular, questions that are sometimes overlooked by a historical approach.

For example, when Fanny finally returns from her punitive stay at Portsmouth, the narration describes her extraordinary happiness in returning to a place where "no sounds of contention, no raised voice, no abrupt bursts, no tread of violence was ever heard; all proceeded in a regular course of cheerful orderliness; every body had their due importance; every body's feelings were consulted."[70] On the surface, the text seems to evince an historical blind spot: here, it appears, Mansfield Park is praised for its pacific and orderly qualities, despite the fact that its wealth rests on the violent exploitation of slave labor. However, the passage is written in free indirect discourse, expressing what Susan Fraiman calls "the conspicuous banality of Fanny's idiom."[71] Allowing us to hear her heroine's thoughts, the narrator clearly distances herself from her character through an irony that reveals a countertruth: Fanny *had* heard sounds of contention when her uncle insisted that she accept Henry Crawford's proposal of marriage. Prior to her entry onto the marriage market, she had never had her due importance considered or her own feelings consulted on any subject. Yet, having identified this narrative irony, this obvious distance between what the character thinks and what the narrator obviously knows, how much more can we assume about the narrator's (not to mention the author's) politics? Does the narrator's knowledge that Fanny is wrong about the nature of Mansfield Park necessarily extend to the perspective that Mansfield Park is morally corrupted by the slave trade?

In fact, the political inclinations of the omniscient, third-person narrator can be inferred only through tonal clues that often indicate severe disapproval of characters like Sir Thomas. At the end of the novel, for example, he congratulates himself that "Fanny was indeed the daughter he wanted. His charitable kindness had been rearing a prime comfort for himself. His liberality had a rich repayment, and the goodness of his intentions by her, deserved it."[72] As self-serving as it is inaccurate (what "charitable kindness" coerces a young woman to marry a man she does not love?), this comment attests to Sir Thomas's continual failings as a father. And so, with an eye to the importance of gender roles in the novel, another group of critics focus their attention on the relationship of domesticity and family to empire, often asking as well about links between themes of racial oppression and gender oppression in the novel. Like the historical critics, these critics also look for evidence of a historical awareness in the text, although they more often identify that awareness as a circulating cultural ideology than as a particular political belief of the author's.

A last set of questions, then, involves the relationship of *Mansfield Park* to emerging ideas about colonialism and the British Empire: independently of what we know of the author's biography, does the novel support or censure emerging colonial and imperial ideologies? Several critics discover connections between Fanny and slavery, connections that seem to intimate an oblique resistance to an imperialist agenda. For instance, Maaja Stewart highlights the economic similarities between the position of women in the novel and that of West Indian slaves who were "central in generating the surplus capital essential to the new economy at the same time that they remained anomalies in the liberal discourse of self-determined actors."[73] For both Joseph Lew and Marcus Wood, Fanny's position powerfully resembles that of a slave, with her connection to Sir Thomas suggesting the tie between the master and the bond servant. For Wood, Fanny is "both exemplar of white female beauty and sexual modesty, and of the overtly displayed charms of the quadroon on the auction block."[74] For many of these critics, Austen's own status as a woman writer is directly relevant to the issue of her imperial complicity. Returning us full circle to Said's critique, Susan Fraiman rightly questions how Austen comes to bear the burden for imperial travesty: "Women did, of course, help to rationalize imperialism, and Austen is guilty along with the rest. But Said's balance sheet still has her paying more than her share of the bills. This occurs in part, because, like the angel of false peace, she, more than any other single figure, is made to bear the symbolic burden of empire."[75] In summary, what is at stake in the critical controversy over *Mansfield Park* is an ongoing debate over Austen's status as a canonical writer. Knowing what we do about the West Indian slave trade, how should we talk about, teach, or generally regard Austen's novel?

But what happens to questions concerning the historical context, the formal effects, the ideological content, and the canonical weight of *Mansfield Park* when the novel becomes a film? As Rozema asserts, "In the book, Fanny is interpreted through Jane Austen. In the movie, I'm the interpreter."[76] She resolves formal issues concerning Austen's relationship to her own character by collapsing Fanny with one version of the author's narrator during the time of her juvenilia, ranging from *Love and Freindship* [sic] (1789) to *Northanger Abbey* (begun in 1798). In those early works, Austen's youthful narrator is perspicacious and astute. Her wit is acerbic and her targets—including hypocrisy, intellectual pretension, and literary convention—are clear and specific. As Claudia Johnson writes in her highly positive review, "By weaving in Austen's uproarious early writings, Rozema transforms Fanny into a version of the Austenian narrator we love."[77] This choice of an updated Austenian narrator enhances the work of the film as pastiche, but it also leads to several contradictions in the screenplay: a Fanny who knows what she thinks and is willing to express herself is unlikely, for instance, to stand by and watch silently as Mary Crawford rides away on her horse.[78] In addition, it is less than convincing that a Fanny who enjoys the spotlight as an author—and who enthusiastically playacts the part for her sister, Edmund, and the camera—later declares "To be truthful, I live in dread of audiences."[79]

Rozema's Fanny says what a modern audience expects—or perhaps wants—her to say. For example, commenting on a dissipated, idle lifestyle, she declares life at Mansfield to be "nothing more than a quick succession of busy nothings."[80] And in response to one too many humiliations by her Aunt Norris, she finally delivers a scathing put-down to the older woman:

Mrs. Norris: Just a moment, Fanny, how long are you staying?
Fanny: I'm not certain, Aunt Norris. And how long are you staying?[81]

Throughout the film, Fanny's voiceovers—many of them taken verbatim from Austen's early works—indicate the exact tenor of Fanny's moral universe, a world in which hypocrisy is always recognized and exposed: upon Maria's wedding, "Her mother stood with salts in her hand, expecting to be agitated . . . and her aunt tried to cry."[82] This portrayal of Fanny as an arch, incipient feminist dissolves the distance not only between Austen and her character but also between the contemporary viewer and Fanny. However, this tension between Fanny and the reader of the novel potentially makes for the best instructional moments in the classroom. As students articulate what they like about Fanny—or, conversely, what drives them crazy about her—they also come to recognize a series of larger principles and issues that follow from the choice of a "passive" versus an "active" approach to life.

Rozema borrows from Austen's biographers and makes Fanny, like her author, an enthusiast for abolitionist literature, in particular Thomas Clarkson's two-volume, twelve-hundred-page work. We are meant to believe that, based on her reading, Fanny (like Austen?) knows what we know; the rights and privileges of slaves as human beings are apparently as obvious to her as they are to a contemporary audience. But the discourse of abolition is not the discourse of modern civil rights. Indeed, as Marcus Wood argues in *Blind Memory*, slaves are curiously absent from Clarkson's history, and Fanny would not necessarily have learned much about slavery from a history of the white abolition movement.[83] Film is an economic medium in which shorthand is used to convey larger historical themes; here "Clarkson" stands for modern liberal philosophy on race. However, in implying that Fanny knows what the audience knows, the film suggests that a moral position in preabolition 1806 (the date in which Rozema sets her film) is the same as one in 1999. There appears to be little difference between a late-twentieth-century political perspective and one that would still have been unevenly emerging at the turn of the nineteenth century. Yet erasing that difference entails erasing as well the complicated and painful history: how did an important liberal truth establish itself as irrefutable fact in the face of powerful arguments to the contrary? Similarly, to depict Sir Thomas in the same scene as an obvious and easy target for his clearly mistaken and racist assumptions about mulattoes is to underestimate the power and persuasiveness of those who successfully opposed abolition for so long.

In making Fanny's mind "as hungry as that of any man," Rozema also leaves out important questions concerning the role of gender in imperial expansion. What was the role of women in an age of imperial growth? What was the relationship between their self-definition and various imperial projects? According to Maaja Stewart, the novel acknowledges the West Indies as a male domain, a place likely to be inaccessible to Austen's female readers. For Stewart, the novel creates a binary between imperialism and domesticity, or between male and female culture, a binary paralleled by the worlds of imperial endeavor and metropolitan culture. Although Stewart describes how that binary is often deconstructed by the presence of the female slave whose sexual oppression transgresses against the domestic family, Stewart's historical perspective puts Fanny in one world and her uncle Sir Thomas in entirely another.

Yet Rozema's interest lies in showing Fanny and Sir Thomas in the same world, and she uses Fanny to deconstruct the binary opposition between the West Indies and the domestic English world—until the climatic moment when Tom's sketchbook is discovered, Fanny is the only "slave" we see. (In fact, house servants very rarely appear in the film.) Fanny is the visible reminder that the leisured world of Mansfield Park rests on the labor of others. Although she is kin to the Bertrams, she is more often treated as a social inferior. In the novel Fanny's primary duty is to serve as a companion to Lady Bertram, but in the film she assures her family in Portsmouth that she does much more.[84] She is not meant to share the pleasures of the other girls, and can be humiliated and banished from the room by Mrs. Norris. The film most clearly makes the connection between Fanny and a slave when Sir Thomas returns from the West Indies. As the actor playing Sir Thomas, Harold Pinter conveys a salacious interest in Fanny's "improved" figure. In a later scene, Rozema's blocking has him towering above Fanny, leering at her from above, while she, at the level of his groin, blushes under his scrutiny. Their bodily positions directly mimic those of Sir Thomas and the slave, apparently as a prelude to fellatio, in a drawing that Fanny later discovers in Tom's sketchbook. In this way, Sir Thomas's decision to put Fanny on the marriage market is connected to his decision to trade slaves, as Fanny herself intuits. "I'll not be sold off like one of your father's slaves," she forcefully tells Edmunds.[85] In response to Sir Thomas's bullying authority, she appropriates the language and demeanor of a rebellious slave. "Then you will marry [Crawford]. I will not [beat] Sir," she sneers in reply.[86]

This attention to Fanny's status as surrogate sexual slave is only one in a series of issues intimated by the novel that are made visible, concrete, and explicit in the film. Interviews often cite Rozema's intention to bring into the open what was "hidden" in Austen's works, beginning with the economic system behind a gentrified lifestyle and moving on to a dubious morality. "I show the economic basis of all that leisure," Rozema is reported as having said. "There's evil in the basement of *Mansfield Park*, and I show it. Just to focus on the fineries is half the picture. [This Austen adaptation] is not as fussy; it's more spare; the aesthetic is a little tougher. It's not all floral patterns and puffy sleeves."[87] Examples of this "tougher" approach include allusions to incest (not only between uncle and niece but also between Fanny and her father), hints of a homosexual attraction between Fanny and Mary Crawford, and the on-screen representation of the adultery between Maria Bertram and Henry Crawford. Whereas Austen's narrator reveals only that Maria and Henry have run away to an undisclosed location, Rozema's film depicts the two caught in the act by a shocked and horrified Fanny, who discovers them in bed together at Mansfield Park. It is certainly possible to defend this choice—as Claudia Johnson does—by reminding Austen's readers that the novel itself is "suffused with frustrated, illicit, wayward, or polymorphous sexuality."[88] In addition, on a purely visual level, it might make sense to show the audience how the estate system, with its insistence on property relations over love and affection, led to hypocrisy and deceit. Since Maria's tragedy was the product of Mansfield Park, why not locate it in situ?

Nonetheless, the decision to foreground Maria's adultery means that the film must forgo another theme of social importance. For Austen, the point of Maria's adultery is not only the repressed sexual passion it reflects but also the destructive and devastating consequences of the social scandal set off by the sexual conduct. In the novel, it is not what we see but what we hear talked about that matters. Fanny, for instance, learns about the transgression from a gossip column brought to her attention in Portsmouth, the malicious tone of the comment being as shocking as the possibility it reveals.[89] The film attempts to convey something of the power of social scandal by having Rushworth—trailed by a member of the nineteenth-century paparazzi (who happens to have come in search of a different kind of story)—seek out his wayward wife the morning she has absconded with her lover.

Astute readers of the novel would not have needed visual prompting to recognize where Maria was heading; they would have "seen" this denouement earlier, allegorically displayed in the visit to Sotherton. As the affianced Maria Bertram, Henry Crawford, and Mr. Rushworth confront a locked gate—for which the inept Mr. Rushworth has no key—Maria quotes the caged starling from Sterne's *A Sentimental Journey*: "But unluckily that iron gate, that ha-ha, give me feelings of restraint and hardship. I cannot get out, as the starling said."[90] With Henry's assistance, Maria then passes around the edge of the gate, despite Fanny's protestations that she will hurt herself or tear her dress. Austen's use of Sterne's text enforces her message that in agreeing to marry Rushworth Maria has "caged" herself in an oppressive marriage that is entirely a property arrangement. But the message goes further. Sterne had written the passage—in which the predicament of a caged talking starling leads his narrator to meditate on the evils of slavery—in response to a request from Ignatio Sancho that he write something on the subject of slavery. Yorick's meditation thus functions as a political intervention in response to abolition issues, one whose ironic tone is nonetheless subject to critique. By having Maria quote the caged starling, Austen clearly means to link the oppressive nature of the marriage market and the slave market, while once again alerting her reader to the topicality of the abolition movement.[91]

Thus, in the novel, the scene set in the "wilderness" at Sotherton—as well as the often-discussed theatrical scene at Mansfield Park—conveys a series of ideas and themes through social and religious allegorical symbols. It is worth considering the role of allegory in the novel version of *Mansfield Park*. As an alternative way of "making visible" what is otherwise unseen, allegory is a very old and traditional way of making demands on the viewer, asking that we do the interpreting, that we move from visual clue to additional meaning. Allegory also risks what the film does not; readers of allegory can fail to get the point (as classroom teachers of *Mansfield Park* know too well).[92] Thus, it is inaccurate to imply that things are not "seen" in Austen's novel; to the contrary, they are already visible to the reader who takes an active part in an alternative kind of reading.

To see the difference between Rozema's and Austen's approaches to visualization, consider the representation of Mary Crawford. Early in the novel, Austen plays with her character on two levels: her narrator makes clear that Mary is sexy, cosmopolitan, and appealing, but she also indicates that Mary has a dubious moral character. Mary's famous off-color pun concerning "rears and vices" in Chapter Six, as well as her callous unresponsiveness to the situation of an agrarian community that cannot serve her needs by immediately transporting her harp, are two early examples of her inferior moral character.[93] During the allegorical visit to Sotherton, the narrator casts Mary as a modern-day Eve who tempts Edmund along a "serpentine course" in a "wilderness" on the estate. With flagrant disregard for the law, expressing little interest in being disciplined by time ("I cannot be dictated to by a watch"[94]), Mary Crawford exists on the boundary of an illicit feminine "wild zone." Centuries before the revolutionary writings of French feminists such as Catherine Clément and Hélène Cixous, Austen explores a femininity that resists patriarchal control. Rather than insist that we reject Mary's values, the narrator instead leads her readers to see gradually how Mary's lifestyle—a life resistant to patriarchal morality, structure, and control—can only lead to dire consequences. Like Edmund weighing Mary's considerable charms, the reader enjoys the brief seduction, only then to consider what such seduction entails. Meanwhile, the narrator herself holds back from explicit comment, judgment, or assessment of Mary's character, allowing Mary's actions to speak for themselves.

In the film version, Rozema signals Mary's "badness" through obvious visual clues: her Mary Crawford plays billiards, bums a cigarette from a brother, and wears her "spider-woman" dress, a black sheath with weblike sleeves. More obviously, she vamps a dangerous lesbian attraction to Fanny. In one scene she playacts a love scene with Fanny, whom she has cast in the male role, while suggestively spanning her waist with her hands. In another scene she undresses a rain-soaked Fanny, wiping and admiring her wet, glistening body. Yet arguably such scenes serve a homophobic purpose. Why should the intimation of Mary's moral dereliction depend on the notion that she is "kinky" at best and gay at worst? What is Rozema saying here about the connection between Mary's unconventional sexuality and her role as the arch villainess of the film? Should we believe that Mary's later outspoken and shocking sentiments on a series of delicate issues, ranging from the possibility of Tom's death to Maria's adultery, are connected to an "aberrant" and unconventional sexuality? In short, whereas Austen's approach to Mary Crawford relies on indirection, a series of clues to be deciphered and weighed by the reader, Rozema's approach requires the direct and immediate recognition of an evil to be reckoned with. Austen sends her readers to the Old Testament for clues; Rozema sends her viewers to the celluloid closet.

To summarize the analysis so far, Rozema's supporters defend her film on the grounds that it "uncovers" or makes accessible deep or darker truths that the novel aims to repress or hide. I argue that it is more accurate to describe the novel and the film as being invested in *alternative means* of visualizing. Austen's recourse to allegory leads the reader to "visualize" her own connections, making accessible a series of freighted images, moments, and events that demand an interpretation and lead to individual insights. Meanwhile, Rozema's direction—in particular, her blocking, dialogue, and costumes—conveys specific, collective meanings that extract from Austen's text not merely what was "hidden" but something more. The distinction between these two kinds of visualization becomes more significant when we consider the representation of the West Indian slave trade in the film. As we have also seen so far, although biographers point to conclusive evidence that Jane Austen knew about—and was most likely fairly liberal in her opinions on—the slave trade, what *Mansfield Park* says on the subject remains resistant to definitive interpretation. The most we can say is that Austen chooses to leave the subject, as it is discussed by both the narrator and the characters, oblique. The silence that meets Fanny Price's question to her uncle is a silence into which much can be projected, one way or another. Similarly, arguments concerning the ideological inclination of the novel prove irresolvable, as critics differ in the weight they give to gender, politics, and the political climate itself.

Rozema's film resolves the critical controversy surrounding the ideology of the novel by picking up on what Austen probably knew and by demonstrating that the characters in the story surely possess the same knowledge. In the movie, evidence of the slave trade is omnipresent—from Fanny's first encounter with the slave ship to the large map of Antigua on the wall of Sir Thomas's study to the statue of the black "lackey" decorating the family's conservatory. Through a series of visual clues, the film shows us what everybody conveniently denies: that the wealth of the estate depends on the brutal exploitation of slave labor. Rozema develops the character of Tom, the eldest Bertram son, to create a moral tale about the dangers of repressing what should be openly seen and challenged.

In both the novel and the film, Tom is profligate, an alcoholic wastrel who threatens to deplete the family coffers, making the situation tenuous for Edmund as the second son. In the novel, however, the roots of that profligacy lie in the unjust system of primogeniture; as she does elsewhere in her oeuvre, Austen impugns an economic system that unfairly concentrates family wealth in the hands of the oldest son, leaving other, equally deserving male—and female—family members to fend for themselves. In Austen's novels, the practice of primogeniture often leads to filial abuses, as the oldest son exploits the power and privileges given to him by the system. (In *Sense and Sensibility*, for instance, Austen depicts eldest son Robert Ferrars as a man who has nothing better to do than buy himself a silver toothpick case.) In the movie, though, Tom's profligacy is pathological; he represses the brutal reality he has seen and experienced on his father's plantation in Antigua, and this repression results in self-destructive behaviors as he struggles with his father's hypocrisy. Rozema's Tom returns prematurely from his trip to Antigua. Inebriated, he falls off his horse, making accusations about the "lovely people there [who are] paying for this party."[95] He later appears in blackface at the house theatricals, hovering in the shadows. Ultimately, he falls deathly ill as a result, the audience is told, of having been abandoned in a debilitated state by his comrades.

Through Fanny's viewpoint, Rozema intimates that the true source of Tom's illness is his knowledge of his father's iniquities as a brutal slave master. As Fanny nurses Tom late at night, she discovers under his bed a leather sketchbook in which he has recorded the shocking truth about life on the Antiguan plantation. With distress and horror, Fanny flips through the book, noting evidence that the plantation community, and Sir Thomas in particular, have been involved in the torture, rape, and sexual abuse of the plantation slaves. On the soundtrack we hear muffled screams and cries, while the camera tilts. Sir Thomas enters the room, grabs the book, and flings it into the fire. "My son is mad," he bellows as Fanny flees from the room.[96]

An ensuing scene, not found in the novel, conveys the idea that Tom has become the necessary scapegoat for his father's sins. Sir Thomas describes how as a child Tom had often begged him for "a noble mission."[97] Full of self-recrimination and regret, Rozema's Sir Thomas implicitly acknowledges his mistake in having involved his son in the sinister business of slavery. Once the evil that has been plaguing him has been brought out into the open and implicitly addressed, Tom recovers, and, with the errant Maria and the corrupt Mary Crawford displaced from the estate, the plot moves toward its quick resolution. Even Rozema herself does not seem to take this speedy denouement seriously. She allows Fanny a final voiceover in which she makes the arch pronouncement that Sir Thomas "eventually abandoned his pursuits in Antigua. He chose instead to pursue existing new opportunities in Tobacco"—a trade equally reliant on slavery in 1806.[98]

In writing about Fanny's discovery of Tom's drawings, Rozema commented, "That scene was my reason for doing the movie—or at least one of my reasons."[99] But what are the consequences of privileging this highly explicit and shocking portrayal of plantation life? As historically inclined viewers will readily recognize, the images that Fanny sees, although not actual copies, refer to other, well-known representations of slavery. The second image is a simulacrum of William Blake's illustration of "A Negro hung alive by the Ribs to a Gallows" for John Stedman's *Narrative of a Five Year's Expedition Against the Revolted Negroes of Surinam*. Other images are still more shocking. Drawn in a crude and sensational manner, they depict, among other sights, a chain gang in front of a plantation house, a close-up of the tortured face of a chained man, and the brutal rape of a female slave.[100] Although the images allude to late-eighteenth-century representations, they differ in crucial ways. The heavy lines with which they are drawn, for instance, suggest the use of modern felt-tip pens, not the charcoal that might have been used. More important, the drawings evince an "in-your-face" attitude; they are clearly drawn to shock and disgust (and indeed Tom supposedly would have drawn them with this intent). Far more aggressive and less subtle than the eighteenth-century originals, they are in fact blatantly pornographic.

To take the second image as an example: in his illustration for Stedman, Blake's drawing is delicate and technically sophisticated. What you see in Blake's picture, as Marcus Wood points out, is not only the suspended torso but also three skulls, two of which are stuck on poles, and a tiny ship that sails away in the bottom right of the frame. The scale of the suspended body "is defined in relation to both the objects which surround him on land, and to the tiny ship"; paradoxically, Blake makes his attack on the slave trade through the marginalization of the slave ship. Wood

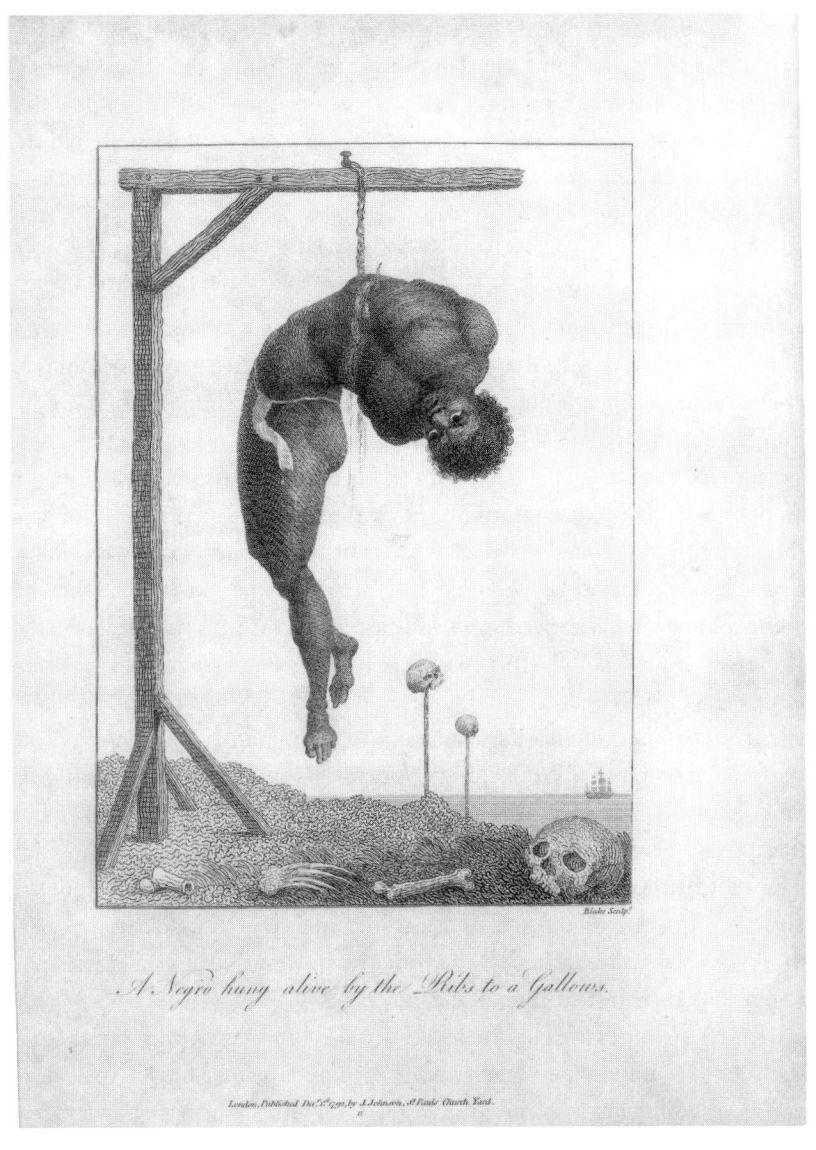

FIGURE 7 "A Negro Hung Alive by the Ribs to a Gallows" from John Gabriel Stedman, *Narrative of a Five Years' Expedition Against the Revolted Negroes of Surinam*. Engraved by William Blake.

Source: Typ 705.96.808F, Department of Printing and Graphic Arts, Houghton Library, Harvard College Library. Reprinted with permission.

further interprets the larger skull on the pole as Death staring toward the tiny slave ship: "the living, but dying, slave stares out toward the audience, which is left to draw its own conclusions about the relationship between the suffering we witness and the little ship which brought the slave to Surinam."[101] For Wood, the subtleties of Blake's engraving place it in a liminal position to high art; such an illustration makes "interpretational demands which more blatantly pornographic, and aesthetically low-grade material, describing slave torture, do not."[102]

By giving her audience only the tortured figure, Rozema thus omits important details that might otherwise offer the audience an opportunity to engage in a significant interpretive act. The image Fanny encounters requires only that we recoil in horror, not that we reflect. Through the combination of camera angles, the soundtrack, and the actress' expression, the scene makes clear what we are to think: plantation slavery is nothing less than the brutal and dehumanizing abuse of power. Sir Thomas is a sadist and a hypocrite, and he deserves to be exposed and excoriated. But the scene also becomes inadvertently complicit with the very racism it decries. Whereas the face of Blake's suspended figure has recognizable human attributes, the black faces and figures that Fanny encounters are blunt caricatures that perpetuate demeaning and dehumanizing stereotypes of slaves.[103] The film, of course, never purports that Tom has Blake's skills (and indeed we are given indications of his otherwise inferior talent), but the impact here goes further. The brutalized figures in Tom's drawings have neither dignity nor agency. As the images pass in rapid succession, the enslaved Africans are more like tortured animals than human subjects. Although the film intends to show its audience the ugly face of slavery, it does so paradoxically by focusing on the ugly faces of the enslaved.

Fanny's feelings are clearly meant to be the focal point here, and what she feels—repulsion and fascination—the audience is meant to feel as well. Her voyeurism becomes our voyeurism. Thus, this scene participates in a larger representational tradition that has been explored by Saidiya Hartman, who has posed a series of questions concerning the frequent representation of slavery as corporeal violence. Asking why pain should function as "the conduit of identification" for white viewers of slave images, she also wonders:

> Does the extension of humanity to the enslaved ironically reinscribe their subjugated status? Do the figurative capacities of blackness en-

able white flights of fantasy while increasing the likelihood of the captive's disappearance? Can the moral embrace of pain extricate itself from the pleasures borne by subjection. . . . Is the act of "witnessing" a kind of looking no less entangled with the wielding of power and the extraction of enjoyment?"[104]

In this way, Hartman prompts us to reflect on the moral purpose behind the kind of visualization that Rozema uses here. Clearly this scene, with its allusions to both the gothic and the horror movie, implicates the viewer in a pleasure that is created out of terror and pain.

Rozema's screenplay juxtaposes this discovery with the next major event in the film. Having been banished from Tom's room by Sir Thomas, Fanny stays upstairs until she hears a noise. Leaving her room, she drops her candle in the dark stairway and stumbles upon the adulterous coupling of Maria Rushworth and Henry Crawford. Both this scene and the previous scene in which Fanny finds Tom's sketchbook illuminate the theme of bringing the hidden into the open. But both scenes also play to a prurient interest by visualizing what is hidden as an illicit sexual act. What Fanny learns in both cases is a perverse "sexual secret" that is—for both her character and the viewer—as titillating as it is morally reprehensible.

In writing about the relationship between slavery and pornography, Marcus Wood explores how, in the work of John Stedman and elsewhere, accounts of slave abuse become "sentimental artefacts" that are designed to be enjoyed as "fantastic spaces, or spaces for fantasy." Citing Edmund Burke's association of blackness with the melancholy and the terrifying, he writes:

> to fantasize about torture, to attempt imaginative subversion in that space, is a Sublime experience. When the reader performs such fantasies around the body of the hanging slave, or the whipping of the "sambo" girl it is also a pornographic experience. Rhetoric can be used to describe horror in any number of ways, there are many pornographies of pain and many arts of violence.[105]

In other words, like Hartman, Wood helps us to see how the film version of *Mansfield Park* leads the viewer to a place of fantasy where the suffering is displaced from the slave who experienced the torture to the viewer who now observes the scene. In addition, Wood allows us to understand that to visualize slavery as pornography is to play to a scopophilic impulse that falls short of advancing a moral purpose. His point proves as true here, in Tom's sketchbook, as it did in *Sacred Hunger*, with its phantasmagoric sexual imagery. Visualizing slavery as horrific, yet erotically charged abuse fails to assert the status of slaves as fully individuated human beings, and it does not help the audience to understand the moral failure of those who denied slaves their humanity.

In sum, whereas Austen's novel allows the reader the opportunity to learn through interpretation, the film not only tells us what to think but structures our thinking in a troubling way. In choosing to present a scopophilic and erotically charged image, it takes the viewer away from the more difficult but necessary work of reflecting on how events such as slavery come to be tolerated in the first place. The novel presents gaps to be filled, leaving important political issues open to debate; the film, however, settles all questions of interpretation, deciding beforehand the message to be gleaned. Finally, Austen's novel initiates a wide-ranging debate concerning ideology, complicity, and resistance, but the film offers us only one point of entry to the issue of the slave trade. Ironically, that point of entry reduces the viewer's experience of slavery to a voyeuristic fantasy.

As we have seen, Tom's illness is a metaphor for his weighty and guilty awareness; as he "vomits" up the vile knowledge gathered during his stay in Antigua, he begins to mend. In deploying this metaphor, Rozema returns her audience to a late-eighteenth-century discourse about slavery, which similarly often saw the slave trade as a "disease" or "infection" weakening the heart of English political life. The trope of infection was often related to a vocabulary of "contamination," whereby colonial trade was thought to bring England into contact with loathsome commodities. Examples of this metaphorical development can be found in a range of texts, from Tobias Smollett's *Humphry Clinker* (1771), in which a tide of luxuries from colonial holdings leads to a diseased and corrupted urban lifestyle, to William Fox's polemical pamphlet *An Address to the People of Great Britain on the Propriety of Abstaining from West Indian Sugar and Rum* (1791), in which eating sugar produced by slaves is equated with the consumption of human flesh.[106] However, the trope of slavery as infection, disease, or contamination serves a variety of political purposes. For abolitionists, for example, it served as a rallying cry for the sugar boycotts of the 1790s; female tea drinkers in particular were urged to avoid the contaminating sweetness of West Indian sugar.[107] For anti-imperialists (who were not

Seeing Slavery and the Slave Trade 177

necessarily abolitionists), the trope generated discussion about the need to draw rigid national boundaries between England and the rest of the world to ensure a militarily strong state. In either case, slavery as illness/disease/contaminating force implies that England loses from contact with the slave trade. The solution is to purge, cut off, or isolate oneself from the corrupting force.

However, this metaphor belies a disturbing historical truth: the slave trade was never Britain's secret "illness." To the contrary, it was a source of robust financial and political health; England grew stronger and more geopolitically powerful as a result of the profits it garnered through the slave trade. It transformed itself into an imperial power on the profits of the trade, as more than a few eighteenth-century citizens would have been proud to attest. For instance, Malachy Postlethwayt, cited in the catalog for *Transatlantic Slavery: Against Human Dignity*, extolled the African slave trade as "'the Great Pillar and Support' of British trade," and he further reveled in the fact that the empire was "a magnificent superstructure of American commerce and [British] naval power on an African foundation."[108] To suggest that slavery was an "illness" is, then, to underestimate the complexity of the historical situation. Evil is not something of which we "purge" ourselves; rather, it is something we have already digested, too late to get rid of but requiring accountability in its aftermath.

If anything, the ironic tone of Austen's novel offers us the more accurate assessment of how such an evil endured for so long. The slave trade and other atrocities may continue not because they "make you sick" but because people live comfortably with them, in no apparent pain and experiencing no apparent ill effects themselves. Austen's *Mansfield Park* suggests that our task is precisely to see what is invisible—not as voyeurs who vicariously take on the suffering ourselves but as sentient beings who are capable of looking deeply, reading between the lines, and understanding how several truths exists in the same silent moment.

In conclusion, we return full circle to the question that began this chapter: what are the politics of making the "invisible" eighteenth-century slave trade visible and seen on screen? I have demonstrated that this question can be answered in a number of ways. For example, in film narratives about family relations, the yearning to make transracial connections is paradoxically most successful when race becomes visibly *invisible*. In addition, when a film provides powerful portraits of black subjectivity and images of black historicity—individuals like Equiano who can be represented as proactive, speaking agents—an important pedagogic purpose is accomplished. However, where the inclination to critique a history of oppression is accompanied by scopophilia—a desire to possess visually what seems erotically charged—then a film representation loses its radical edge. It is difficult to develop an effective political vision when humanistic motive is un-self-conscious or lacks critical self-awareness about the nature of one's relationship to others.

Chapter Four

Transnationalism and Performance in 'Biyi Bandele's *Oroonoko*

In 1999, after a considerable absence from the English stage, the character of Oroonoko returned, in an adaptation for the Royal Shakespeare Company (RSC) by Nigerian-born and London-based playwright 'Biyi Bandele.[1] In the foreword to the play, Bandele cites a Yoruba proverb: "It is said of Eshu, the Yoruba trickster-God, who is the ubiquitous reverse hero of Oroonoko, that 'he threw a rock today, and killed a bird yesterday.'" Bandele explains: "The present, says this paradox, is defined by the future. Eshu, and his metaphor of transcendence [,] has inspired this feast-of-a-war—which is to say jam session between a myth and two myth makers situated three hundred years apart."[2] Unlike the pre-twentieth-century versions of the play *Oroonoko*, which almost always featured white actors, Bandele's 1999 production used a large black cast. The leading role was performed by Nicholas Monu, who was also born in Nigeria and, according to his publicity Web site, is himself actually a prince. "We all feel very honoured to be in this," Monu said. "Probably it means as much to us to be in this as it would to Jewish actors being given the chance to tell the story of the Holocaust. I think it's a wonderfully written play. It isn't just a case of good black people on one side and evil white people on the other, it makes clear that there was good and bad on both sides."[3]

Both Bandele's lyrical foreword and Monu's cheerful endorsement of the Oroonoko story are bound to surprise and challenge the position of twentieth-century academic critics who have responded to an "African" story that was first told in English by Aphra Behn in the late seventeenth century. Wylie Sypher, for example, argues that the Oroonoko character belongs to the "noble-Negro tradition,"[4] and Srivinas Aravamudan has more recently exposed the "pet logic" at work in Aphra Behn's novel.[5] Additionally, feminist critics have debated the nature of Behn's authority, especially in relation to her character's putative origins. But the two Nigerian-born men are cosmopolitans, transnational subjects whose experiences place them in a complicated relationship to both their native countries and their adopted cultures.[6] For both Bandele and Monu, the play illuminates an important aspect of Nigerian history. No doubt theirs is a problematic position—Bandele's comment obscures both the colonial context that generated the original Oroonoko story and the postcolonial context that leads to his own writing in English. He also seems to ignore the role of the RSC as the purveyor of powerful cultural forms. Monu's comment initially seems naive: how could a highly contrived fiction first written down by a seventeenth-century white woman writer possibly convey an authentic story of the African holocaust?

There are three good reasons to take the comments of Bandele and Monu seriously and to explore the Oroonoko story on their terms. First, their statements can lead us toward what can be construed as a global humanism, a position of transcultural recognition and identification that, as Julie Stone Peters has argued, "is not necessarily complicit with an overwhelming hegemonic order."[7] Bandele's adaptation of Behn's text, especially as a response to eighteenth-century versions of the Oroonoko story, cannot simply be dismissed as the result of an "oppressive political and cultural assertion of metropolitan dominance, of centre over margin."[8] Rather, Bandele's *Oroonoko* belongs to what Paul Gilroy has called the black Atlantic: "an ex-centric, unstable, and asymmetrical cultural ensemble that cannot be apprehended through the manichean logic of binary coding."[9] Indeed, Bandele's foreword suggests that the playwright seeks to release the Oroonoko story and its variations from a simple, causal chain of events moving inexorably in only one direction. By using a Yoruba proverb, he disrupts the idea that First World culture is always already present. In addition, by evoking a theological grounding for the story of Oroonoko, he tellingly situates his play neither in opposition to Aphra Behn's late-seventeenth-century text nor as a corrective to her work. Instead, he places both himself and Behn in a "jam session," a musical dialogue *with* a mythic version of Oroonoko: his reference to jazz turns his version of the story and Behn's improvisations into hybrid works that are something very different.

A jazz riff belongs to neither the originator of the tune nor the musician through whom it passes in its moment of transformation; similarly, neither Bandele nor Behn can be said to possess the story of the African prince. Bandele implicitly argues that, just as fragments of melody travel freely across national, racial, and ethnic boundaries, so too can seminal narratives. Thus, his foreword redirects the debate over the Oroonoko story as intellectual property—a debate that often stalls over questions of race and gender—toward a more fluid understanding of cultural forms. Or, as Julie Stone Peters reminds us, nobody "owns" a culture. "When one inherits, one inherits a global collective web . . . which one is meant, indeed bound, to reweave. The point is to recognize the ways in which the documents of history may be the documents of barbarism, and to repossess them differently."[10]

Second, following Monu's lead, we can consider how the Oroonoko story embeds a circum-Atlantic story—a story of the "diasporic and genocidal histories of Africa and the Americas, North and South, in the creation of the culture of modernity."[11] Bandele's version returns us to the diasporic underpinnings that have always been at the heart of the Oroonoko story, which, despite everything that has been written about it, remains a story of violent dispersal, trauma, and suffering. In the play's best moments—especially in its keen attention to issues of gender politics and language–Bandele's *Oroonoko* accomplishes the highest purpose of diasporic art: to move its audience first through and then beyond human suffering to a place that not only conveys the scope of the human tragedy but also facilitates meaningful conversations about guilt, responsibility, reconciliation, and future cross-cultural contact. Bandele's drama thus culminates a list of similar projects aiming to represent the story of the African holocaust to a broad-based, popular audience in England at the end of the twentieth century. Like the museum exhibits and walking trails in Liverpool and Bristol, and like the novels, films, and documentaries also taking up the subject of Britain's slave trade, it exemplifies a moral inclination that functions under consumerist pressure. However, despite its status as a story to be sold, this play allows us to see how the theater can be a useful space in which to historicize, explore, and contest racial characteristics.

Third, the staging of the Oroonoko story at the turn of the twenty-first century provides a powerful bridge between earlier expressions of eighteenth-century transnationalism and later versions of the same phenomenon. A term that is often employed to describe a prevailing effect of a globalized economy, *transnationalism* has been neatly defined by Aihwa Ong as "the condition of cultural interconnectedness and mobility across space."[12] Thus, transnationalism refers to a range of social and cultural effects created by accelerated mobility. These effects occur when people are no longer rooted in their birthplace—for example, when, as a result of migration, immigration, or forced exile, they find themselves struggling between national identities, languages, or cultures. A number of controversial issues arise in relation to this concept. For example, two cultures brought into contact may not be equal in political or economic power, leading to a situation in which, for instance, a local, indigenous, and traditional culture may seem to lose its bearings against a modernizing tide. Others worry that transnationalism yields homogenized culture, a world of "McDonaldization." On the other hand, as Malcolm Waters writes, global contact can "revive [cultural] particularisms in so far as it relativizes and in so far as it releases them from encapsulation by the nation-state-society." Moreover, "as people become more implicated in global cultural flows they also become more reflexive."[13] Paradoxically, then, the greater the contact with the rest of the world, the greater the awareness of what makes one's own culture unique, special, and worth preserving.

However, while transnationalism is one powerful effect of globalization, globalization itself is arguably not a new phenomenon. Roland Robertson and other scholars trace an earlier, "germinal" period of global expansion to the period between 1400 and 1750. Immanuel Wallerstein finds traces of a "European world system" or a "modern world system" in the late fifteenth and early sixteenth centuries. Similarly, Robertson cites several factors as evidence of early globalizing trends, including the "collapse of Christendom, the development of maps and maritime travel, the rise of the nation-state, global exploration, colonialism, the creation of citizenship, passports, [and] diplomacy and the rise of international communication."[14] All these events are early historical circumstances precipitating the kind of intercultural contact that characterizes transnationalism. In a similar vein, Paul Gilroy argues that the black Atlantic—the mobile black culture that developed as a result of and in relation to eighteenth-century transatlantic slavery—engenders transnationalism in another paradigmatic form. Other exemplary discussions of transnationalism in earlier periods include Joseph Roach's *Cities of the*

Dead: Circum-Atlantic Performance, a book exploring intercultural contact in eighteenth-century London and nineteenth-century New Orleans; Srinivas Aravamudan's *Tropicopolitians: Colonialism and Agency, 1688–1804*; and *Picturing Imperial Power: Colonial Subjects in Eighteenth-century British Painting*, by Beth Fowkes Tobin.[15] Transnational scholars borrow much of their vocabulary and method from postcolonial studies, frequently marking the violent, destructive legacy of colonialism, but they also explore the performative potentialities occurring in the moment when cultures collide. They recognize as well (to borrow a phrase from Tobin) the possibility of a "fragile middle ground of intertwined identities and shared space," albeit a middle ground whose existence is often transitory.[16]

In this chapter, then, I am interested in questions of appropriation and revision from a transnational perspective. These questions have special relevance because Bandele recuperates a theatrical history of racial impersonation during a scholarly debate about eighteenth-century perceptions of race. Surveying racial counterfeit on the eighteenth- and early nineteenth-century stage, Felicity Nussbaum points out how "inconsistencies and confusions are *characteristic* of racial discourse and related cultural practice in eighteen-century England rather than the exception." Moreover, she concludes, "Racial categories, closely aligned with anomaly, are highly adaptable within England in the eighteenth century, in spite of the pronounced and enormously significant rise of racial slavery in the New World and elsewhere."[17] Nussbaum expands on the work of Roxann Wheeler, who has argued that "eighteenth-century Britons' understanding of complexion, the body, and identity was far more fluid than ours is today" and that "the assurance that skin color was the primary signifier of human difference was not the dominant conception until the last quarter of the eighteenth century, and even then individuals responded variously to nonwhite skin color."[18] Wheeler further explains:

> There was an uneven, not a cumulative, development of racial ideology. Moreover, skin color, even in the case of black Africans, was not the primary issue when the British considered human differences in the first half of the eighteenth century. Racial ideology forms mainly around English responses to certain customs, dress, religion, and trading—in short around a concept of civility. It was through these means that early eighteenth-century ideology encouraged a keen sense of the visibility of differences, both of the British themselves and of others.

> Early eighteenth-century British narratives about Africa did not tend to link slavery to skin color.[19]

Although Wheeler does not pinpoint the moment at which a binary black–white understanding begins to operate, she intimates that it does not occur until sometime in the second half of the eighteenth century.[20]

This new scholarship prompts several questions concerning the performance of race on the eighteenth-century stage. Given that race was not yet necessarily linked to skin color, how did eighteenth-century white actors understand the task of embodying a black African like Oroonoko? How was race represented on the eighteenth-century stage? Property lists from the sixteenth century suggest that fine lawn fabric, and later black stockings, masks, and wigs, may have once been used to disguise white actors.[21] Engravings from the earlier centuries provide further evidence of characteristic costuming and blocking used in early productions of *Othello*.[22] Also, some actors apparently "blacked up," most often using burnt cork (an event that is brilliantly recreated in the opening scenes of Spike Lee's *Bamboozled*). However, most of what theater historians know about the performance of race comes from nineteenth-century theatrical records, particularly from the minstrel tradition.[23] Because the ideology of race was so different by then, and racial categories were more fixed and contemporary attitudes more immediately racist (in the modern sense of that word), it does not seem wise to read backward.[24] Before race was codified as skin color, were there particular physical gestures that coincided with, or signified, black (or "African") embodiment? Were there characteristic postures or poses of blackness? These questions are made more difficult by the fact that the eighteenth-century stage was more self-consciously "theatrical." It employed a range of acting styles that differ considerably from a twentieth-century "method" approach to representing a character. Illuminated throughout most of the century by chandeliers, theaters were not conducive to the silent specular intensity that characterizes a present-day audience's experience.[25] Although eighteenth-century audiences were capable of being spellbound by a particularly thrilling performance, they tolerated a great deal of distraction, and they often audibly expressed skepticism about a weak or unconvincing performance. Given the obstacles, then, how was the *impression* of blackness presented and sustained on the eighteenth-century stage?

In *The Limits of the Human*, Felicity Nussbaum emphasizes how flexible, yet fleeting, the eighteenth-century performance of blackness must have been: plays with black roles "allowed white men to inhabit the putative bodies of black men, to shape and mold the culture's perceptions of them, while simultaneously implying through racial simulation that race is ephemeral." Yet in the end she argues that eighteenth-century blackface must have worked against a genuinely transracial connection, ensuring only the persistence of whiteness: "The core beneath the racial counterfeit, and perhaps even the core of black men themselves, is imagined as 'white.'"[26] Nussbaum's interpretation is useful and suggestive, but it depends on imagining the traces of a highly elusive medium, in which we can only guess the nature of the actor's experience. It cannot cover the number of interpretations introduced by individual performances, nor can it reconstruct audience reception. Bandele's twentieth-century return to an eighteenth-century theatrical tradition challenges us to consider the full range of possibilities that any given performance puts into play. Until we have explored how performance works both through—and potentially against—a given text, it may be premature to make assumptions about racial ideology on the eighteenth-century stage.

Before turning to the question of what it means to stage the Oroonoko story on both the eighteenth- and late-twentieth-century stages, this chapter briefly reviews the publication and production history of that story. After situating Bandele's text in relation to Behn's novel and Thomas Southerne's play version of the story, it explores four issues of special importance to a transnational reading of the play, including the deployment of an "African" setting for the prequel as a strategy for counteracting an abstract universalism; the place of anachronism, especially in the representation of gender relations; and Bandele's use of English as a means of conveying Yoruba culture. Fourth, I will return to the question of what it means to "sell" Oroonoko to a wide audience at this historical juncture. How does Bandele's *Oroonoko* participate in broader trends of commodifying the experience of the eighteenth-century transatlantic slave trade?

Originally published in 1688, Aphra Behn's *Oroonoko; or, The Royal Slave* is the story of a noble African prince from Coramantien (or a Gold Coast slave trading station) who is tricked into slavery and taken to Suriname. There he leads an unsuccessful rebellion and is captured, tortured, and finally executed in an especially gruesome way: beginning with his genitals, bits of his trussed-up body are "hacked off" and thrown into a fire. Throughout this ordeal Oroonoko calmly smokes his pipe, until at last he dies. The romance plot of the novel involves the princess Imoinda, whom Oroonoko loved while in Coramantien but who was chosen by Oroonoko's grandfather. She is sold into slavery as a punishment for carrying on a relationship with Oroonoko. The lovers are reunited in Suriname, where she becomes pregnant. But after the failed rebellion led by Oroonoko, he kills Imoinda and mutilates her body. A character who may or may not be the actual author herself and who claims to have personally known Oroonoko narrates the story.

In recent years, *Oroonoko* has become an enormously popular text. Between 1997 and 1999, at least four major paperback editions of Behn's novel—including two critical editions—were made available for classroom use.[27] Meanwhile, an ever-expanding bibliography of criticism has accompanied the circulation of the novel. Perhaps it was inevitable that interest in the dramatic versions of Behn's story would follow (and both critical editions include excerpts from dramatic texts). Once available only in a single paperback edition, the dramatic version of the Oroonoko story currently appears in anthologies of eighteenth-century drama.[28] The play version as first written by Thomas Southerne in 1695 included several important alterations to Behn's novel, among them an added comic subplot concerning the fate of two unmarried sisters. Southerne also rewrote the origin of Imoinda, giving her a white heritage—thereby allowing English actresses to play the part without blackface.[29] In addition, Southerne omitted the spectacular scenes of Oroonoko's dismemberment as well as other violent acts. When John Hawkesworth (together with David Garrick) revised Southerne's dramatic script in 1759, he excised the comic subplot, which is now deemed inappropriate and in questionable taste. A subsequent dramatic adaptation by Francis Gentleman appeared in 1760, followed by an abolitionist version entitled The *Prince of Angola* by John Ferriar in 1788.[30] After the first production of Southerne's version in 1695, the play appeared on the boards at least once every season in London until 1801, often in a staging of Hawkesworth's revised text.[31]

This complicated history of reproduction and production demonstrates that the Oroonoko story was, long before Bandele's recent consideration, already an improvised text, one that saw major transformations in both form and content.[32] Southerne was the first to raise the question of whether the Oroonoko figure properly belonged to the page or the stage. In his dedicatory preface, Southerne puzzles why Behn, who "had a great command of the stage," buried "her hero in a novel when she might have revived him in the scene." He opines:

> She thought either that no actor could represent him, or she could not bear him represented. And I believe the last when I heard from a friend of hers, that she always told his story more feelingly than she writ it. Whatever happened to him at Surinam, he has mended his condition in England. He was born here under [The Duke of Devonshire's] influence and that has carried his fortune farther into the world than all the poetical stars I could have solicited for all success.[33]

In a gesture simultaneously deferential and aggressive, Southerne implicitly steals Oroonoko away from Behn and situates him on English soil. Yet Southerne's retelling of Behn's story also becomes a different kind of political statement, one that sets aside a highly specific colonial history of violence and mutilation "in favor of a much more assimilable account of great human, that is, transcultural, tragedy," as Suvir Kaul contends.[34]

By the same token, several feminist critics have been troubled by the ease with which Southerne and the later, eighteenth-century male playwrights were able to appropriate the female playwright's creation. Jane Spencer, for one, notes how on the eighteenth-century stage the Oroonoko play gradually evolved into a "vehicle for anti-slavery sentiment," but one that unfortunately coincided with "a tendency to play down the significance of Behn as narrator and author."[35] For other feminist critics, any discussion of the Oroonoko story must address the gender of Behn's narrator, as this persona raises crucial questions concerning the narrator's and author's complicity with colonialist ideologies, their attitudes toward slavery, their erotic inclinations toward Oroonoko, and their intentions toward Oroonoko's wife, Imoinda.[36]

As the Oroonoko story moves from its fictional to dramatic forms, these issues do not cease to matter. Indeed, they may well be intensified by Southerne's decision to leave out the female narrator and to create instead a white Imoinda, a heroine who, in the words of one feminist critic, "facilitates the erasure of African women from Oroonoko and colonial cultures deeply troubled by the sexual implications of white men's supremacy for the social welfare of white women."[37] Nonetheless, it must be noted that to rewrite and then stage the Oroonoko story without Behn's highly autobiographical female narrator is to give the tale a different thematic center, one that focuses above all on the story of the male African protagonist. Although this gesture may initially trouble those interested in the gender politics of the story, it can also—as I explain below—effectively serve a feminist purpose. In addition, to rewrite a fictional romance as a dramatic tragedy is to place the story in additional sets of hands altogether—those of the actors who interpret the character as well as those of their live audiences.

For the most part, then, Bandele's version of the Oroonoko story belongs to an eighteenth-century theatrical tradition, despite his direct references to Behn in his foreword; his most immediate source is Hawkesworth's 1759 dramatic text, with some important alterations.[38] To begin, the action that occurs over five acts in the Hawkesworth version is collapsed into only two acts, resulting in a more economic unfolding of the plot. Bandele writes a significant "prequel" (his word), a new act that explores Oroonoko's formative years and obviates the need for lengthy exposition. He alters and cuts the white roles that predominated in the eighteenth-century production, and he returns Imoinda to her blackness. He also collapses two white roles—the Governor and Stanmore—into one character, Byam, and renames two others. In addition, Bandele's version alters Hawkesworth's cultural allusions and returns to the characters their indigenous beliefs. Instead of praying to the sun, Oroonoko invokes Eshu. In another scene, Aboan and other slaves invoke Shango, god of thunder, justice, and fair play.

With an eighteenth-century dramatic text as his immediate source, why does Bandele conjure up the ghost of Aphra Behn in his foreword? His gesture introduces several important points of comparison between himself and Behn, as well as possible points of identification. In her novel Behn situates herself—not unlike Bandele—between two cultures, in her case, England and colonial Suriname.[39] Her narrative persona identifies herself as a gentlewoman who is left without a dowry when her father dies en route to Suriname. In Suriname, her social status remains ambiguous. Lacking the power enjoyed by elite colonial men, she nonetheless experiences a form of authority over her fictional creation. Later that authority is challenged and contested. Bandele is also perceived as an outsider, and, as a purveyor of cultural forms he remains open to challenge and contestation, as some reviews of his play in the conservative English press suggest. By identifying with Behn, Bandele signals his awareness of an ongoing attempt to mark him as a peripheral figure, despite his commission at the RSC. At the same time, his identification with Behn eclipses the accomplishments of successful white male dramatists, even while it suggests a desire to share in their success.

However, despite Bandele's apparent desire to align himself with Behn the novelist, the nature of his dramatic accomplishment is best seen in light of a stage history that unfolds for the most part in the eighteenth century, because this is the event that his version recreates. What, then, accounted for the extraordinary popularity of the dramatic version of the Oroonoko story during the eighteenth century? And what does it mean for it to reappear at the beginning of the twenty-first century? Eighteenth-century scholars have several explanations for the successful stage history of the "royal captive." For example, in an age that preceded the introduction of naturalist acting styles, Southerne's drama, as well as Hawkesworth's adaptation, is thought to have been a showcase for the exaggerated theatrical gestures popular on the contemporary stage. The stage version of *Oroonoko* subtly manipulated the possibilities of spectacle and invited tragic actors to showcase their thespian spirits. Quite simply, it appears that in the eighteenth century "the play rose and fell on the talents of the actor."[40]

Thus, the play Bandele takes up has always showcased the performer. In his version, the story provides multiple opportunities for a theatricality that invokes African—in particular Yoruba—performance history. For example, in Scene 2, a "teenage" Oroonoko is exhorted by his peers to "play the sage"—in other words, to display his talents as an actor and mime despite the fact that their task is to engage in militaristic exercises. As Oroonoko imitates the actions of an infirm wise old sage, he invokes Yoruba ritualistic play. Accompanied by drumming and the chants of his friends, the imitation evolves into a spirited dance, a highly entertaining distraction from their work:

>   ALL: You danced, Old Sage,
>   You definitely danced!
>   OROONOKO: Look at my feet,
>   I can hardly walk!
>   ALL: You danced, you danced!
>   You definitely danced![41,42]

With its display of Yoruba performance traditions, Bandele expands possibilities that were set into motion by Behn's telling of the Oroonoko story. We have already seen how, coming to London via Nigeria, Bandele interprets Behn's Englishness through a Yoruba proverb. He thereby not only deracinates her but also resituates himself in relation to Western tradition. What matters in his foreword is not the race or national identity of either author but their synchronic connection. For Bandele, the geographic indeterminacy of the Oroonoko story—an indeterminacy resulting from both slavery and colonialism—is not an obstacle but rather testimony to a cosmopolitan impulse. In this way, Bandele dissipates geographic boundaries and imagines himself and Behn in the same metaphoric space. The eighteenth-century place known as Coramantien may have existed in Ghana, writes Bandele in his foreword, but "Behn's Coramantien is a notional one." Claiming that the names of Behn's characters may have been recognizably Yoruba, Bandele sets his play in what is now known as Nigeria. He adds, " Ultimately, though, Coramantien, our fabled kingdom, is born of a distilled evocation of a metaphorical megalopolis of intersecting universal dreams."[43] This comment simultaneously echoes Fred D'Aguiar's comment (discussed earlier) that "the creative imagination knows no boundaries" and breaks down a binary distinction between England and Africa.

Nonetheless, in a gesture designed to evoke African origins, Bandele provides a prequel to Behn's European narrative. Behn covers Oroonoko's early years, his romance and aborted marriage to Imoinda—in effect, his formative experiences as a young warrior and husband—in relatively few pages, but Bandele uses nearly half of his two-hour-and-forty-minute play to present the same material. He offers his audience an Africa simultaneously mythical and culturally precise, historically specific and deliberately anachronistic. As the stage lights come up, the audience finds itself situated in the main court of the palace of Kabiyesi, king of the Coramantien. In the opening scene, a series of diplomatic negotiations quickly lead to the offstage decapitation of Ibn Sule, an ambassador who has been sent to exact obedience from the Coramantiens.

The first scene leaves the viewer with several impressions: Coramantien is neither a pastoral paradise nor a primitive tribal scene, but a developed military culture in which ruthlessness and political shrewdness prevail. Bandele's play script carefully instructs the costume designer to make certain the audience understands the conflict between the different

West African cultures represented here—the visitors, Ibn Saeed and Ibn Sule, wear turbans and "other accoutrements of the desert farer" whereas the people of Coramantien are "dressed in the coastal Yoruba style of 'agbada' and 'dashiki.'"[44] Such visual clues deessentialize the category of "Africa" by reminding the audience that important geographic and cultural differences preceded the creation of national boundaries. Bandele's changes are especially significant because they inject a kind of cultural specificity into a dramatic text that, as several critics have noted, previously worked to render the Oroonoko story a "timeless" tale.

Yet what, then, is the historical reality to which Bandele refers, especially since his source is an eighteenth-century adaptation of a late seventeenth-century English text? On the one hand, he seems to take seriously Catherine Gallagher's claim that Behn was "the first English author who attempted to render the life lived by sub-Saharan African characters on their own continent"[45]—that is, to accept the original, novelistic account as a valuable historical record. On the other hand, Bandele necessarily comes to Behn's sources from a late-twentieth-century vantage point. Thus, his text contains at least two levels of mimesis: the first is a late-seventeenth-century reflection of an African "reality" and the second is a modern, cosmopolitan reflection of a Nigerian "reality." In production, deliberate anachronisms puncture the illusion that the audience has been transported back to a genuine, historical African past. For example, in Act Two, Orombo, referring to a Western commodity that might only recently have been imported to Africa, jokes about the new invention called soap, claiming that his wives have come to "swear by it."[46] In the RSC production, Gregory Doran's direction further emphasized this double consciousness through gestures and blocking, for example, by showing a solider snapping to attention like a modern American marine.[47] Thus, the illusion of a precise historical context coexists with a consciousness of modernity. The effect is paradoxical: Bandele succeeds in demonstrating how Afrocentric constructions of Africa are *real* constructions. As such, they are fictions rooted in precise, geopolitical circumstances, and they have real dimensions. In this way, Bandele counteracts a pseudouniversalism—a Eurocentric representation purported to be universal—in favor of a more precise understanding of how Africa represents itself in the face of Western representation.[48]

This linkage of historical rendering and modern awareness is especially apparent in Bandele's treatment of Imoinda. Feminist critics of

Behn's novel have long debated how to interpret Imoinda in Behn's novel, as well as how to decipher the woman narrator's conflicted relationship to her female African creation. Previous arguments have centered on a range of issues, from Imoinda's bodily status as a possession and an "erotic, powerful agent"[49] to her silencing as an "inarticulate hysteric."[50] As mentioned, in the eighteenth-century dramatic version, Southerne rewrote Imoinda's origins in order to give her a white patrilineage, thereby enabling white actresses to play her without blackface. According to Joyce MacDonald, this eighteenth-century white, Desdemona-like Imoinda functioned as a mechanism triggering the construction of a European female subjectivity.[51] Restored to her blackness, Bandele's Imoinda resembles Behn's heroine more than Southerne's or Hawkesworth's. Yet Bandele gives his Nigerian heroine powers of self-articulation beyond those possessed by the original Imoinda, as well as greater agency. The character he has created offers a significant opportunity for a black actress to express an indigenous female identity, one that struggles dramatically against patriarchal abuse.

Having been given the "royal veil of invitation" by the lecherous yet impotent King Kabiyesi, Imoinda finds herself in the bath with him, coerced to perform fellatio. She responds by slashing his penis with a mirror, an act that brings dire consequences: shortly afterward, she is brutally raped (offstage) by the palace guards. Even then her status as "victim" is carefully balanced by her fierce determination to resist her oppressors. In the next scene, she contemplates taking her own life but is thwarted by Orombo, adviser to the king, who tells her that if she wants to kill herself, "have the decency/To wait until the white man has paid/For you."[52] If this Imoinda's physical strength and endurance can be traced back to Behn's heroine, her expression is entirely original to Bandele's reworking, as becomes apparent at the celebration of her betrothal to Oroonoko, just before Kabiyesi's unwanted invitation.

Whereas both Behn and Southerne gave Imoinda a patrilineage but no significant matrilineage, Bandele gives her the powerful Lady Onola. Loosely based on Behn's creation Onahal, Bandele's Lady Onola serves as Imoinda's mother figure and mentor. On the eve of her engagement to Oroonoko, Imoinda celebrates her upbringing:

> Let everybody thank my mother:
> She did not allow me to borrow dresses

FIGURE 8 Mrs. Hartley as Imoinda.

Source: Courtesy of the Victoria and Albert Museum, Theatre Collection. Reprinted with permission.

FIGURE 9 Nadine Marshall as Imoinda.

Source: Photography by Jonathan Dockar-Drysdale. Copyright Royal Shakespeare Company. Reprinted with permission.

From those who would turn around and abuse me.
She dressed me in clothes so rich
I could confuse a god.[53]

Onola as fairy godmother not only clothes Imoinda but empowers her to speak on her own behalf. Here Imoinda speaks of her marriage to Oroonoko as an opportunity to regain what has been lost to her:

I look right, and left,
I look behind and in front of me.
But I see nobody
Who resembles my other parents,
The ones who birthed me.
What kind of god created me
In a sickly world
To make my mother die like rotten yam?
What kind of god created me
In a violent world
To make my father die in war?

If luck is not against me
I shall have them back with me
In my husband's house.
If luck is not against me
They shall reenter the world
Through me.[54]

In this way, Imoinda hopes to retain possession of her own body and direct the course of her own life. She hopes as well to reinstitute familial lines and further the generations of an African family.

However, the unfolding of patriarchal power relations thwarts her efforts to protect herself. When Imoinda reappears as a slave in the second part of the play, her power has been curtailed. Yet even then, Bandele's text affords her enslaved body much dignity. In the original version of the story, Behn describes Imoinda as having a spectacularly tattooed, erotic body, which Oroonoko later ritualistically dismembers.[55] In Southerne's play, eighteenth-century actresses played the death scene, revised to omit the dismemberment, at center stage. In hooped skirts and a big wig,

Southerne's Imoinda stabbed herself in a dramatic, suicidal gesture. In Bandele's production, Imoinda's death is staged in a simple and intimate manner that is nonetheless capable of eliciting a genuine gasp of horror from the audience. Bandele's stage directions indicate that "As [Imoinda] makes to stab herself, OROONOKO stays her hand, takes the dagger away, and grabs her in a tight embrace. They hold on to each other as if for dear life. Then, in one swift move, OROONOKO breaks her neck."[56] The scene is unbearably sad, testimony to a deep and abiding affection whose only recourse against the power of slavery is self-destruction; the allusions here are closer to *Beloved* than they are to *Othello*.

Thus, although it is true that gender politics are inextricably altered by the excision of the female narrator from the story, and it is equally true, as Jane Spencer argues, that Bandele's play has no roles for white women, his play offers a sustained critique of African political relations that takes a decidedly feminist turn.[57] Here traditional African patriarchy is exposed for its obsessive focus on phallic power, a power that is ironically impotent. In Act Two, the King's entrance is heralded with the verbal play of the court drummer, who celebrates his procreative power:

> His Highness—long may he reign—
> Fathered a child in Liverpool
> While emptying his testicles
> In Coramantien![58]

The tragedy of a phallic power that spawns slaves in England seems to be lost on Orombo, the king's chief adviser, who remains invested in the idea of the king's potency. The drummers continue their salacious celebration of the king's sexual dalliances:

> 2ND ROYAL DRUMMER: He entered deeply, deeply.
>   He touched the base of his cock—
>   —Was it asleep? Was it fatigued?
> 2ND ROYAL DRUMMER: He found that his cock, the fearless Rogue, was not fatigued.
> 1ST ROYAL DRUMMER: It was thrusting, thrusting.[59]

This sort of salacious language might be seen as drawing from a racist perception of black prowess, but here it works quite differently, participating in a playful expression of sexuality that characterizes many folk traditions, including that of the trickster. More important, it contributes to an explicit attack on the phallocentric nature of Coramantien monarchy, as expressed by Lady Onola, who criticizes the king for his obsessive pursuit of sex at the expense of his other royal duties.

> I did not come here to listen to the
> Idle prattle of jesters and eunuchs. As for
> The King—if you want my opinion—
> The problem with His Highness is that
> His brain is in his penis. More's
> The pity, since he has no penis.[60]

In Lady Onola's account, the king's only efficacy lies in his sexual performance, and his inability to copulate becomes a metaphor for his inability to rule over Coramantien.

Her arch feminist commentary on political relations in Coramantien accomplishes two purposes. First, it returns the viewer to the theme of African complicity. Here, the King's exclusive focus on his own sexual pleasure prevents him from thinking about his kingdom's best interests; oblivious to the fate of his offspring, he fathers a child in Liverpool while emptying his testicles in Coramantien. However, another construction of paternity—for example, one resembling that evoked by Caryl Phillips in his frame for *Crossing the River*—might have rendered him responsible and accountable for his children. In other words, another understanding of paternity might have prevented African collusion with the slave traders. As Bandele pointed out at an Aphra Behn conference in November 2000, his larger intention was to "demystify British blacks' views of the nature of the slave trade, to point out, perhaps, that there was complicity, and in a way agency, not just passivity and victimization."[61] Second, through Lady Onola, Bandele denounces phallocentrism itself, implying that the roots of human oppression can be traced back to deleterious gender constructs. For this idea, he seems to return to Behn's text, because Behn's narrator similarly hints that oppressive colonial politics must be traced in part to distorted understandings of male privilege and authority.[62] Neither Bandele nor Bhen recommends the return to an essential "female" to counter the weight of oppressive patriarchal power. Rather, both suggest that men and women alike would benefit from an alternative understanding of gender, one wherein masculinity ceases to be defined by aggressively phallic acts.[63]

Bandele's anachronistic, feminist depiction of gender politics depends on his access to English as his chosen means of expression. On the surface, his choice to write in English appears ironic, a former colonial subject's resort to the language of the colonial oppressor. His play (indeed, all his works) appears to support a polemic against a powerful globalizing impulse that deprives native cultures of their indigenous tongues and cultural expression and forces them to tell their stories in words that are at once alien and alienated from their formative experiences.[64] However, instead of abrogating English as a language of colonial oppression, Bandele adapts and expands its linguistic potential, infusing it with the rhythms of his indigenous speech. Discussing the difficulty he faced finding a language for the play, he explains that he wrote the additional speeches for Parts One and Two in poetry because "I imagined the conversation happening in Yoruba, a highly rhetorical language. I felt the best way to capture the poetry when translating it into English was to keep it in poetry."[65] Instead of sublimating his Yoruba linguistic origins, Bandele calls attention to them. Although not an explicit criticism of linguistic domination, the language he produces for the RSC realistically expresses how one culture negotiates another, and how it seeks to make itself resonant and to signal its differences—and foregrounds additional possibilities within English itself. The play, then, participates in a movement to resist "English" by offering one counterexample of what Chinua Achebe has called "englishes."[66] Moreover, by offering his audience a hybrid English that moves from a culturally peripheral to a central position, Bandele implicitly demonstrates how the friction created by the confrontation between black and white societies "was cruel, but it was also creative."[67] His text further reminds the audience that English has always responded to new vocabularies and new modes of expression. On this point he returns us, once again, to Behn's version of the story, as for her also contact with a new culture means expanding English vocabulary and expression.[68]

A good example of this linguistic positioning occurs in Part One, where Lady Onola celebrates Oroonoko's return from his brave military exploits. As T. J. Cribb points out, Bandele borrows a selection from Ulli Beier's *Yoruba Poetry*, giving the lines to Onola to allow her to celebrate the moment.[69] Spoken in context, her words suggest the Yoruba linguistic conventions that permeate important social contacts, but they also demonstrate how the possibilities of English can be extended:

> Ladies. My friends and workers.
> Sisters, let me present to you the
> Mighty Oroonoko, in praise of
> Whose patron God, Eshu, the God
> Of fate, it has been said that:
>
> When he stands up
> Even a day-old suckling
> Beggars him in height.
> But when he lies down, the world
> Clambers mountains to catch
> Sight of his face.
>
> Eshu slept in the house—
> But the house was too
> Small for him.
>
> Eshu slept out in the open—
> But the open was too
> Small for him.
> Eshu slept in a nut—.
> At last he could stretch himself![70]

Here the god Eshu confounds calculation: how do you measure a god who is so small when he is so big? As Cribb further explains, the paradoxes express "the impossibility of enclosing Eshu within logic of whatever kind . . . Eshu is unpredictable, not to be defined by whatever state of affairs or beliefs happen to be current. He is the most unpredictable of the gods and in that sense a sort of degree zero of divinity."[71] Eshu thus defies logical measurement and implicitly refutes rational, Westernized accounts of his power. Yoruba ideas are translated in a way that preserves and simulates their paradoxical structure.[72]

In return, Oroonoko answers Lady Onola with another series of metaphors that celebrate her power as maternal principle:

We thank you, our mother.
You are—
The thorn in the rhino's foot.
The pebble that breaks the leopard's tooth.
The rope that drags the elephant along.
The back that carries its brother.
The leaf that is bigger than a forest.
The hare that climbs a mountain running.
The sea that cannot be emptied.
The flood that struts through fire.
The silence that births a song.
We salute you, mothers of our land.[73]

Oroonoko's metaphors implicitly encourage native speakers of English to notice how indirection and ceremonial circumlocution convey meaning as precisely as direct expression. The passage initiates reflection on the workings of normative, contemporary English itself and reminds native speakers how often standard English is circumscribed in its expressions of gratitude and hospitality. No doubt English itself once included the ceremonial possibilities demonstrated here—perhaps in the language of Elizabethan courtiers, for example—but it now benefits anew from contact with another rhetorical tradition.

Whereas Part One of Bandele's *Oroonoko* offers a distinct construction of Africa, Part Two evokes no particular place. Although the action is set at "a portside slave-hold in Surinam" and later at two nameless plantations, no effort is made to evoke the geographic specificity of the British seventeenth-century slave system. Only the costumes of the actors—in Doran's production, the foppish duds of a cavalier for the whites, head rags and breeches for the slaves—situate the action historically. The suggestion is that Suriname could have been any number of colonial locations, over a wide span of time. This sense of spatial and temporal dislocation is appropriate in a drama in which the actions unfolds as if through the eyes of those who have been taken from their native culture. But it also part of Bandele's technique for decentralizing the play's European roots. Suriname for Behn is an important location in the struggle for colonial dominance in the region, but for Bandele it is merely the backdrop of his character's tragedy.[74]

But why stay so close to an eighteenth-century text popular precisely at the moment when Britain was expanding its colonial holdings? Perhaps the answer lies, as I suggested earlier, in the diasporic underpinnings of the play, which can be exposed when we remember that a script is only an occasion for an interpretation, for a particular live performance occurring at a distinct historical moment on a precise historical stage. As performance theorists remind us, a full understanding of any production history depends on our access to important physical details, including objects such as props that may have been used to create meaning in now untraceable ways.[75] Yet because we have no access to the characteristic gestures or the blocking that marked racial difference on stage, it is difficult for us to theorize *Oroonoko*'s interconnected histories of performance and racialized experience, as Mita Chodhury has pointed out.[76] We do have brief yet suggestive stories about actors who achieved varying results playing the part of Oroonoko, beginning with Jack Verbruggen, who was Southerne's own choice despite the actor's relative inexperience.[77] Also, David Garrick made his debut as an actor in a provincial production of *Oroonoko* in 1741, yet he later failed in the starring role in a 1759 London production. As Thomas Davies records, "the lustre of his eye was lost in the shade of the black color; nor was his voice so finely adapted to the melting and passionate addresses of the lover as to the more violent emotions of the heart."[78] In contrast, the African American actor Ira Aldridge was apparently quite successful in an early-nineteenth-century English production. His biographers cite Southerne's language as important to Aldridge's portrayal; although the blank verse was "stilted and artificial," it allowed for "moments of passion and protest." Moreover, unlike in later melodramas, in Aldridge's production "neither Oroonoko nor any of the Negroes spoke in any accent or phraseology of the West Indies or U.S.A." Yet black actor Ignatius Sancho had had no luck with the same play in the 1760s, apparently owing to the fact that he lisped.[79]

Complicating this elusive performance history is an equally elusive history of audience reception. With rare exception, we do not know how live spectators received a particular performance, how they internalized—or perhaps resisted—a play's complicated messages. In one often-cited incident, the African prince Annamaboe (as Wylie Sypher writes, "he has no other name"), the son of a Fantin chief who had been taken in slavery, then ransomed and brought to London—wept at the sight of the tragedy.[80] Once again, Peters is helpful, for she reminds us that "each performance has its own valences: each engages its own terms, its own representations, its own versions of power relations."[81] Yet how do we imagine such valences? Even if we had greater access to eighteenth-century histories of spectatorship (an unlikely capability), we still lack appropriate theoretical models for interpreting a history of performance. Perhaps something like Wolfgang Iser's theory of the "implied reader" could be adapted to a hypothesis of the "implied viewer," allowing us to think about how actual viewers either embody or resist their subject positions.[82] The staging of Bandele's *Oroonoko* at the end of the twentieth century is therefore important precisely because, as a recent, live performance, it allows us to imagine how, in the right circumstances, certain actors might have successfully conveyed the genuine anguish brought on by violent and forced removal from one's homeland, thus evoking the moral outrage that ought to accompany such atrocity.

Thus, it may be the case that Bandele is willing to leave the eighteenth-century text intact because within it lies the *potential for performing* an ennobled response to a diasporic experience. Indeed, Bandele makes only those changes in the eighteenth-century text that facilitate the actors' full engagement with the themes of forced removal. He omits the aspects that diminish Oroonoko's reason for rebellion, while preserving and focusing on speeches that can be understood to speak to Oroonoko's motivations. Although this Oroonoko is still recognizably elite, he only reluctantly accepts his leadership role. Whereas Hawkesworth had Oroonoko galvanized by the thought that he might lose Imoinda to the governor's salacious advances, Bandele's Oroonoko dwells neither on this nor on the thought that his unborn son will be born into slavery. Instead, he responds to Aboan's reminder that he was "born for the good of other men."[83]

Bandele also changes Oroonoko's motivation from personal to political. Here and in Part Two he excises the *Othello* allusions that permeate the eighteenth-century text. By distinguishing Oroonoko from the "noble Moor" and by freeing him from a representational tradition that freezes him as a tragic, misguided husband, Bandele emphasizes the idea of Oroonoko as agent. In the RSC production, Monu's carriage, as well as his phrasing, transformed the traditional Oroonoko into a character who was not only more modern but also more complexly motivated. When Aboan taunts him with his captivity, Oroonoko responds using the same words that he had in the eighteenth century:

> Remember this, Aboan, if we are
> Slaves, these planters did not make us slaves.
> They were not to know of Stanmore's treachery.
> They bought us in a honest way of trade
> As we have done before them, bought
> And sold many a wretch and never
> Thought it wrong. They paid our price
> For us and we are now their property.[84]

Initially it appears that these words contribute to the theme of Oroonoko as the "royal captive," a man so motivated by "honor" that he is not able to save himself or anyone else. They might also be read as defending slavery as a legitimate form of commerce. However, in the RSC production, Monu's emphasis on the word *if* undermined the apologetic tone of the passage; his phrasing suggested that his captivity is only provisional and that his mental capacities and understanding allow him to transcend his physical circumstances. In addition, on the RSC stage Monu was blocked and backlit in a way that isolated him as a leader.[85] Monu's performance was an important reminder of the power of an actor to alter in performance what seems problematically rendered in theatrical tradition or the play script.

At the conclusion of the Part Two, Bandele chooses irony over sentimentality. Immediately after Oroonoko breaks Imoinda's neck, Trefry, a white colonist who has been Oroonoko's advocate throughout the play, arrives to announce that Oroonoko has been freed by the newly arrived lord governor. Oroonoko attempts to kill himself, and when Trefry tries to prevent him Oroonoko rushes toward him in a way that forces Trefry to shoot him. Instead of leaving his audience with the sad vision of Oroonoko's dead body, Bandele confronts them with the possibility of their own involvement. Trefry might not have wanted to kill Oroonoko, and—like the white members of the audience—he might have seen himself as Oroonoko's supporter. However, he kills Oroonoko because it is ultimately impossible for him to befriend him in a world where the economic business of slavery has placed them in an inimical relationship to each other. Despite its Nigerian opening and its initial decentering of a Western framework for the story, Bandele's *Oroonoko* closes with a white frame, for the play ends with the largely white audience of the RSC contemplating Trefry, who, according to Bandele's stage directions, "remains standing in the same spot, looking suddenly very tired."[86] This final gesture reflects the white audience back to itself, in a framing that simultaneously reintroduces the theme of white complicity and ironically forecloses the question of white, liberal intervention.

Thus, the ending of Bandele's *Oroonoko* reminds us of the institutional pressures that "whiten" the story of the African holocaust. Perhaps the spectacle of Oroonoko's dead body eclipses themes of African agency and resistance and sells the story to a white audience who must see the story in terms of its direct relevance to them. Moreover, some might argue that it is ironic how the transatlantic slave trade now "sells" as readily as black bodies did. Critics might further lament how marketable the topic of slavery has become—in museum sites that can be integrated into tourism, in popular novels, and in lavish Hollywood-type spectacles. Isn't Bandele's project also compromised by the fact that it must be sold to a white audience?[87] However, as I have previously argued, the representation of black experience for a white audience is a complex endeavor with several aspects to be considered. First, we return to the connection between Bandele and Behn. Bandele's recourse to a text authored by a seventeenth-century white woman writer—his very willingness to engage in a dialogue with her, despite profound differences in their subject positions—suggests that he is not merely making a marketable product but actually positioning himself in relation to white literary tradition in a way that denies its primacy. *Oroonoko* may be a Western generated myth of blackness, but it can also be reclaimed under a Yoruba literary tradition and then rerepresented to a white audience. In this view, Bandele's *Oroonoko* suggests the give and take of cross-cultural connections. Despite the colonial history of the text—and the obvious framing of the story within the nationalistic, institutional framing of the RSC—Bandele successfully adapted the play to make an original contribution to a discussion of interracial relations.

Second, to answer the charge that Bandele's play "sells" the transatlantic slave trade to a white audience, I turn to another example in which the African holocaust appears to have been co-opted by corporate intent. In 1994, the McDonald's corporation awarded as a prize to ninety-six U.S. citizens (eighty-nine of whom were African American) a "heritage tour" to historical slave ports in Senegal and Gambia. After participating in the tour, ethnologist Paulla Ebron provided an intricate and instructive account. She concluded that the contest winners appeared to have had meaningful experiences as African Americans, even within the structure of a commodified event. How did McDonald's become an enabler of minority cultural identities? Refuting the binary opposition between a "real" self and an identity compromised by contact with consumer culture, Ebron claims that deeply felt personal identities and commercial campaigns are not oppositional but mutually constitutive. She argues that, for better or worse, "oppositional identities no longer appear to be autonomous from global commerce, even to their most radically passionate adherents; instead they are inescapably intertwined."[88] Ebron's observations imply that it is counterproductive, for either a black audience in search of its heritage or a white audience eager to make amends, to seek representations of diasporic experience that lie "outside of" commodification. Although we may dream of achieving social justice beyond the reaches of globalized capitalism, we can better initiate meaningful change by mobilizing the transnational community created by globalism. As Ebron suggests, we do best to focus on the moments when diasporic culture successfully taps familiar images, symbols, and narratives and creates transformative personal experiences, which can then become the basis for a shared project of political restitution.

In conclusion, when Bandele as a playwright lauds the potential of the Oroonoko story, or when Monu as an actor celebrates its diasporic potential, these are positions worth weighing seriously. Bandele's reweaving of the Oroonoko story into a modern, cosmopolitan story of the African holocaust need not be viewed as a capitulation or as a sign of his cultural bad faith. Instead, his investment in Oroonoko can be considered an important step toward interracial conversation. Yasmin Alibhai-Brown has recently advocated just such a conversation:

> Somehow we need to break away from the foolish idea that we are all forever fated to remain disconnected; to shout across ravines and canyons at one another or gripe amongst ourselves about those on the other side. Maybe one day we will find the courage and wisdom not to deny, in face of all truth and evidence, that our lives overlap, and that they share most of what it means to be human.[89]

Although a deeply troubling legacy of unequal power might appear to make black and white dialogue impossible, Alibhai-Brown and other writers urge us to move beyond a current political impasse. In this chapter I have argued that the Oroonoko story—because it first appeared when binaristic racial categories were not yet fixed and immutable—is a crucial text for any interracial conversation addressing the eighteenth-century transatlantic slave trade. Looking more closely at its long history of improvisation, adaptation, performance, and production, we discover possibilities of transnational connection and identification, some of which may have been in place in the eighteenth century. Finally, as one more voice speaking about what it means to be British at the beginning of the twenty-first century, Bandele does not merely retell an old story. Instead, he offers his audience a creative and significant meditation on diasporic experience, performance history, and the future of transcultural contact.

Conclusion

This book surveys a range of artistic and cultural attempts to remember publicly a traumatic event in British history that had been largely forgotten or ignored in popular memory. As I argue in the Introduction, although historians had long since documented the fact of British involvement in the transatlantic slave trade, until the latter decades of the twentieth century the economic facts, the full repercussions, and, most of all, the human toll of transatlantic slavery had rarely received attention in broadly accessible public forums. This public silence was broken in the 1980s and 1990s, as artists, filmmakers, novelists, and major cultural institutions—responding to the political realities of burgeoning multiculturalism and to new movements in social history and cultural studies—committed themselves to remembering transatlantic slavery and to facilitating local and national conversations on its legacy. As this book shows, the project of remembering the transatlantic slave trade was not without its perils, especially when many of those who were being enjoined to remember slavery felt neither connected to nor responsible for the trade. Asked to "experience" a trauma that was not their own, many may have initially resented the collective guilt called up by the task of commemoration. In addition, those calling for commemoration faced a daunting challenge: how is it possible to educate people about the utterly dehumanizing effects of slavery without playing into stereotypes of dehumanized slaves, ineffectual subjects rendered passive, weak and silent through their enslavement?

Further quandaries arose as those committed to commemoration considered the representation of human suffering itself. How does one convey the extraordinary human affliction brought on by transatlantic slavery in general and the Middle Passage in particular without reducing that suffering—that is, without potentially cheapening the experience or suggesting that it can be vicariously assumed? How, as well, can one avoid the scopophilic impulses of so many older representations of slavery, especially those that crossed the line into pornography?

The last challenge was how to foster respect among all those who would have to converse with one another: how does one create an awareness of a shared humanity without shrinking from the task of tracing responsibility on the one hand and without polarizing communities on the other? This last task has special urgency in a multiracial and multicultural society in which hybridity operates. How does hybridity itself resist being co-opted into the state of things? How does hybridity continue to be the state of coexisting differences that challenge racist assumptions about irreconcilable human dissimilarities?

Surveying a broad field of commemorative sites, novels, films, and a play, I have argued that the solutions to these questions lie, in part, in an ethnographic understanding of human subjectivity in which we recognize how individuals are experiencing bodies situated in time and place. It is a mistake to think that we live "after" those who came before us; we live *with* them on a historical continuum that links our behaviors to theirs and allows us to learn from them. Thus, the question is not whether we assume their guilt but whether we learn valuable moral lessons through our connectedness to them. In thinking about a historical atrocity like the transatlantic slave trade, ethical responsibility demands not that we take on the suffering of another but that we reflect on the conditions that created the suffering and that we act to prevent similar abuse. At the same time, it is imperative to acknowledge the full humanity of those who were enslaved and to recognize them as agents of history.

The most successful artistic and cultural forms remain self-conscious about themselves as expressions. Resisting a realistic style that creates a false sense of complacency, the impression that "it has all been worked out," successful hybrid fictions on page and stage encourage readers to think for themselves. Often they acknowledge the institutional and economic pressures that influence their own production. They self-consciously call into question their own authority while eliciting participation from their audiences. Successful commemorative art gives us flawed, fallible, and even contradictory human beings whose stories are all the more valuable for the ongoing nature of their struggles. Finally, successful forms of commemoration resist a vocabulary of property and ownership and instead offer themselves as shared forms of expression, as contested sites of human creativity.

The Preface of this book, set in the streets of Bath in 2002, described early postmillennial indications that vibrant and livable multicultural communities could thrive in the United Kingdom. Such communities would have to be built on a revised British history, one in which the facts of the eighteenth-century transatlantic slave trade, as well as the full story of the further implications of imperial expansion for all citizens of the commonwealth, would be commonly acknowledged. Yet such communities would also need to make that history the basis for a communal vision for the future. As of early 2005, the signs that healthy public conversation on the subject of British hybridity were omnipresent. New, popular cultural representations do not necessarily represent historical slavery or the transatlantic slave, but they reflect the aftermath and the legacy of violent contact and upheaval associated with the trade. While proposing the work that remains to be done, these representations suggest how new histories are being integrated into the fabric of British life.

In January 2005, for example, the Whitbread Prize, a popular honor given to an author chosen by the Booksellers Association of Great Britain and Ireland and funded by Whitbread PLC, was awarded to Andrea Levy's *Small Island*, a novel that had won the prestigious Orange Prize in 2004.[1] Levy's novel chronicles two British couples, one black and the other white, whose lives intersect in Earls Court in 1948, just after the arrival of the *Windrush*. Flashbacks to a time "before" chronicle the lives of Gilbert Joseph and his bride, Hortense Roberts, in their native Jamaica and of Queenie Bligh and her husband, Bernard, in England. Flashbacks also present the experiences of the two men during the Second World War. Gilbert, as a member of the supposed black Royal Air Force (the airmen were actually never permitted to fly) experienced extraordinary racism, especially from the American GIs, and Arthur endured the physical hardships and military cruelties of a soldier's life in India.

Like Zadie Smith in *White Teeth* (2001) and Monica Ali in *Brick Lane* (2003), Levy writes a fictional meditation on "the future of multi-ethnic Britain." Although her characters live in a recent past, they carry within them the traces of their nation's historical engagement with discourses on race and ethnicity. They struggle with the racism that informs their existence—either by circumscribing the sort of lives they can live or by limiting their capacity to connect on a human level. But a novelistic exploration of national identity such as Levy's does not dominate the headlines, nor does it elicit impassioned letters to the editor. Instead, it is consumed by an audience grown accustomed to the idea of British multiculturalism. Hers is an audience that might also have read, in the Winter of 2005, an insert in the *Guardian* entitled "London: the world in one city: a special celebration of the most cosmopolitan place on earth." In the lead article for the section, "Every race, colour, nation and religion on earth," Leo Benedictus chronicles the presence of "Turks in Green Lane, Congolese in Tottenham, Somalis in Wembley, and Koreans in New Malden."[2] Levy's novel ends as post-war London begins to assume the form that Benedictus describes: when Hortense and Gilbert move out of their rooming house in Earls Court to establish a home of their own, they take with them Queenie's half-black son (fathered by Michael, Queenie's first love back in Jamaica) to raise him in the diasporic community that is just beginning to take shape. Levy's treatment of hybridity shares the caution we saw earlier in *Crossing the River* by Caryl Phillips. For both novelists, the idea that the white and black community will "connect" through their progeny appears tentative at best.

Also in January 2005, novelistic attempts to work through the issues of multiculturalism were being matched elsewhere in London, in the exhibit halls of the Victoria and Albert Museum and on the stage of National Theatre. Following its very successful show "Cinema India: The Art of Bollywood" in 2002, the Victoria and Albert filled an upstairs gallery from fall 2004 through the early winter of 2005 with an exhibition entitled "Black British Style." For the curators, the story begins with the *Windrush* era: "The migration of black people from Africa and the Caribbean after the Second World War changed the visual landscape of the 'mother country.'" After surveying the impact of Caribbean and African migration, the Rastafarian and black power movements, Pentacostalism and Evangelicalism, hip-hop, and designer fashion on black style, the exhibit culminated in an uneasy tension, as "the issue of compatibility between blackness and 'Englishness' remains."[3]

At the same time, that same tension was apparent across town in a new play by Kwame Kwei-Armah, *Fix Up*.[4] Kwei-Armah's first drama for the National Theatre, *Elmina's Kitchen* (2003), although set in modern-day London, directly evoked in its title the European settlement on the Gold Coast notorious for its role in the slave trade. *Fix Up* takes place in a London bookshop run by Brother Kiyi, a man who has built a shrine to black history, culture, and the arts out of the books he lovingly collects. Yet, ironically, his vision has no recourse against more powerful commercial interests at work in his neighborhood; at the end of the play, Brother Kiyi has lost the lease for his shop, which is destined to become a store selling hair products to black customers. The main action of the drama revolves around the appearance of a young teacher named Alice, still another biracial Briton whose existence symbolizes the failure of black and white affiliation.

It is possible to argue that such an artistic and cultural calendar, with these events happening within two months, would not be possible had there not already been broad adjustments to the national story Britons are willing to tell themselves. At the beginning of the twenty-first century, the idea articulated in *The Parekh Report* that "Britain is not and never has been the unified conflict-free land of the popular imagination" appears to have become a truism. "Telling the untold" is now a phrase employed to cover a myriad of historical events—not merely an account of transatlantic slavery but the full circumstances of the British empire, the impact of colonial and imperial expansion on individuals around the globe.[5] Entire literary genres, chief among them the postcolonial novel, commence in the moment when untold stories must be rendered in their fullest historical context.[6]

For children born in the third millennium, the kind of historical recovery that has been the subject of this book may one day seem curious; unlike their parents, these children across Western Europe increasingly experience diversity and heterogeneity as a fact of everyday existence. In the United Kingdom, state-owned broadcasting for young people is especially invested in presenting to preschoolers and school-aged children a world in which multiethnicity and multiculturalism are unquestioned facts of daily existence. Witness a representative show for the preschool set on the cable channel CBeebies: set on the Isle of Mull in the town of Tobomory, *Balamory* features a rainbow cast, including Archie, a Scot in a kilt; Spencer, a black American painter; a black sports enthusiast called Josie Jump; and Penny, a woman who helps run the store and cafe from her wheelchair. In addition to its multihued puppets, the channel also regularly features human beings of different races and ethnicities. Critics might well argue that this type of programming skews the facts; most British children living outside of a few major metropolitan centers will never encounter on a daily basis the range of racial and ethnic types represented. But the issue is less one of access than one of tolerance. Many parents who grew up without ever seeing a black face on television may well prefer that their children grow up comfortable with the idea of Britain's diversity, even within the bounds of a Scottish fishing village.

When seen against a broader national agenda of tolerance and respect for diversity, the history of transatlantic slavery cannot remain an untold story. Both the racism and the unspeakable human cruelty that made the trade possible must be identified and condemned. However, the story of transatlantic slavery must also be told in a manner that allows people to recognize both the human capacity for evil and the human ability to retain agency—either on one's own behalf despite one's victimization or on behalf of another who suffers an injustice, even when doing so entails risks. In the new century, individuals and communities will need to continue to find appropriate forms of commemoration and to expand on and clarify the work that has been done so far. Far from being an untold story, the eighteenth-century transatlantic slave trade is an event that is driving British society forward in the twenty-first century.

Notes

Preface

1. For a collection that captures the full range of newcomers' experiences, see *Extravagant Strangers: A Literature of Belonging*, edited by Caryl Phillips (New York: Random House, 1997).

Introduction

1. *The Future of Multi-Ethnic Britain: The Parekh Report* (London: Profile Books, 2000).

2. According to its Web page, the Runnymede Trust was founded in 1968 as an independent, privately funded think tank focused on ethnicity and cultural diversity. The trust expresses a commitment to "challenging racial discrimination and to promoting a successful multi-ethnic Britain." Its funding comes from a wide range of sources, including large corporations such as the Bank of England, British American Tobacco, and Marks and Spencer; church-affiliated groups such as the Council of Churches and the Church's Commission for Racial Justice; charitable organizations, including the Sainsbury Family Charitable Trust; and individuals such as Mohammed Al Fayed, the Egyptian-born owner of Harrods. With a goal of advising the UK policy community, the Runnymede Trust "fulfills its mandate through timely, high-visibility, leading-edge policy research" ("Who We Are," http:// www .runnymedetrust.org, accessed January 19, 2004).

3. "Wrapped Up in the Flag": letters to the editor by Jennifer Griffin, Barnaby Brocklehurst, and Clare Hartley, *The Guardian*, October 12, 2000, p. 21 (http://www.guardian.co.uk/letters/story/0,3604,380896,00.html, accessed April 15, 2004).

4. Roz Coward, "A Question of Identity," *The Observer*, October 15, 2000 (http://observer.guardian.co.uk/comment/story/0,,382755,00.html), accessed April 15, 2004).

5. This kind of retrospection culminated in "The 1940s House," a reality show that was broadcast in early 2001, in which a contemporary English family "time-traveled" back to endure such wartime experiences as rationing and nightly trips to an Anderson bomb shelter.

6. *The Parekh Report*, p. 2.

7. *The Parekh Report*, p. 3.

8. Ibid.

9. Stuart Hall, "A Question of Identity" (II), *The Observer*, October 15, 2000 (http://observer.guardian.co.uk/comment/story/0,,382756,00.html, accessed April 15, 2004).

10. Mike Phillips and Trevor Phillips, *Windrush: The Irresistible Rise of Multi-racial Britain* (London: HarperCollins, 1998), p. 6.

11. Sarah Lawson Welsh, "(Un)belonging Citizens, Unmapped Territory: Black Immigration and British Identity in the Post-1945 Period," in *Not on Any Map: Essays on Postcoloniality and Cultural Nationalism*, ed. by Stuart Murray (Exeter: University of Exeter Press, 1997), p. 44.

12. For an appreciative response to this point in the report, see Kevin Robbins, "Endnote to London: The City Beyond the Nation," in *British Cultural Studies*, ed. by David Morley and Kevin Robbins (Oxford: Oxford University Press, 2001), pp. 483–484.

13. *The Parekh Report*, p. 26.

14. *The Parekh Report*, p. 22.

15. *The Parekh Report*, p. 10.

16. Raphael Samuel, *Island Stories: Unravelling Britain, Theatres of Memory*, Vol. 2 (New York: Verso, 1998), p. 201.

17. James Walvin, *Black and White: The Negro and English Society, 1555–1945* (London: Penguin, 1973).

18. James Walvin, *Black Ivory: A History of British Slavery* (London: HarperCollins, 1992).

19. Walvin, p. 233.

20. Walvin, p. 336.

21. F. O. Shyllon, *Black Slaves in Britain* (London: Institute for Race Relations and Oxford University Press, 1974).

22. Folarin Shyllon, *Black People in Britain, 1555–1833* (London: Institute for Race Relations and Oxford University Press, 1977).

23. Peter Fryer, *Staying Power: The History of Black People in Britain* (London: Pluto Press, 1984), p. ix.

24. Fryer, p. 1.

25. Fryer, p. 399.

26. Additionally indispensable historical work on slavery written between 1970 and 1990 in the United Kingdom includes: Hugh Thomas, *The Slave Trade: The Story of*

the Atlantic Slave Trade, 1440–1870 (New York: Simon and Schuster, 1997); Barbara Bush, *Slave Women in Caribbean Society, 1650–1838* (Kingston: Heinemann, 1990); and Robin Blackburn, *The Making of New World Slavery: From Baroque to the Modern, 1492–1800* (London: Verso, 1997). Gretchen Gerzina's *Black England: Life Before Emancipation* is a crossover book that compiles much of the scholarship previously published by Walvin, Shyllon, Fryer, Dabydeen, and others. Widely reviewed in both the United Kingdom and the United States when it appeared in 1999, Gerzina's book opens with a description of how, when she entered a "well-known London bookshop," she was rebuffed in her efforts to purchase a paperback copy of Fryer's book by a saleswoman, who sternly told her, "Madam, there *were* no black people in England before 1945" (*Black England: Life Before Emancipation*, London: Allison and Busby, 1999, p. 10).

27. David Dabydeen, *The Black Presence in English Literature* (Manchester: Manchester University Press, 1985). For a discussion of Powell's remarks, their context, and the aftermath, see *Imagining the New Britain* by Yasmin Alibhai Brown (New York: Routledge, 2001), Chapter 2.

28. Dabydeen, p. ix.

29. David Dabydeen, *Hogarth's Blacks: Images of Blacks in Eighteenth-century English Art* (Athens, Georgia: University of Georgia Press, 1989) and *Black Writers in Britain, 1760–1890: An Anthology*, ed. by Paul Edwards and David Dabydeen (Edinburgh: Edinburgh University Press, 1991). For a discussion of Dabydeen's creative reworking of one image from Hogarth, that of the black boy appearing in plate II of "A Harlot's Progress," see Chapter Two below.

30. In this context, Wylie Sypher's *Guinea's Captive Kings: British Anti-Slavery Literature of the XVIIIth Century* remains a remarkable book both for the early date of publication (1942), a time when few literary scholars wrote on the topic of slavery, and for the influential nature of his arguments (1942; rpt., New York: Octagon Books, 1969). For a fuller discussion of Equiano in the classroom, see Chapter Three below.

31. *Black British Cultural Studies: A Reader*, ed. by Houston A. Baker, Jr., Manthia Diawara, and Ruth H. Lindeborg (Chicago: University of Chicago Press, 1996), p. 10.

32. *Black British Cultural Studies*, p. 4.

33. *Black British Cultural Studies*, p. 2.

34. *Black British Cultural Studies*, p. 13.

35. *Black British Cultural Studies*, p 11.

36. Prabhu Guptara, *Black British Literature: An Annotated Bibliography* (Oxford: Dangaroo Press, 1986), p. 14.

37. Helge Nowak, "Black British Literature—Unity or Diversity?," in *Unity in Diversity Revisited: British Literature and Culture in the 1990s*, ed. by Barbara Korte and Klaus Peter Muller (Tübingen: Gunter Narr, 1998), pp. 73–74.

38. Nowak, p. 72.

39. Alibhai-Brown, p. xii. Similarly, Peter Fryer uses the term *Black* to cover all nonwhite people of England. Nonetheless, his book is limited primarily to the history of those of African descent.

40. Fred D'Aguiar, "Against Black British Literature," in *Tibisiri: Caribbean Writers and Critics*. ed. by Maggie Butcher (Sydney: Dangaroo Press, 1989), p. 106.

41. D'Aguiar, p. 107.
42. D'Aguiar, pp. 108 and 109.
43. Stuart Hall, "New Ethnicities," in *Black British Cultural Studies: A Reader*, p. 164.
44. Hall, p. 166.
45. Paul Gilroy *'There Ain't no Black in the Union Jack': The Cultural Politics of Race and Nation* (1987 rpt., Chicago: University of Chicago Press, 1991), pp. 11 and 12.
46. Gilroy, p. 39.
47. Gilroy, p. 149.
48. Gilroy, p. 27.
49. Gilroy, p. 150.
50. See also James Clifford's essay "Diasporas" in *Cultural Anthropology* (1994), 9: 302–338. The concept is discussed in relation to Equiano, below.
51. Gilroy, p. 154.
52. Gilroy, p. 217.
53. Paul Gilroy, *The Black Atlantic: Modernity and Double Consciousness* (Cambridge, MA: Harvard University Press, 1993), p. 19.
54. For an astute critique of Gilroy's ideas about diaspora, see Jacqueline Nassy Brown, "Black Liverpool, Black America, and the Gendering of Diasporic Space," in *Cultural Anthropology* (1998), 13 (3): 291–235.
55. A full bibliography defining postcolonial theory is beyond the scope of my project. However, most studies of the field would begin with Bill Ashcroft, G. Griffiths, and H. Tiffin, eds., *The Empire Writes Back: Theory and Practice in Post-Colonial Literatures* (London: Routledge, 1989). See also Stuart Hall, "When was 'The Post-Colonial'?: Thinking at the Limit," in *The Post-Colonial Question: Common Skies, Divided Horizons*, ed. by Iain Chambers and Lidia Curti (New York: Routledge, 1996), pp. 242–260.
56. Catherine Hall, "Histories, Empires and the Post-Colonial Moment," in *The Post-Colonial Question: Common Skies, Divided Horizons*, pp. 69–70.
57. *The Parekh Report*, pp. 38–39.
58. *The Parekh Report*, p. 57.
59. The "List of Works Cited" includes Anderson but not Samuel, although it appears clear that the kind of historical recovery work envisioned here owes much to Samuel's oeuvre.
60. Marcus Wood, *Slavery, Empathy, and Pornography* (New York: Oxford University Press, 2002) and *Blind Memory: Visual Representations of Slavery in England and America 1780–1865* (New York: Routledge, 2000); Vivian M. Patraka, *Spectacular Suffering: Theatre, Fascism, and the Holocaust* (Bloomington: Indiana University Press. 1999); and Saidiya Hartman, *Scenes of Subjection: Terror, Slavery, and Self-Making in Nineteenth-Century America* (New York: Oxford University Press, 1997).
61. For two illustrative examples of eighteenth-century scholarship that incorporate new critical approaches and challenge the idea of period boundaries, see Joseph Roach, *Cities of the Dead: Circum-Atlantic Performance* (New York: Columbia University Press, 1996) and Srinivas Aravamudan, *Tropicopolitans: Colonialism and Agency, 1688–1804* (Durham, NC: Duke University Press, 1999).

62. Fred D'Aguiar, "The Last Essay About Slavery," in *The Age of Anxiety*, ed. by Sarah Durant and Roy Porter (London: Virago Press, 1996), p. 142.

63. The American Civil War is sometimes played out in England; for example, I witnessed a mock American Civil War battle, between the members of SOSKAN ("Southern Skirmish Association") and the "Union" army—both groups of British enactors of the American Civil War—on the grounds of the American Museum in Bath, on September 5, 1999.

64. Steven Mintz, "Spielberg's *Amistad* and the History Classroom," in *The History Teacher* (1998), 31: 370.

65. For two essays on American commemoration, see Allison Blakely, "Remembering Slavery in the United States," pp. 102–108, and Seymour Drescher, "Commemorating Slavery and Abolition in the United States of America," pp. 109–112, both in *Facing Up to the Past: Perspectives on the Commemoration of Slavery from Africa, the Americas and Europe*, ed. by Gert Oostindie (Kingston, Jamaica: Ian Randle, 2001).

66. Oostindie, p. 9.

67. Yasmin Alibhai Brown. p. 94.

1. Commemorating the Transatlantic Slave Trade in Liverpool and Bristol

1. Madge Dresser and Sue Giles, eds. *Bristol and Transatlantic Slavery: A Catalogue of the Exhibition "A Respectable Trade? Bristol and Transatlantic Slavery"* (Bristol: Bristol Museums and Art Gallery with the University of the West of England, 2000), p. 7.

2. For a critique of the discursive construction of the violence in Britain's black communities in the 1980s, including the St. Paul events, see Chapter 3 of Paul Gilroy, *'There Ain't no Black in the Union Jack': The Cultural Politics of Race and Nation* (Chicago: University of Chicago Press, 1987), pp. 72–113.

3. This population is currently calculated at approximately 4 per cent of the city's total population. This community is of mixed African and European descent and is the longest-standing black community in England. See Stephen Small, "Racialized Relations in Liverpool: A Contemporary Anomaly," *New Community* (1991), 11: 511–537. However, as Roger Anstey and P. E. Hair point out, it seems unlikely that any part of this community is "descended from ancestors who arrived on Merseyside before 1807" (Introduction to *Liverpool, the African Slave Trade, and Abolition*, ed. by Roger Anstey and P. E. H. Hair [Bristol, UK: Western Printing Services, 1976], p. 5.)

4. Alissandra Cummins, "Caribbean Slave Society," in *Transatlantic Slavery: Against Human Dignity*, ed. by Anthony Tibbles (London: HMSO/National Museums and Galleries on Merseyside, 1994), p. 54.

5. Writing retrospectively, curator Anthony Tibbles explains that, in the earlier exhibit, "The slave trade was placed in the context of the overall trade of the port and because of this its significance was underplayed. We also hurried the brief and were unaware of recent research. On reflection our treatment was woefully inadequate and not surprisingly we were criticized for it" ("Against Human Dignity: The Development

of the Transatlantic Slavery Gallery at Merseyside Maritime Museum, Liverpool," *Proceedings, Ninth International Congress of Maritime Museums* [1996], p. 95).

6. See, for example, Celeste-Marie Bernier "Exhibition Review" in *Journal of American History* (2001–2002), 88 (3–4): 1010. Bernier's comment that "any comparison of these two exhibits would confirm the superiority of Liverpool's Transatlantic Slavery" proved controversial, especially because she apparently did not see the Bristol exhibit in its original and entire form.

7. Vivian M. Patraka, *Spectacular Suffering: Theatre, Fascism, and the Holocaust* (Bloomington: Indiana University Press. 1999), p. 122.

8. Marcus Wood, *Blind Memory: Visual Representations of Slavery in England and America 1780–1865* (New York: Routledge, 2000), p. 11. Compare Stuart Hall: "There are certainly very close relations between the Black diaspora and the Jewish diaspora—for example, in the experience of suffering and exile, and the culture of deliverance and redemption, which flow out of it" ("The Formation of a Diasporic Intellectual: An Interview with Stuart Hall by Kuan-Hsing Chen," in *Stuart Hall: Critical Dialogues in Cultural Studies*, ed. by David Morley and Kuan-Hsing Chen [New York: Routledge, 1996], p. 491). Some Afrocentric scholars have argued that the African holocaust might more appropriately be called *Maafa*, the Kiswahili word for disaster.

9. Wood, *Blind Memory*, p. 7.

10. Christine Chivallon, "Bristol and the Eruption of Memory: Making the Slave-Trading Past Visible," *Social and Cultural Geography* (2001), 2: 349.

11. Kirk Savage, *Standing Soldiers, Kneeling Slaves: Race, War, and Monument in Nineteenth-Century America* (Princeton: Princeton University Press, 1997), pp. 210 and 8.

12. Jennifer L. Eichstedt and Stephen Small, *Representations of Slavery: Race and Ideology in Southern Plantation Museum*s (Washington, DC: Smithsonian Institution Press, 2002), pp. 3 and 105.

13. Richard Handler and Eric Gable, *The New History in the Old Museum: Creating the Past at Colonial Williamsburg* (Durham, NC: Duke University Press, 1997), pp. 84–93. But Handler and Gable also note the important work of the all-black Department of African-American Interpretation and Presentation (AAIP) at the museum. Allison Blakely discusses the museum's effort to include the reenactment of an actual slave auction in her piece "Remembering Slavery in the United States," in *Facing Up to the Past: Perspectives on the Commemoration of Slavery from Africa, the Americas and Europe*, ed. by Gert Oostindie (Kingston, Jamaica: Ian Randle, 2001), pp. 105–106. By 2002, Williamsburg had taken up the topic of slavery by incorporating actors portraying the lives of slaves, as reported in the *New York Times* ("Where the Past Lives, Undisturbed by the Present," by Francis X. Clines, May 17, 2002, section A, p. 10).

14. In the field of museum studies, the work of Susan Pearce is indispensable. See both her own seminal essays and others she edited in two collections: *Material Studies in Material Culture* (London: Leicester University Press, 1989) and *New Research in Museum Studies 1: Objects of Knowledge* (London: Athlone Press, 1990). See also Susan Pearce, *Archaeological Curatorship* (Washington, DC: Smithsonian Institution Press, 1990). Also suggestive is *Dream Spaces: Memory and the Museum,* by Gaynor Kavanagh (London: Leicester University Press, 2000). For a history of ethnographic practice in museums, see

Brian Durrans, "The Future of the Other: Changing Cultures on Display in Ethnographic Museums," in *The Museum Time Machine*, ed. by Robert Lumley (London: Routledge, 1988), pp. 144–169. The work of Eilean Hooper-Greenhill is also helpful for a survey of the field. See *Museums and their Visitors* (London: Routledge, 1994) and a collection she edited entitled *Museum, Media, Message* (London: Routledge, 1995).

15. Dwight Conquergood, "Rethinking Ethnography: Towards a Critical Cultural Politics," in *Communication Monographs* (1991), 58: 184.

16. Conquergood, p. 187. Italics added.

17. Caryl Phillips, *The Atlantic Sound* (London: Faber and Faber, 2000), pp. 90–91 and 93.

18. Roger Anstey and P. E. H. Hair, *Liverpool, the African Slave Trade, and Abolition: Essays to Illustrate Current Knowledge and Research* (Bristol, UK: Western Printing Services, 1976), pp. 1–2.

19. Anstey and Hair, p. 2.

20. See, for instance, his inexpensive brochure *The Bristol Slave Traders: A Collective Portrait*, reprinted by the Bristol Branch of the Historical Association at the University of Bristol in 1997.

21. David Richardson, "Liverpool and the English Slave Trade," in *Transatlantic Slavery: Against Human Dignity*, p. 73.

22. Richardson, "Liverpool and the English Slave Trade," p. 75.

23. Richardson, "Liverpool and the English Slave Trade," p. 76.

24. Tim Burke, "'Humanity is Now the Pop'lar Cry': Laboring-class Writers and the Liverpool Slave Trade, 1787–1789," in *The Eighteenth Century: Theory and Interpretation* (2001), 42: 248.

25. Peter Moores, Foreword to *Transatlantic Slavery*, p. 9.

26. Ivan Karp, "Culture and Representation," in *Exhibiting Cultures: The Poetics and Politics of Museum Display* edited by Ivan Karp and Steven D. Lavine (Washington, DC: Smithsonian Institution Press, 1991), p. 2.

27. Helen Coxall, "Speaking Other Voices," *in Cultural Diversity: Developing Museum Audiences in Britain*, ed. by Eilean Hooper-Greenhill (Leicester: Leicester University Press, 1997), p. 104. For a fuller articulation of the issues of writing museum text, see her essay "How Language Means: An Alternative View of Museum Text" in *Museum Languages: Objects and Texts*, ed. by Gaynor Kavanagh (Leicester: Leicester University Press, 1991), pp. 85–99.

28. Coxall, "Speaking Other Voices," p. 107–108.

29. Coxall, p. 110.

30. Coxall, p. 112.

31. In a review of the exhibit, David Devenish comments on the characters: "They make the story unnecessarily complicated. Why not follow the careers of documented slaves, some of whom actually appear in the displays as well?" ("Slavery in the Grip of Prejudice,?" in *Museums Journal*, March 1995: 21). See also Ratan Vaswani, "A Respectable Trade" (*Museums Journal*, May 2000: 16–18).

32. Barbara Kirshenblatt-Gimlett, "Objects of Ethnography," in *Exhibiting Cultures*, p. 414.

33. Mary E. Modupe Kolawole, "An African View of Transatlantic Slavery and the Role of Oral Ceremony in Creating a New Legacy," in *Transatlantic Slavery*, p. 107.

34. *Transatlantic Slavery: Against Human Dignity* (pamphlet) (Liverpool: National Museums and Galleries on Merseyside, n.d.), p. 7.

35. Tibbles, "Against Human Dignity," p. 98.

36. Peter Manning, "The Impact of the Slave Trade on the Societies of West and Central Africa," in *Transatlantic Slavery*, p.97.

37. For a critique of the use of such objects as "artefacts," see Peter Gathercole, "The Fetishism of Artefacts," in *Museum Studies in Material Culture*, pp. 73–81.

38. Or, as Marcus Wood writes, "The Africa we are shown looks foreign because it is foreign" (Wood, p. 299). For a full-scale critique of the use of time in ethnography, see Johannes Fabian, *Time and the Other: How Anthropology Makes its Object* (New York: Columbia University Press, 1983). On the subject of museums, Adrienne L. Kaeppler argues polemically, "It is time to place peoples of the world in historical settings. It is time to show how a society's cultural past influences how that society operates in the modern world. It is time to show how all nations of the world are culturally and socially equal—with no implication that some societal groups are somehow the remnants of earlier stages of civilization" ("Museums of the World: Stages for the Study of Ethnohistory," in *Museum Studies in Material Culture*, p. 87).

39. Svetlana Alpers, "The Museum as a Way of Seeing," in *Exhibiting Cultures*, p. 29. See also Barbara Kirshenblatt-Gimlett, "Objects of Ethnography," in *Exhibiting Cultures*, p. 390.

40. Brian Durrans, "The Future of the Other: Changing Cultures on Display in Ethnographic Museums," in *The Museum Time Machine*, p. 145.

41. George W. Stocking, Jr., "Essays on Museums and Material Culture," in *Objects and Others: Essays on Museums and Material Culture*, ed. by George W. Stocking, Jr. (Madison: University of Wisconsin Press, 1985), p. 4.

42. As Annie Coombes points out, the artifacts are most often made from an alloy of copper, zinc, and lead. See *Reinventing Africa: Museums, Material Culture and Popular Imagination in Late Victorian and Edwardian England* (New Haven: Yale University Press, 1994), p. 228, note 1.

43. *Nature* (July 7, 1889), p. 224. Cited by Coombes, p. 25.

44. See Coombes, chapter one.

45. Stephen Small charges that many museums in the United Kingdom displaying the bronzes "emphasize punishment for uninvited wrongdoing and completely ignore, or significantly downplay, the economic and political interests of the British. Visitors come away with partial and biased perspectives" ("Contextualizing Black Presence," in *Cultural Diversity*, p. 56). Brian Durrans offers the radical suggestion that "just as some kinds of objects tend to be shown in display cases, while others make more sense in a 'reconstructed' setting, so visitors' experience of almost everything shown in museums would be enhanced by highlighting the 'transactional' history that brought a particular object or collection into its current, museum context. This narrow history could be linked not only with wider historical experiences such as explorations or colonial relations but also with earlier uses and presentations of the material

by previous generations of anthropologists and curators, emphasizing the value of reinterpreting collections" (p. 162).

46. Tibbles, *Transatlantic Slavery*, p. 112.

47. Wood, *Blind Memory*, p. 216.

48. Wood, *Blind Memory*, pp. 219–220.

49. For a comprehensive coverage of the topic, see *Black Imagination and the Middle Passage*, ed. by Maria Diedrich, Henry Louis Gates, and Carl Pedersen (New York: Oxford University Press, 1999).

50. Wood, *Blind Memory*, p. 19.

51. This linking results in unintentional ironies, such as the fact that the last room of the exhibit is entitled "1833: Emancipation and Death," as if the end of Wilberforce's life were also the end of the story of emancipated Africans.

52. At the National Maritime Museum in Greenwich, an October 1999 exhibit reduced the representation of slavery to a single, manacled black hand rising up from a cargo hatch, which lay beneath the feet of an elegant white female tea drinker. But the exhibit was soon withdrawn, after public outcry. See Ratan Viswani, "A Respectable Trade," in *Facing Up to the Past*, ed. by Gert Oostindie (Kingston, Jamaica: Ian Randle Publishers, 2001), p. 139.

53. Tibbles, "Against Human Dignity," p. 100. Marcus Wood asks what it means to simulate an event like the middle passage. He concludes, "Museum parodies of the experience of the middle passage, which claim to 'put us there,' may well do more harm than good. You cannot merchandize, advertise, and package the middle passage, and if you try to do these things where are the limits?" (*Blind Memory*, p. 300).

54. Tony Forbes, exhibition text, "A Respectable Trade? Bristol and Transatlantic Slavery," Bristol Industrial Museum.

55. Raphael Samuel, *Theatres of Memory, Vol. I: Past and Present in Contemporary Culture* (London: Verso, 1994), p. 196.

56. Samuel, p. 8.

57. David Richardson, *The Bristol Slave Traders: A Collective Portrait* (Bristol: Bristol Branch of the Historical Association, The University, Bristol, 1997), pp. 2 and 1.

58. David Richardson, pp. 4–5.

59. Madge Dresser, *Slavery Obscured: The Social History of the Slave Trade in an English Provincial Port* (New York: Continuum, 2001). Although commonly said to run third, behind Liverpool and London, in the volume of trade, Bristol may well have been first. Dresser writes, "In this early [18th century] period, Bristol was a more important slaving port than Liverpool and even, for a brief time, surpassed London, to become the nation's number one slaving port" (p. 8).

60. Alan Richardson, "Darkness Visible? Race and Representation in Bristol Abolitionist Poetry," in *Romanticism and Colonialism: Writing and Empire, 1780–1830*, ed. Tim Fulford and Peter Kitson (Cambridge, UK: Cambridge University Press, 1998), pp. 131–132.

61. Richardson, p. 131.

62. *Bristol Racial Equality Newsletter*, December 1996/January 1997, p. 5. Cited by Chivallon, p. 352.

63. See, for instance, http://myweb.ecomplanet.com/phip8366/mycustompage 0006.html. Accessed January 15, 2004.

64. This is according to the research of David Small and Christine Eickelmann. See http://www.englandpast.net/education/legacy2.html. Accessed January 15, 2004.

65. *Bristol and Transatlantic Slavery.* Catalog of the exhibition "A Respectable Trade?: Bristol and Transatlantic Slavery" (Bristol, UK: University of the West of England, 2000), p. 120.

66. The script remains available on a website: http://www.hotwells.freeserve.co.uk/georghouse.html. Accessed February 15, 2004.

67. Michel de Certeau, *The Practice of Everyday Life*, trans. by Steven Rendall (Berkeley: University of California Press, 1984), p. 117.

68. de Certeau, p. 118. Patraka gives a very useful account of the difference between de Certeau's uses of space and place, p. 109.

69. de Certeau, pp. 117–118.

70. *Slave Trade Trail around Central Bristol* by Madge Dresser, Caletta Jordan, and Doreen Taylor (Bristol: Bristol Museum and Art Gallery, 1998).

71. *Slave Trade Trial*, p. 11.

72. *Slave Trade Trial*, p. 2.

73. *Slave Trade Trial*, p. 10.

74. *Slave Trade Trial*, p. 17.

75. *Slave Trade Trial*, p. 16.

76. *Portsmouth Black Heritage Trail: A Self-Guided Walking Tour* (n.p. 1999), p. 1.

77. http://www.afroammuseum.org/trail.html. Accessed March 1, 2004.

78. In *Time and the Other*, Fabian defines *coevalness* as sharing the same time. The denial of coevalness, in contrast, entails "a persistent and systematic tendency to place the referent(s) of anthropology in a Time other than the producer of anthropological discourse." He further writes, "For human communication to occur, coevalness has to be *created*. Communication is, ultimately, about creating shared Time" (his italics) (pp. 30–31).

79. Richard Schechner, *Between Theater and Anthropology* (Philadelphia: University of Pennsylvania Press, 1985), pp. 1–6.

80. Schechner, p. 6.

81. de Certeau, p. 108.

82. de Certeau. p. 93.

83. de Certeau, p. 97.

84. de Certeau, pp. 97–98.

85. *Slave Trade Trial*, p. 10.

86. *Slave Trade Trial*, p. 9.

87. *Slave Trade Trial*, p. 26.

88. *Slave Trade Trial*, p. 11.

89. See Dresser, pp. 96–128.

90. Felecia Davis, "Uncovering Places of Memory: Walking Tours of Manhattan," in *Sites of Memory: Perspectives on Architecture and Race*, ed. by Craig E. Barton (New York: Princeton Architectural Press, 2001), p. 27.

91. Pinney, for instance, is on record as having corresponded from Nevis: " Since my arrival I have purchased 9 Negroes at St. Kitts and can assure you I was shocked at the first appearance of human flesh, exposed for sale. But surely God ordained them for ye use and benefit of us; otherwise his Divine will would have been made manifest by some particular sign or token" *(Bristol and Transatlantic Slavery*, p. 115).

92. Patraka, pp. 3–7.

93. Patraka, p. 4.

94. Patraka, p. 7.

95. Dresser, p. 3.

96. *Slave Trade Trail*, p. 21.

97. Forbes, exhibition text, *Bristol and Transatlantic Slavery*.

98. *Slave Trade Trail*, p. 18.

99. Raymond Williams, *The Long Revolution* (New York: Columbia University Press, 1961), pp. 48–49.

100. Mark O'Neill, "Curating Feelings: Issues of Identity in Museums," unpublished paper delivered at the Canadian Art Gallery Education Group Conference, November 1994, cited by Gaynor Kavanagh, *Dream Spaces*, p. 2.

2. Fictionalizing Slavery in the United Kingdom, 1990–2000

1. Caryl Phillips, *Cambridge* (New York: Random House, 1991); Barry Unsworth, *Sacred Hunger* (London: Penguin Books, 1992); Caryl Phillips, *Crossing the River* (New York: Alfred A. Knopf, 1994); Graeme Rigby, *The Black Cook's Historian* (London: Constable, 1993); Fred D'Aguiar, *The Longest Memory* (London: Chatto and Windus, 1994); Philippa Gregory, *A Respectable Trade* (London: HarperCollins, 1995); S. I. Martin, *Incomparable World* (London: Quartet Books, 1996); Fred D'Aguiar, *Feeding the Ghosts* (London: Chatto and Windus, 1997); and David Dabydeen, *A Harlot's Progress* (London: Jonathan Cape, 1999).

2. Bénédicte Ledent, "Remembering Slavery: History as Roots in the Fiction of Caryl Phillips and Fred D'Aguiar," in *The Contact and the Culminations: Essays in Honor of Hena Maes-Jelinek*, ed. by Marc Delrez and Bénédicte Ledent (Liege, Belgium: Liege Literature and Language, 1997), p. 272. Ledent also remarks: "Without unduly generalizing, one can indeed say that slavery has rarely been tackled head-on by the older generation [of Caribbean writers], though its pervasive presence may be felt throughout their writing" (p. 271). Referring to the poetry of Edward Brathwaite and Derek Walcott, Gail Low qualifies this assertion: "This is not to say that slavery has entered the imagination only recently" ("The Memory of Slavery in Fred D'Aguiar's *Feeding The Ghosts*," in *Postcolonial Literatures: Expanding the Canon*, ed. by Deborah Madsen, [London: Pluto Press, 1999], p. 104).

3. See Richard Todd, *Consuming Fictions: The Booker Prize and Fiction in Britain Today* (London: Bloomsbury, 1996).

4. Bénédicte Ledent, "Remembering Slavery," p. 272.

5. Gail Low, "The Memory of Slavery in Fred D'Aguiar's *Feeding The Ghosts*," p. 117.

6. Ledent, p. 274.

7. Robert Young, *Colonial Desire: Hybridity in Theory, Culture, and Race* (New York: Routledge, 1994), pp. 6 and 26. On the historical shift of the term—including a discussion of the fact that "hybrids are, in biological terms, often sterile"—see Jonathan Friedman, "Global Crises, the Struggle for Cultural Identity and Intellectual Porkbarrelling: Cosmopolitans versus Locals, Ethnic and Nationals in an Age of De-Hegemonization," in *Debating Cultural Hybridity: Multi-Cultural Identities and the Politics of Anti-Racism*, ed. by Pnina Werbner and Tariq Modood (London: Zed Books, 1997), pp. 70–89. For an exploration of the theme of hybridity specifically in the works of Caryl Phillips, see Brad Buchanan, "Caryl Phillips: Colonialism, Cultural Hybridity and Racial Difference," in *Contemporary British Fiction*, ed. by Rod Mengham and Philip Tew (Malden, MA: Blackwell, 2003), pp. 174–190.

8. For instance, in *The Location of Culture*, Bhabha refers to hybridity as "in-between the designation of identity" (New York: Routledge, 1994, p. 4). For a critique of Bhabha's view of hybridity, see Antony Easthope, "Bhabha, hybridity, and identity," in *Textual Practice* (1988), 12 (2): 341–358.

9. "Tracing Hybridity in Theory," in *Debating Cultural Hybridity: Multi-Cultural Identities and the Politics of Anti-Racism*, pp. 257 and 259.

10. Sara Ahmed, *Strange Encounters: Embodied Others in Post-Coloniality* (New York: Routledge, 2000), p. 13.

11. Stuart Hall, "When was 'The Post-Colonial'?: Thinking at the Limit" in *The Post-Colonial Question: Common Skies, Divided Horizons*, ed. by Iain Chambers and Lidia Curti (New York: Routledge, 1996), p. 250.

12. Maria Frias, "Building Bridges back to the Past: An Interview with Fred D'Aguiar," in *Callaloo* (2002), 25 (2): 420.

13. Hall, p. 244.

14. Hall, p. 247.

15. Hanif Kureishi, *"My Beautiful Laundrette" and "The Rainbow Sign"* (London: Faber and Faber, 1986), p. 38.

16. Kureishi, p. 31.

17. Vlatka Velic, "Postmodern and Postcolonial Portrayals of Colonial History: Contemporary Novels about the Eighteenth Century," in *Tennessee Philological Bulletin* (2001), 38: 46. As Todd points out on p. 215, there is the possibility that this story is the one that Clive Benson, another Unsworth protagonist, was struggling to write in *Sugar and Rum*, published in 1988.

18. *Sacred Hunger*, p. 361.

19. *Sacred Hunger*, p. 568.

20. *Sacred Hunger*, pp. 328 and 618.

21. *Sacred Hunger*, p. 629.

22. *Sacred Hunger*, p. 2.

23. Cf. Todd, who also writes, "The knowledge the reader gains as to Luther's 'place,' his identity and origins, his construction of his identity through language, is presented, with arbitrary omniscience, as parallel to an act of reconstruction by the narrator from the fragmentary remains of the historical record" (pp. 215–216).

24. *Sacred Hunger*, p. 149.
25. *Sacred Hunger*, pp. 511–523.
26. Todd, 216.
27. *Sacred Hunger*, p. 130.
28. *Sacred Hunger*, p. 490.
29. Paul Sharrad, "Speaking the Unspeakable: London, *Cambridge* and the Caribbean," in *De-scribing Empire: Post-colonialism and Textuality*, ed. by Chris Tiffin and Alan Lawson (New York: Routledge, 1994), p. 216.
30. *Sacred Hunger*, p. 142.
31. *Sacred Hunger*, p. 365.
32. See "A Warning Voice: Bryan Podmore Talks to Barry Unsworth" for Unsworth's own comments on Conrad's influence on his oeuvre (http://www.historicalnovelsociety.org/solander%20files/warningvoice.html, accessed February 2, 2004).
33. *Sacred Hunger*, p. 251.
34. A good place to dip into the controversies is *"Heart of Darkness": An Authoritative Text, Background, and Sources*, ed. by Robert Kimbrough (New York: W. W. Norton, 1988).
35. *Sacred Hunger*, pp. 199–200.
36. *Sacred Hunger*, pp. 203–204.
37. *Sacred Hunger*, p. 204.
38. *Sacred Hunger*, p. 205.
39. Ahmed, p. 123–124.
40. *Sacred Hunger*, p. 417.
41. *Sacred Hunger*, p. 419.
42. Ibid.
43. Mary Birkett, *A Poem on the African Slave Trade, Addressed to her Own Sex* (Dublin: J. Jones, 1792). On women and the sugar boycott, see Clare Midgely, *Women Against Slavery: The British Campaigns, 1780–1870* (New York: Routledge, 1992) and Charlotte Sussman, *Consuming Anxieties: Consumer Protest, Gender, and British Slavery, 1713–1833* (Palo Alto, CA: Stanford University Press, 2000).
44. For further discussion of the link between slavery and pornography, see Marcus Wood, *Slavery, Empathy and Pornography* (New York: Oxford University Press, 2002) and my discussion of *Mansfield Park* below.
45. Frias, p. 421.
46. For a comprehensive analysis of water, fire, and wood imagery in the novel, see Carol Low, "The Memory of Slavery in D'Aguiar's *Feeding the Ghosts*," pp. 104–119.
47. Cf. Carole Froude-Durix: "Through his character Mintah, D'Aguiar explores how memory may be retained through the written word" in "Anonymity, Naming, and Memory in Fred D'Aguiar's *Feeding the Ghosts*: Islands of Fiction in a Sea of History," in *Commonwealth Essays and Studies* (1998), 21: 52.
48. *Feeding the Ghosts*, p. 155.
49. *Feeding the Ghosts*, p. 156.
50. *Feeding the Ghosts*, p. 169.
51. *Feeding the Ghosts*, p. 193.

52. *Feeding the Ghosts*, p. 194.
53. http://stjohnbeachguide.com/Isert.html, accessed February 13, 2004.
54. See Gronnisaw's narrative as reproduced in *Unchained Voices: An Anthology of Black Authors in the English Speaking World*, ed. by Vincent Carretta (Lexington: University of Kentucky Press, 1996). Gronnisaw appears to have been fluent in both Dutch and English.
55. *Feeding the Ghosts*, p. 206.
56. *Feeding the Ghosts*, p. 175.
57. *Feeding the Ghosts*, p. 11.
58. Hall, p. 247.
59. *Feeding the Ghosts*, p. 195.
60. Saidiya Hartman, *Scenes of Subjection: Terror, Slavery, and Self-Making in Nineteenth-Century America* (New York: Oxford University Press, 1997), p. 6.
61. Jenny Sharpe, *Ghosts of Slavery: A Literary Anthology of Black Women's Lives* (Minneapolis: University of Minnesota Press, 2003), p. 106.
62. Sylvie Chavanelle, "Caryl Phillips's *Cambridge*: Ironical (Dis)empowerment?" in *The International Fiction Review* (1998), 25: 78. See Chavanelle also on parallels between content and form and for an analysis of Cambridge's speech patterns (pp. 79–81).
63. Evelyn O'Callaghan, "Historical Fiction and Fictional History: Caryl Phillips's *Cambridge*," in *Journal of Commonwealth Literature* (1993), 29: 39.
64. For example, compare Janet Schaw: "We proceeded to our lodgings thro' a narrow lane; as the Gentleman told us no ladies ever walk in this Country. Just as we got into the lane, a number of pigs run out at the door, and after them a little parcel of monkeys. This not a little surprised me, but I found what I took for monkeys were negro children, naked as they were born" (*Journal of a Lady of Quality*, ed. by Evangeline Walker Andrews [New Haven: Yale University Press, 1923], p. 78) with *Cambridge*, pp. 23–24: "However, on resettling my position, I discovered that what I had taken for monkeys were nothing more than negro children, naked as they were born, parading in a feral manner to which they were not only accustomed, but in which they felt comfortable."
65. O'Callaghan, p. 39.
66. O'Callaghan, p. 42.
67. *Cambridge*, p. 156.
68. Bénédicte Ledent, *Caryl Phillips* (Manchester: Manchester University Press, 2002), p. 84.
69. Ledent, *Caryl Phillips*, pp. 85–90.
70. Chavanelle, p. 84
71. Ledent, *Caryl Phillips*, p. 94.
72. Ledent, *Caryl Phillips*, p. 100.
73. Ledent, *Caryl Phillips*, p. 102.
74. Paul Smethurst, "Postmodern Blackness and Unbelonging in the Works of Caryl Phillips," in *Journal of Commonwealth Literature* (2002), 37 (2): 13.
75. Ledent, *Caryl Phillips* , p. 98.

76. Todd, p. 199.
77. Chavanelle, p. 88.
78. Cf. Gail Low: "The juxtaposition of these narratives forces the reader to mediate between the self-contained realities of their different worlds and provides rich opportunities for the ironic exposure of the willful self-delusion of the slave-owning communities" ("'A Chorus of Common Memory': Slavery and Redemption in Caryl Phillips's *Cambridge* and *Crossing the River*" *Research, in African Literatures* (1998), 19: 123.)
79. Richard Wolin, *Walter Benjamin: An Aesthetics of Redemption*, cited by Low, p. 130.
80. Frias, p. 421.
81. *The Longest Memory*, p. 9.
82. *The Longest Memory*, p. 46.
83. *The Longest Memory*, p. 64.
84. *The Longest Memory*, p. 106.
85. *The Longest Memory*, p. 114.
86. *The Longest Memory*, p. 134.
87. Frias, p. 419
88. *The Longest Memory*, pp. 14–15.
89. Ibid.
90. *The Longest Memory*, p. 26.
91. *The Longest Memory*, p. 34.
92. *The Longest Memory*, pp. 34–35.
93. *The Longest Memory*, pp. 70–71.
94. Ledent, "Remembering Slavery," p. 279
95. Ledent, "Remembering Slavery," p. 278.
96. Frias, p. 419–420.
97. Fred D'Aguiar, "The Last Essay about Slavery," in *The Age of Anxiety*, ed. by Sarah Dunant and Roy Porter (London: Virago Press, 1996), p. 139.
98. Alessandra Di Maio, "Diasporan Voices in Caryl Phillips's *Crossing the River*," in *Multiculturalism and Hybridity in African Literature*, ed. by Hal Wylie and Bernth Lindors (Trenton, NJ: African World Press, 2002), p. 367.
99. *Crossing the River*, p. 13.
100. *Crossing the River*, p. 61.
101. *Crossing the River*, p. 29.
102. *Crossing the River*, p. 11.
103. *Crossing the River*, pp. 62–63.
104. It does, however, draw attention to this fact in a later scene, in which Madison, another former slave whom Edward had molested, being no longer under the control of the enfeebled white man, resists Edward's sexual advances (p. 68).
105. *Crossing the River*, p. 56.
106. *Crossing the River*, p. 69.
107. Young, p. 5.
108. *Crossing the River*, p. 57.
109. On the significance of the title, and in particular the river image, see Ledent, *Caryl Phillips*, pp. 110–112.

110. *Crossing the River*, p. 108.
111. *Slavery, Empathy, and Pornography*, pp. 54, 59, 64, and 54, respectively.
112. Low, p. 137.
113. *Crossing the River*, p. 87.
114. *Crossing the River*, p. 91.
115. Low, p. 136.
116. *Crossing the River*, p. 134.
117. *Crossing the River*, p. 145.
118. Of course, having "no race" is impossible, and so Phillips's portrayal raises an interesting question concerning the reader's mental picture of Travis prior to the discovery that he is black: do some readers see him as white?
119. *Crossing the River*, p. 149.
120. *Crossing the River*, p. 162.
121. *Crossing the River*, p. 167.
122. *Suture*, directed by David Siegel and Scott McGehee, MGM/UA, 1996.
123. *Crossing the River*, p. 202.
124. *Crossing the River*, p. 163.
125. *Crossing the River*, pp. 231–232.
126. Maya Jaggi, "Crossing the River: Caryl Phillips talks to Maya Jaggi," in *Wasafiri* (1994), 20: 26.
127. *Crossing the River*, p. 237.
128. Ledent, *Caryl Phillips*, p. 124.
129. *Radio Times* April 18–24, 1998: 4.
130. *Radio Times*, May 2–8, 1988: 72.
131. *A Respectable Trade*, p. 109.
132. For a selection of Pringle's writings, see Alan Richardson, ed. *Slavery, Abolition and Emancipation: Writings in the British Romantic Period*, Vol. 4: verse (London: Pickering and Chatto, 1999), pp. 342–343.
133. See Douglas Hall's edition of the historical Thistlewood's manuscript: *Miserable Slavery: Thomas Thistlewood in Jamaica, 1750–1786* (London: Macmillan, 1989).
134. *A Harlot's Progress*, p. 1.
135. *A Harlot's Progress*, p. 2.
136. *A Harlot's Progress*, p. 256.
137. *A Respectable Trade*, p. 1.
138. *A Respectable Trade*, p. 5.
139. *A Respectable Trade*, pp. 5–6.
140. *A Respectable Trade*, pp. 279–283.
141. I am thinking here of the work of Janet Radcliffe Richards in *The Skeptical Feminist* (London: Routledge, 1980) and Elizabeth Wilson in *Adorned in Dreams* (Berkeley: University of California Press, 1985).
142. See Deidre Shauna Lynch, *The Economy of Character: Novels, Market Culture, and the Business of Inner Meaning* (Chicago: University of Chicago Press, 1998).
143. *A Respectable Trade*, p. 102.
144. *A Respectable Trade*, p. 119.

145. *A Respectable Trade*, p. 349.
146. Ibid.
147 Ibid.
148 Janice Radway, *Reading the Romance: Women, Patriarchy, and Popular Literature* (Chapel Hill: University of North Carolina Press, 1984), p. 69.
149. *A Respectable Trade*, p. 254.
150. Radway, p. 83.
151. *A Respectable Trade*, p. 310.
152. James Walvin, *Black Ivory: A History of British Slavery* (London: HarperCollins, 1993), p. 221.
153. *A Respectable Trade*, p. 140.
154. *A Respectable Trade*, p. 178.
155. *A Respectable Trade*, p. 468.
156. *A Respectable Trade*, p. 486.
157. Valerie Smith, "Black Feminist Theory and the Representation of the 'Other,'" in *Changing Our Own Words*, ed. by Cheryl Wall (New Brunswick, NJ: Rutgers University Press, 1989), p. 46.
158. *A Harlot's Progress*, p. 57.
159. *A Harlot's Progress*, p. 69.
160. Ibid.
161. *A Harlot's Progress*, p. 50.
162. *A Harlot's Progress*, p. 70.
163. *A Harlot's Progress*, p. 71.
164. *A Harlot's Progress*, p. 75.
165. Ibid.
166. *A Harlot's Progress*, p. 184.
167. *A Harlot's Progress*, p. 168.
168. *A Harlot's Progress*, p. 169.
169. *A Harlot's Progress*, p. 136.
170. *A Harlot's Progress*, p. 70.
171. *A Harlot's Progress*, pp. 271–272.
172. *A Harlot's Progress*, pp. 259–260.
173. *A Harlot's Progress*, pp. 252–253.
174. *A Harlot's Progress*, pp. 30–31.
175. Ibid.
176. *A Harlot's Progress*, p. 33.
177. *A Harlot's Progress*, p. 123.
178. *A Harlot's Progress*, p. 164.
179. *A Harlot's Progress*, p. 19.
180. *A Harlot's Progress*, pp. 237–242.
181. *A Harlot's Progress*, p. 256
182. Ibid.
183. *A Harlot's Progress*, p. 258.
184. *A Harlot's Progress*, pp. 279–280.

230 Notes

185. I am borrowing here, of course, from Paul Gilroy's concept of *The Black Atlantic*.

3. Seeing Slavery and the Slave Trade

1. All quotations from the novel are from *Mansfield Park*, ed. by Kathryn Sutherland (New York: Penguin Books, 1996). Moira Ferguson, *Colonialism and Gender Relations from Mary Wollstonecraft to Jamaica Kincaid* (New York: Columbia University Press, 1993), p. 85. Marcus Wood, *Slavery, Empathy, and Pornography* (New York: Oxford University Press, 2002), p. 300.

2. Jane Austen's *Mansfield Park: A Screenplay by Patricia Rozema* (New York: Talk Miramax Books, 2000), scene 61, p. 60.

3. Juliana Pidduck provides a deft analysis of the role of movement in films about Austen's heroines in "Of Widows and Country Walks: Frames of Space and Movement in 1990 Austen Adaptations," in *The Postcolonial Jane Austen*, ed. by You-me Park and Rajeswari Sunder Rajan (London: Routledge, 2000), pp. 116–168.

4. For a reading that explores how Rozema "recasts the positive power of literature into a more social mode, a celebration of the liberating force against the repressions of social structure" (p. 189), see "The Mouse that Roared: Patricia Rozema's *Mansfield Park*," by Linda Troost and Sayre Greenfield, in *Jane Austen in Hollywood*, 2nd ed., ed. by Linda Troost and Sayre Greenfield (Lexington: University of Kentucky Press, 2001), pp. 188–204.

5. *Mansfield Park: A Screenplay*, scene 5, p. 15.

6. As Joseph Lew points out, unlike Liverpool and Bristol, "Portsmouth was largely untainted by the slavers' interest" ("'That Abominable Traffic': *Mansfield Park* and the Dynamics of Slavery," in *Historicizing Gender*, ed. by Beth Fowkes Tobin (Athens, Georgia: University of Georgia Press, 1994), p. 275. See also Keith Windschuttle, who asserts in "Rewriting the History of the British Empire": "To be anywhere near the coast of England, a slave trader would have to be thousands of miles off course" (*New Criterion*, May 2000, 8 [9]).

7. Cf. Rajeswari Sunder Rajan: "Reading Jane Austen postcolonially is not one critical 'approach' among others, uniquely propagated by 'postcolonial critics,' but rather, an inescapable historical imperative in our times" ("Austen in the World: Postcolonial Mappings," in *The Postcolonial Jane Austen*, p. 3).

8. *A Son of Africa: The Slave Narrative of Olaudah Equiano* (1995). Aimimage Productions for BBC Education, 28 minutes. Executive producer, Chris Lent; producer, Hugh Williams; director, Alrick Riley; writer, Danny Padmore; starring Hakeem Kae-Kazim as Equiano. All quotations have been transcribed from the videotape.

9. *A Respectable Trade* (1998). Video produced by WGBH Boston, two tapes. Director, Suri Krishnamma; writer, Philippa Gregory. All quotations have been transcribed from the videotape.

10. *Britain's Slave Trade: Telling the Untold*. Made by Pepper Productions and Brook Lapwing for Channel 4. Producers, Trevor Phillips and Phillip Whitehead. Broadcast

October 3, 10, 17, and 24, 1999. All quotations have been transcribed from the videotape in the collection of the British Film Institute, London.

11. I borrow this distinction from Andrew Higson, *English Heritage, English Cinema: Costume Drama Since 1980* (Oxford: Oxford University Press, 2003). p. 12.

12. Pam Cook, *Fashioning the Nation: Costume and Identity in British Cinema* (London: British Film Institute, 1996).

13. For this list of publications, I am indebted to Brygchan Carey's indispensable Web site on Equiano: http://www.brycchancarey.com/equiano (accessed February 20, 2004). This site is also the best source for the large bibliography of secondary sources on Equiano. For a full discussion of the evidence concerning Equiano's birth, see Vincent Carretta, "Questioning the Identity of Olaudah Equiano, or Gustavus Vassa, the African," in Felicity Nussbaum, ed. *The Global Eighteenth Century* (Baltimore: John Hopkins University Press, 2003), pp. 226–235. For a lively discussion of pedagogical issues arising from Equiano's text, see "A Forum on Teaching Equiano's *Interesting Narrative*," with pieces by Adam Potkay, Srinivas Aravamudan, and Roxann Wheeler, in *Eighteenth-century Studies* (2001), 34: 601–619.

14. *The Interesting Narrative of the Life of Olaudah Equiano, or Gustavus Vassa, Written by Himself: A Norton Critical Edition*, ed. by Werner Sollors (New York: W. W. Norton, 2001), pp. 2–5.

15. I take these characteristics from James Clifford's essay "Diasporas," in *Cultural Anthropology* (1994), 9: 302–338.

16. *Narrative of the Life of Olaudah Equiano*, pp. 21–22.

17. *Narrative of the Life of Olaudah Equiano*, p. 23.

18. Catherine Obianju Acholonu, "The Home of Olaudah Equiano—A Linguistic and Anthropological Search," in *The Interesting Narrative of the Life of Olaudah Equiano*, ed. by Sollors, pp. 351–361.

19. See Vincent Carretta, Introduction, in *Olaudah Equiano: The Interesting Narrative and Other Writings* (New York: Penguin Books, 2003), p. xi. Or see his essay "Questioning the Identity of Olaudah Equiano, or Gustavus Vassa, the African."

20. Comments by Carretta in response to a student's question, April 24, 2003, Boston College, Chestnut Hill, MA.

21. *Narrative of the Life of Olaudah Equiano*, p. 26.

22. *Narrative of the Life of Olaudah Equiano*, p. 126.

23. *Narrative of the Life of Olaudah Equiano*, p. 177.

24. *Narrative of the Life of Olaudah Equiano*, p. 111.

25. *Narrative of the Life of Olaudah Equiano*, p. 155.

26. *Narrative of the Life of Olaudah Equiano*, p. 137.

27. *Narrative of the Life of Olaudah Equiano*, pp. 126–127.

28. *Narrative of the Life of Olaudah Equiano*, p. 127.

29. *Narrative of the Life of Olaudah Equiano*, p. 128.

30. *Narrative of the Life of Olaudah Equiano*, p. 137.

31. See Vincent Carretta's discussion entitled "Appendix B: A Note on the Illustrations," pp. 315–316 in the 2003 Penguin edition.

32. *Narrative of the Life of Olaudah Equiano*, p. 57.
33. *Narrative of the Life of Olaudah Equiano*, p. 136.
34. *Narrative of the Life of Olaudah Equiano*, p. 137
35. See John Corner, *The Art of Record: A Critical Introduction to Documentary* (Manchester: Manchester University Press, 1996).
36. Paul Gilroy, *'There Ain't no Black in the Union Jack': The Cultural Politics of Race and Nation* (Chicago: University of Chicago Press, 1987), p. 12.
37. *Amistad* (1997). 157 minutes. Director, Steven Spielberg; writers, David H. Franzoni and William Owens; starring: Morgan Freeman, Nigel Hawthorne, Anthony Hopkins, Djimon Hounsou, Matthew McConaughey, David Paymer, Pete Postlethwaite, Stellan Skarsgård, Razaaq Adoti, Abu Bakaar Fofanah, Anna Paquin, and Tomas Milian.
38. Sally Hadden, "Review of Amistad" (http://www.tntech.edu/history/amistadr.html, accessed March 4, 2004). See also her piece "How Accurate is the Film?" in a special section on "*Amistad*: Controversy about the Film and its Use," in *The History Teacher* (1998), 31 (3): 374–379.
39. Steven Mintz, "Spielberg's *Amistad* and the History Classroom" in "*Amistad*: Controversy about the Film," p. 372.
40. For instance, a visit of the ship to Boston on October 25, 2003, sponsored by the Massachusetts Conference of the United Church of Christ, offered an opportunity for interracial conversation and dialogue, as the event brought together individuals from Boston's black and white communities. A published program for the event encouraged participants to "Continue the Amistad Legacy! Take an Active Stand Against Racism" and suggested specific strategies for doing so (Program: Massachusetts Conference of the United Church of Christ, Amistad Celebration Day). See also *The Amistad Affiliate*, Fall/Winter 2000, published by Mystic Seaport, Mystic, Connecticut. Similar educational work is being done at the Historical Museum of Southern Florida through the artifacts of the slave ship *Henrietta Marie*.
41. Robert Hewison, *The Heritage Industry: Britain in a Climate of Decline* (London: Methuen, 1987). Raphael Samuel, *Patriotism: The Making and Unmaking of British National Identity* (London: Routledge, 1989), Vol. 1; Pam Cook, *Fashioning the Nation: Costume and Identity in British Cinema* (London: British Film Institute, 1996). Higson's very useful summary occurs on pp. 47–76 of *English Heritage, English Cinema: Costume Drama Since 1980* (Oxford: Oxford University Press, 2003).
42. Higson, p. 75.
43. Higson, p. 29. But cf. Cook, who also argues that costume dramas from an earlier period characteristically "present a picture of a nation in crisis, with shifting and unstable boundaries" (p. 89).
44. Higson, p. 77.
45. Ann Jones and Peter Stallybrass, *Renaissance Clothing and the Memory of Material* (Cambridge, UK: Cambridge University Press, 2000), pp. 17 and 20.
46. Higson, p. 42.
47. Higson, p. 79.

48. Although the novel tells us that Mehuru is initially physically repulsed by Frances, the actor can, at best, only resort to suggestive looks to indicate any adverse response to her.

49. Bill Nichols, *Representing Reality: Issues and Concepts in Documentary* (Bloomington: Indiana University Press, 1991), p. 31.

50. Trevor Phillips and S. I. Martin, *Britain's Slave Trade* (London: Channel 4 Books, 1999), p. 4.

51. Phillips, p. 5.

52. Michael Renov, "Introduction: The Truth about Non-Fiction," in *Theorizing Documentary*, ed. by Michael Renov (New York: Routledge, 1993), p. 2.

53. Phillips, p. 7.

54. Pnina Werbner, "Introduction: The Dialectics of Cultural Hybridity," in *Debating Cultural Hybridity: Multi-Cultural Identities and the Politics of Anti-Racism*, ed. by Pnina Werbner and Tariq Modood (London: Zed Books, 1997), p. 14

55. See *Britain's Slave Trade*, pp. 82–83. The actual number of slaves executed is still in dispute.

56. Nichols, p. 31.

57. *Secrets & Lies* (1996). A CiBy 2000/Thin Man Production, 142 minutes. Producer, Simon Channing-Williams; director and writer, Mike Leigh; starring Brenda Blethyn, Marianne Jean-Baptiste, Timothy Spall, Phyllis Logan, and Claire Rushbrook. Screenplay published by Faber and Faber, 1997.

58. *Narrative of the Life of Olaudah Equiano*, p. 72.

59. *Narrative of the Life of Olaudah Equiano*, p. 100.

60. For a comparison of two film versions of *Mansfield Park*, see Jan Fergus, "Two Mansfield Parks: Purist and Postmodern," in *Jane Austen on Screen*, ed. by Gina Macdonald and Andrew F. Macdonald (Cambridge, UK: Cambridge University Press, 2003), pp. 69–89.

61. Edward Said, *Culture and Imperialism* (New York: Alfred Knopf, 1993), pp. 93–97. Said's comments on Austen had appeared earlier in *Raymond Williams: Critical Perspectives*, ed. by Terry Eagleton (Cambridge, UK: Polity, 1989), pp. 150–164, and in *Contemporary Marxist Literary Criticism*, ed. by Francis Mulhern (London: Longmans, 1992), 97–113.

62. Joseph Lew, "'That Abominable Traffic: *Mansfield Park* and the Dynamics of Slavery," in *Historicizing Gender*, p. 282. See also Brian Southam "The Silence of the Bertrams," in *"Mansfield Park": A Norton Critical Edition*, ed. by Claudia A. Johnson (New York: W. W. Norton, 1998), pp. 493–498 (reprinted from *Times Literary Supplement*, February 17, 1995), and Ruth Perry, "Jane Austen and British Imperialism," in *Monstrous Dreams of Reason: Body, Self, and Other in the Enlightenment*, ed. by Laura J. Rosenthal and Mita Choudhury (Lewisburg, PA: Bucknell University Press, 2002), pp. 231–254.

63. See R. W. Chapman, *The Novels of Jane Austen: The Text Based on Collation of the Early Editions*, 5 vols. (London: Oxford University Press, 1923), III: 553–556. See also Perry, pp. 246–248.

64. See Appendix II to *Jane Austen: A Life*, by Claire Tomalin (New York: Penguin Books, 1998), pp. 291–294.

65. Ferguson, p. 70.

66. Perry, p. 251.

67. Michael Steffes, "Slavery and *Mansfield Park*: The Historical and Biographical Context," *English Language Notes* (1996), 34: 24.

68. Southam argues—based on books that appear on Fanny's table in Chapter 16 (including Crabbe's *Tales in Verse*, published in 1812)—that "Austen fixes the month and year of Sir Thomas's return as October 1812," though "October 1813 is theoretically possible" (p. 494). See also Wood, pp. 317–319 for a discussion of what abolition might have meant for Sir Thomas.

69. Ferguson, p. 74.

70. *Mansfield Park*, p. 39.

71. Susan Fraiman, "Jane Austen and Edward Said: Gender, Culture, and Imperialism," in *Janeites: Austen's Disciples and Devotees*, ed. by Deidre Lynch (Princeton: Princeton University Press, 2000), p. 210.

72. *Mansfield Park*, p. 389.

73. Maaja A. Stewart, *Domestic Realities and Imperial Fictions: Jane Austen's Novels in Eighteenth-Century Contexts* (Athens, Georgia: University of Georgia Press, 1993), p. 135.

74. Lew, p. 312; Wood, p. 313.

75. Fraiman, p. 220.

76. James Berardinelli, "The Darker Side of Jane Austen: Patricia Rozema Talks about *Mansfield Park*," interview, November 15, 1999 (http://movie-reviews.colossus.net, accessed May 10, 2003).

77. Claudia Johnson, *Times Literary Supplement*, December 31, 1999, p. 16.

78. This and other contradictions in Rozema's portrayal of Fanny were discussed by Pam Bromberg in a paper, "A Commentary on *Mansfield Park*: A New Film by Patricia Rozema," delivered to the Jane Austen Society, Boston, March 12, 2000.

79. *Mansfield Park: A Screenplay*, scene 52, p. 52.

80. *Mansfield Park: A Screenplay*, scene 35, p. 34.

81. *Mansfield Park: A Screenplay*, scene 135, p. 23.

82. *Mansfield Park: A Screenplay*, scene 73, p. 70.

83. Marcus Wood, *Blind Memory: Visual Representations of Slavery in England and America: 1780–1865* (New York: Routledge, 2000), pp. 1–11.

84. In scene 104, Fanny tells her mother, "I do a lot myself. I'm the right hand of Lady Bertram and Mrs. Norris" (p. 97). But most often we see Fanny involved in recreational activities such as playing cards or riding.

85. *Mansfield Park: A Screenplay*, scene 63, p. 63.

86. *Mansfield Park: A Screenplay*, scene 91, p. 88.

87. Steve Wiecking, "Loving the Longing: The Yearnings of Patricia Rozema's *Mansfield Park*" (http://thestranger.com/1999–11–25/flm.html, accessed May 10, 2003).

88. Claudia Johnson, *Times Literary Supplement*, December 31, 1999, p. 17.

89. *Mansfield Park*, p. 363.

90. *Mansfield Park*, p. 83.

91. I owe this insight concerning the connection between Sterne and Sancho to Alan Richardson. For a critique of the passage in Sterne, see Wood, *Blind Memory*, pp. 12–18. According to Wood, "above all Sterne uncovers the appropriative, and experientially leveling, drive undermining the desire to 'feel for the slave,' to feel 'pity' for the poor Africans'" (p. 13). In the movie, Henry Crawford reads the text, affectedly but with no irony, directly to Fanny, while Maria spies on the two of them from around the corner. For viewers who know the text, the allusion reinforces the idea that Fanny is in danger of "being caged," while it obviates questions concerning the tone of Sterne's original passage.

92. On the other hand, as Angus Fletcher writes, "The whole point of allegory is that it does not *need* to be read exegetically; it often has a literal level that makes good sense by itself" (*Allegory: The Theory of a Symbolic Mode* [Ithaca: Cornell University Press, 1964]), p. 7.

93. Mary's pun has generated considerable controversy over whether Austen herself would ever have made such a dirty joke. See the Penguin edition, p. 396n.

94. *Mansfield Park*, p. 80.

95. *Mansfield Park: A Screenplay*, scene 48, p. 45.

96. *Mansfield Park: A Screenplay*, scene 141, p. 128.

97. *Mansfield Park: A Screenplay*, scene 158, p. 139.

98. *Mansfield Park: A Screenplay*, scene 166, p. 144.

99. Berardinelli, "The Darker Side of Jane Austen."

100. Rozema's screenplay refers to a slightly different set of images from the ones that appear in the film. The screenplay mysteriously also refers to texts—"Oroonoko's wrists," for example, to accompany a detail of severely chafed wrists and "Equiano's Last Day" to accompany the Blake etching (scene 142, p. 128).

101. Wood, *Blind Memory*, pp. 39–40.

102. Wood, *Slavery, Empathy, Pornography*, p. 95.

103. Wood points out that the face of the slave in the Blake engraving is "inverted, foreshortened and carries an expression of bemused concentration. Like a contortionist the victim holds his impossible, broken-backed position, frozen in the laborious web of the graver's labor, as if for applause" (*Blind Memory*, p. 231).

104. Saidiya V. Hartman, *Scenes of Subjection: Terror, Slavery, and Self-Making in Nineteenth-Century America* (New York: Oxford University Press, 1997), pp. 20 and 22.

105. Wood, *Slavery, Empathy, Pornography*, p. 140.

106. For more on this topic, see Charlotte Sussman's essay, "Lismahgo's Captivity: Transculturation in *Humphry Clinker*," *ELH* (1994), 61: 597–618.

107. As Charlotte Sussman argues, "women's political power . . . lay in their ability to regulate the domestic space, keeping its contents separate from the economic dynamic of colonial trade" ("Women and the Politics of Sugar, 1792," *Representations* [1994], 48: 65).

108. Malachy Postlethwayt, *The African Trade, the Great Pillar and Support of the British Plantation Trade in America* (London, 1754), cited by David Richardson, "The Rise of the

Atlantic Empires," in *Transatlantic Slavery: Against Human Dignity*, ed. by Anthony Tibbles (London: HMSO, 1994), pp. 27–28.

4. Transnationalism and Performance in 'Biyi Bandele's *Oroonoko*

1. *Aphra Behn's Oroonoko*, in a new adaptation by 'Biyi Bandele, premiered at the Royal Shakespeare Company, The Other Place, Stratford Upon Avon, April 7, 1999. It opened at the Barbican, in The Pit, on December 15, 1999. Amber Lane Press published the play text in London in 1999.

2. Bandele's *Oroonoko*, p. 5.

3. Nicholas Monu, "A Brief History" (http://www.nickmonu.com/a_brief_history.html, accessed May 2002).

4. Wylie Sypher, *Guinea's Captive Kings: British Anti-Slavery Literature of the Eighteenth Century* (1942 rpt., New York: Octagon Books, 1969), pp. 108–121.

5. Srinivas Aravamudan, *Tropicopolitans: Colonialism and Agency, 1688–1804* (Durham, NC: Duke University, 1999), pp. 29–70.

6. Monu was schooled in England and the United States (at American University), trained at Webber Douglas, and has appeared on the stage in London, Manchester, Liverpool, Nigeria, and Berlin. Bandele was born in Kafancahn, Nigeria, in 1967. His career began when, after attending the University of Ife in Nigeria, he was invited to England for the National Student Drama Festival in 1990. Stephen Jeffreys and Alan Ayckbourn subsequently supported him, and he settled in London (Jeremy Kingston, "*Oroonoko* Flows Again," *Times* [London], April 27, 1999, p. 38). For an insightful exploration of the issues associated with cosmopolitanism, see Kwame Anthony Appiah, "Cosmopolitan Patriots," in *Cosmopolitics: Thinking and Feeling Beyond the Nation*, ed. by Peng Cheah and Bruce Robbins (Minneapolis: University of Minnesota Press, 1998), pp. 91–114.

7. Julie Stone Peters, "Intercultural Performance, Theatre, Anthropology, and the Imperialist Critique: Identities, Inheritances, and Neo-Orthodoxies" in *Imperialism and Theatre: Essays on World Theatre, Drama, and Performance*, ed. by J. Ellen Gainor (London: Routledge, 1995), p. 207.

8. Bill Ashcroft, Gareth Griffiths, and Helen Tiffin, *The Empire Writes Back: Theory and Practice in Post-Colonial Literatures* (New York: Routledge, 1989), p. 11.

9. Paul Gilroy, *The Black Atlantic: Modernity and Double Consciousness* (Cambridge, MA: Harvard University Press, 1993), p. 198.

10. Peters, p. 210. My discussion of Oroonoko as intellectual property can be read against Laura J. Rosenthal's essay exploring the issues raised by "ownership" of Oroonoko in the seventeenth and eighteenth centuries. See "Owning Oroonoko: Behn, Southerne, and the Contingencies of Property," in *Troping Oroonoko from Behn to Bandele* edited by Susan B. Iwanisziw (New York: Ashgate, 2004), pp. 83–107. Rosenthal is particularly helpful for her discussion on Behn's anxiety over ownership of *Oroonoko*: "The narrator's disclaimers not only express the uneasiness with which an English woman inhabits the position of ownership, but they also recognize and prob-

lematize Behn's own position in a literary economy. If the author owns *Oroonoko*, then she participates in the same economy as the men who own Oroonoko" (p. 90).

11. Joseph Roach, *Cities of the Dead: Circum-Atlantic Performance* (New York: Columbia University Press, 1992), p. 4.

12. Aihwa Ong, *Flexible Citizenship: The Cultural Logics of Transnationality* (Durham, NC: Duke University Press, 1999), p. 4.

13. Malcolm Waters, *Globalization* (New York: Routledge, 1995), pp. 196 and 226.

14. Here I borrow from Paul Jay's summary of the debate over the origins and beginnings of globalism in "Beyond Discipline? Globalization and the Future of English, in *PMLA* (2001), 116: 35. As Jay points out, both Anthony Giddens and David Harvey disagree with the idea that globalization should be traced back before the twentieth century (pp. 35–36).

15. Beth Fowkes Tobin, *Picturing Imperial Power: Colonial Subjects in Eighteenth-century British Painting* (Durham, NC: Duke University Press, 1999).

16. Tobin, p. 109.

17. Felicity Nussbaum, *The Limits of the Human: Fictions of Anomaly, Race, and Gender in the Long Eighteenth Century* (New York: Cambridge University Press, 2003), pp. 139 and 254.

18. Roxann Wheeler, *The Complexion of Race: Categories of Difference in Eighteenth-Century British Culture* (Philadelphia: University of Pennsylvania Press, 2000), pp. 5 and 7.

19. Wheeler, p. 92.

20. See also Nancy Stepan, *The Idea of Race in Science: Great Britain 1800–1960* (London: Macmillan, 1982).

21. Ruth Cowhig, "Blacks in English Renaissance Drama and the Role of Shakespeare's *Othello*," in *The Black Presence in English Literature*, ed. by David Dabydeen (Manchester: Manchester University Press, 1985), p. 1.

22. On the oddness of James Quin's "magpie" appearance as Othello, see Virginia Mason Vaughan, *Othello: A Contextual History* (Cambridge, UK: Cambridge University Press, 1994), p. 95. See also Anthony Barthelemy, *Black Face, Maligned Race: The Representation of Blacks in English Drama from Shakespeare to Southerne* (Baton Rouge: Louisiana State University Press, 1987), and Julie Ellison *Cato's Tears and the Making of Anglo-American Emotion* (Chicago: University of Chicago Press, 1999), pp. 48–73.

23. Two often-cited works on nineteenth-century blackface are Eric Lott, *Love and Theft: Blackface Minstrelsy and the American Working Class* (New York: Oxford University Press, 1993), and W. T. Lhamon, *Raising Cain: Blackface Performance from Jim Crow to Hip Hop* (Cambridge, MA: Harvard University Press, 1998).

24. In the early nineteenth century, Henry Crabb Robinson reportedly responded to Edmund Kean's portrayal of Oroonoko. Although he appreciated the actor's performance, he was offended and disgusted by the sight of "a whole stage filled with blacks." About Kean's performance, Hazlitt similarly wrote, "The negroes in it (we could wish them out of it, but then there would be no play) are *ugly customers* upon

the stage" (his emphasis, cited by Arthur Richard Nichols, in "A History of the Staging of Thomas Southerne's *The Fatal Marriage* and *Oroonoko* on the London Stage from 1694 to 1851," Ph.D. dissertation, University of Washington, 1971, pp. 187–188).

25. On eighteenth-century acting styles, see Earl Wasserman, "The Sympathetic Imagination in 18th-century Theories of Acting," in *Journal of English and Germanic Philology* (1947), 46: 264–272, and Shearer West, *The Image of the Actor: Verbal and Visual Representation in the Age of Garrick* (New York: St. Martin's Press, 1991). On the theater-going experience, see Peter Stallybrass and Allon White, *The Politics and Poetics of Transgression* (Ithaca: Cornell University Press, 1986), Chapter Two.

26. Nussbaum, p. 219.

27. *Oroonoko: A Norton Critical Edition*, ed. by Joanna Lipking (New York: W. W. Norton, 1997), and *"Oroonoko": A Bedford Cultural Edition*, ed. by Catherine Gallagher (Boston: Bedford/St Martin's, 2000).

28. Thomas Southerne, *Oroonoko*, edited by Maximillian E. Novak and David Stuart Rodes (Lincoln: University of Nebraska Press, 1976). The play also appears in *The Broadview Anthology of Early Eighteenth-Century Drama*, ed. by J. Douglas Canfield (Orchard Park, NY: Bedford, 2001).

29. Nussbaum devotes an entire chapter to the possible explanations for Imoinda's whiteness (pp. 151–188). See also Jenifer B. Elmore, "'The Fair Imoinda': Domestic Ideology and Anti-Slavery on the Eighteenth-Century Stage," in *Troping Oroonoko from Behn to Bandele*, pp. 35–58. Elmore argues that a white Imoinda "occupies the moral center of the 18th-century theatrical adaptations, visually and verbally collapsing discourses of sentimentalism, domesticity, and anti-slavery into a spectacle of suffering white womanhood.... Compelled by their own ideology and a powerfully emotive drama to admire a heroine who is at once a slave, the miscenegous wife of a black slave and a virtuous white matron, 18th-century audiences were placed in a position in which tolerating slavery was incompatible with middle-class British virtue and some degree of anti-slavery sentiment seemed to be simply a 'natural' family value" (p. 36).

30. Francis Gentleman, *Oroonoko: A Tragedy Altered from Southerne* (Glasgow: n.p., 1790), and John Ferriar, *The Prince of Angola* (Manchester: n.p., 1788).

31. On the dating of Southerne's *Oroonoko*, see John Wendell Dodds, *Thomas Southerne, Dramatist* (New Haven, CT: Yale University Press, 1933), p. 128. Dodds also surveys the performance history of the play. Although *Oroonoko* has only recently become part of the literary canon, as Laura Brown points out, "Historians of slavery have never neglected Oroonoko" ("The Romance of Empire: Oroonoko and the Trade in Slaves," in *The New Eighteenth-century*, ed. by Felicity Nussbaum and Laura Brown [New York: Methuen, 1987], p. 42). For a detailed reading of crucial changes made to the story during its long history, see Rhoda M. Trooboff, "Reproducing *Oroonoko*: A Case Study in Plagiarism, Textual Parallelism, and Creative Borrowing" in *Troping Oroonoko*, pp. 108–139. Also useful in the same collection is the essay of Susan B. Iwanisziw, "The Eighteenth-Century Marketing of *Oroonoko*: Contending Constructions of Maecenas, the Author and the Slave," pp. 141–173. Iwanisziw argues that "Southerne's *Oroonoko* challenged Behn's novella for precedence not because it more

accurately or astutely depicted slavery and colonial torture but because it was more accessible, both in the theater and in print" (p. 167).

32. In her essay "Reviving Oroonoko 'In the Scene': From Thomas Southerne to 'Biyi Bandele," Jessica Munns reads the *Oroonoko* story through the paradigm of "surrogation," as defined by Joseph Roach, as "the process of standing in for someone or something else" (in *Troping Oroonoko*, pp. 174–197).

33. Southerne, p. 4.

34. Suvir Kaul, "Reading Literary Symptoms: Colonial Pathologies and the Oroonoko Fictions of Behn, Southerne, and Hawkesworth," in *Eighteenth-Century Life* (1994), 18: 89.

35. Jane Spencer, *Aphra Behn's Afterlife* (Oxford: Oxford University Press, 2000), pp. 237 and 233.

36. For more on these debates, see Margaret Ferguson, "News from the New World: Miscegenous Romance in Aphra Behn's *Oroonoko* and *The Window Ranter*," in *The Production of English Renaissance Culture*, ed. by David Miller, Sharon O'Dair, and Harold Weber (Ithaca: Cornell University Press, 1994), pp. 151–189; Laura Brown, "The Romance of Empire: *Oroonoko* and the Trade in Slaves," in *The New Eighteenth-century*, pp. 41–61; Suzanne Z. Andrade, "White Skin, Black Masks: Colonialism and the Sexual Politics of *Oroonoko*," in *Cultural Critique* (1994), 27: 189–214; and Charlotte Sussman, "The Other Problem with Women: Reproduction and Slave Culture in Aphra Behn's *Oroonoko*," in *Rereading Aphra Behn: Theory and Criticism*, ed. by Heidi Hutner (Charlottesville: University of Virginia Press, 1993), pp. 212–233.

37. Joyce Green MacDonald, "The Disappearing African Woman: Imoinda in *Oroonoko* After Behn," *ELH* (1999), 66: 75.

38. In the program notes for the RSC version, as well as in his preface to the play text, Gregory Doran refers to the Hawkesworth text as the [David] Garrick version.

39. On this issue, see Robert Chibka's essay "'Oh! Do Not Fear a Woman's Invention': Truth and Fiction in Aphra Behn's *Oroonoko*" in *Texas Studies in Language and Literature* (1988), 30: 510–537.

40. Nichols, p. 190.

41. Bandele's *Oroonoko*, p. 20.

42. For a fuller discussion of Yoruba performance tradition, see Margaret Thompson Drewal, *Yoruba Ritual: Performers, Plays, Agency* (Bloomington: Indiana University Press, 1992). For an exploration of Yoruba worldview in the work of several playwrights, including Ama Ata Aidoo and Wole Soyinka, see B. M. Ibitokum, *African Drama and the World View* (Ibadan: Ibadan University Press, 1995). Jenny Davidson also remarks on Oroonoko as a comic or parodic actor in her unpublished essay "Aphra Behn's *Oroonoko*: 'Biyi Bandele, Thomas Southerne and the Return of the Repressed," delivered at the annual meeting of the Northeast American Society for 18th-Century Studies, New York, October 19, 2002.

43. Bandele's *Oroonoko*, p. 5.

44. Bandele's *Oroonoko*, p. 15.

45. Gallagher, *"Oroonoko": A Bedford Cultural Edition*, p. 15.

46. Bandele's *Oroonoko*, p. 27.

47. T. J. Cribb, "*Oroonoko* and *Happy Birthday, Mister Deka D*, by 'Biyi Bandele." *African Literatures* (2000) 31: 174.

48. Kwame Anthony Appiah makes a point similar to Bandele's: "Recent historiography has stressed again and again the ways in which the 'national heritage' is constructed through the invention of traditions; the careful filtering of the rough torrent of historical event into the fine stream of official narrative; the creation of a homogeneous legacy of values and experience" ("Topologies of Nativism," in *Literary Theory: An Anthology* edited by Julie Rivkin and Michael Ryan [New York: Blackwell, 1988], p. 951).

49. Sussman, p. 215.

50. Ros Ballaster, "New Historicism: Aphra Behn's *Oroonoko*: The Body, the Text, and the Feminist Critic" in *New Feminist Discourses: Critical Essays in Theories and Texts*, ed. by Isobel Armstrong (London: Routledge, 1992), p. 293.

51. MacDonald, p. 82.

52. Bandele's *Oroonoko*, p. 67.

53. Bandele's *Oroonoko*, p. 53.

54. Bandele's *Oroonoko*, p. 53–54.

55. Several feminist critics have analyzed this scene as having crucial importance for the gender politics of the fiction. Margaret Ferguson, for example, argues that "Behn as author uses Imoinda's death scene to inscribe the authority and the agency of the *white woman writer*, figured in the narrator, as a function of a set of finely calibrated *differences* from the female 'other' embodied in Imoinda" (Ferguson, p.181, italics in the original).

56. Bandele's *Oroonoko*, p. 103.

57. Spencer, p. 233, note 27.

58. Bandele's *Oroonoko*, p. 29.

59. Ibid.

60. Bandele's *Oroonoko*, p. 30.

61. This is according to Jessica Munns in "Reviving Oroonoko 'In the Scene,'" p. 190.

62. It should be noted that, through the subplot involving the two sisters Charlotte and Lucy Welldon, Southerne also sets in motion such potentially feminist themes as the injustices of the marriage market for women. However, when Hawkesworth omitted the subplot from his adaptation, that aspect of the story disappeared. See Nussbaum's discussion of this point, pp. 173–175.

63. For a similar critique of phallocentrism in an African setting, see Chinua Achebe's *Things Fall Apart*, in which much of the unfolding tragedy in precolonial Africa can be traced to Okonkwo's compulsion to express his manhood. For instance, the murder of Ikemefuma, necessitated by patriarchal law runs contrary to the deep affection that Okonkwo feels for the surrogate son. At the same time, patriarchal obsessions prevent the father from recognizing the superior strengths and virtues in his daughter Ezinma. Or, as Kwadwo Osei-Nyame asks, "May we not read the story of [the female characters] and the displaced Okonkwo with all its insistent re-orderings

of significations of gender and authority as being of cardinal importance to Achebe's construction of the contested nature of power and authority within the clan?" ("Chinua Achebe Writing Culture: Representation of Gender and Traditions in *Things Fall Apart*," in *African Literatures* [1999], 30: 159).

64. For one version of such a polemic, see Ngugi Wa Thiong'o, *Decolonizing the Mind: the Politics of Language in African Literature* (Portsmouth, NH: Heinemann, 1986).

65. Kingston, p. 38.

66. See Chinua Achebe, "The African Writer and the English Language," in *Morning Yet on Creation Day* (London: Heineman, 1975), pp. 55–62.

67. Edward Brathwaite, *The Development of Creole Society in Jamaica, 1720–1820* (Oxford: Clarendon Press, 1971), p. 307.

68. See *Oroonoko*, as edited by Lipking, pp. 8–10, or as edited by Gallagher, pp. 38–40.

69. Cribb, p. 176.

70. Bandele's *Oroonoko*, pp. 36–37.

71. Cribb, p. 176.

72. For a different attempt to bring to English the Yoruba "relationship between the dynamics of speech and the dynamics of action," see M. Nourbese Philip, *The Genealogy of Resistance* (New York: Mercury, 1977), pp. 201–223.

73. Bandele's *Oroonoko*, pp. 37–38.

74. According to Jessica Munns, the shift of mise-en-scène during the second half of the play, with its heavy reliance on Hawkeworth's text, was due to the fact that Bandele was "not interested in writing the Surinam section." Moreover, the dramaturge and director liked "the strong contrast between the colorful first part and the drab world of slavery" ("Reviving Oroonoko 'In the Scene,'" p. 190).

75. This is a central assertion in a seminal work entitled *The Stage Life of Props* by Andrew Sofer (Ann Arbor: University of Michigan Press, 2003).

76. Mita Chodhury, *Interculturalism and Resistance in the London Theatre, 1660–1800: Identity, Performance, Empire* (Lewisburg, PA: Bucknell University Press, 2000), p. 162.

77. Roach, p. 157.

78. Cited by Nichols, pp. 174–175.

79. Herbert Marshall and Mildred Stock, *Ira Aldridge: The Negro Tragedian* (Carbondale: Southern Illinois University Press, 1968), pp. 54–55. Nussbaum also discusses Aldridge's career, pp. 214–238.

80. Sypher, p. 167. Laura Brown analyzes this incident as "an influential cultural fable . . . that takes on the problem of cultural difference and transforms it into identification" in *Fables of Modernity: Literature and Culture in the English Eighteenth Century* (Ithaca: Cornell University Press, 2001), p. 179.

81. Peters, p. 201.

82. The work of Kenneth Krauss, in *Private Readings/Public Texts: Playreader's Constructs of Theatre Audiences* (Cranbury: Associated University Press, 1993) suggests the kind of work that might be done by integrating reader response theory into performance theory.

83. Bandele's *Oroonoko*, p. 92.

84. Bandele's *Oroonoko*, p. 82.

85. All of this is captured on a videotape in the Theatre Museum in London (director, Gregory Doran): *Oroonoko* by 'Biyi Bandele, adapted from Aphra Behn, performed by Nicholas Monu, The Other Place, Stratford Upon Avon (National Video Archive of Stage Performance, 1999).

86. Bandele's *Oroonoko*, p. 105.

87. Here arises another interesting series of connections between Behn and Bandele. Both appear alert to the power of the marketplace over the outcomes of their stories. As Ferguson writes, "In *Oroonoko* Behn constructs an ambiguous reflection on the role of intellectual producers and consumers in [a late-seventeenth-century] international market" (Ferguson, p. 176).

88. Paulla A. Ebron, "Tourists as Pilgrims: Commercial Fashioning of Transatlantic Politics," *American Ethnologist* (1999), 26 (4): 912 and 928.

89. Yasmin Alibhai-Brown, *Imagining the New Britain* (New York: Routledge, 2001), p. 17.

Conclusion

1. Andrea Levy, *Small Island* (London: Review Books, 2004).

2. Leo Benedictus, "Every Race, Colour, Nation and Religion on Earth—Part Two," *The Guardian*, January 21, 2005, section G2, pp. 2–5.

3. Victoria and Albert Museum, exhibition guide, "Black British Style."

4. Kwame Kwei-Armah, *Fix Up*. Director, Angus Jackson. Opened in the Cottesloe Theatre, December 16, 2004.

5. The phrase is equally appropriate, for example, to describe the work of the British Empire and Commonwealth Museum, which describes as itself offering "the first serious attempt in the United Kingdom to present a publicly accessible history of the British empire and to examine its continuing impact on Britain and the rest of the world." The museum further announces its mission: "The guiding principle is to allow people, whatever their faith or background, access to a unique shared history. To enable them to make sense of who they are, where they come from, in order to move confidently into the future. It is an attempt to invoke a clearer notion of an individual and collective identity" (http://www.empiremuseum.co.uk/aboutus/index.html, accessed January 2005).

6. For a discussion of the fictional representation of hybrid communities in London in particular, see John McLeod, *Postcolonial London: Rewriting the Metropolis* (London: Routledge, 2004).

Index

abolition, critique of, 40, 135
abolitionist poetry, 32, 48
absence, 60
Achebe, Chinua, 198, 240n63
Acholonu, Catherine Obianju, 131
acting, eighteenth-century, 184
African American history, Manhattan, 57
Ahmed, Sarah, 69, 78
Aldridge, Ira, 201
Alibhai-Brown, Yasmin, 10–11, 23, 205
allegory, 168
Alpers, Svetlana, 37
Amistad (film), 139–40
Amistad (ship), 140, 232n40
Anderson, Benedict, 16
Annamahoe, 201–202
Anstey, Roger, 31
anti-racism, politics of, 13
Ariyon, Bakare, 110, 140
    as Mehuru, 144–147
Aravamuden, Srinivas, 180, 183, 216n61
Austen, Jane
    Mansfield Park, 125
        colonialism, 160–161
        Fanny as heroine, 125
        formal reading, 163–164
        primogeniture, critique of, 171
        slavery, 161–162

Bandele, 'Biyi, 179–181, 197, 236n6
    Oroonoko, 179–206
        Africa, 190–191
        Behn, relation to, 108–9, 197–198, 204
        diasporic themes, 181
        ending, 203–204
        Imoinda, 191–196
        Lady Onola, 192–193
        performance, 189–190, 202–203
        phallocentricism, 196–197
        prequel, 188, 190
        Suriname, 200
        women, 187–188
        Yoruba, relation to, 179, 180, 190, 198–200
Barker, Dennis, 152–153
Barker, Francis, 152
Bath, City of, ix–xi
Beckford, Robert, 155–156
Behn, Aphra, 179, 180
    Bandele and, 188–189
    Oroonoko, 185–186
Benedictus, Leo, 210

244   Index

Benin bronzes, 38
binary oppositions, 62–63, 70, 105
biraciality, 69–70
Birkett, Mary, 79–80
black Atlantic, 14, 180, 182
Black British Cultural Studies, 9–11
Black British Style, 210
Black History Trail (Boston), 54
Blackburn, Robin, 148, 215n26
blackface, 184
blackness, definition of, 9–11
Blake, William
    A Negro hung alive by the ribs to the gallows, 172–174
    Song of Innocence and *Songs of Experience*, 116
Boston Freedom Trail, 32
Bristol, city of
    enslaved Africans living in, 59
    1996 commemoration, 25, 43–45
    St. Paul district, 25
    slave trade, 31–32, 47–48
    walking trail—See *Slave Trade Trail around Central Bristol*
Bristol City Museum and Art Gallery, 26
Bristol Industrial Museum, 45
Bristol Slave Trade Action Group (BSTAG), 26, 48
Bristol and Transatlantic Slavery: The Story of the City's Role in the 18th Century Slave Trade, 45
Britain, idea of, 2–3, 4, 15–16
Britain's Slave Trade: The Untold Story, 148–156
British black identity, 11–13
British Empire and Commonwealth Museum, 242n5
British identity, 71
Brown, Laura, 238n31, 241n80
Buchanan, Brad, 224n7
Burke, Tim, 32
Bush, Barbara, 215n26

Cabot, John, 25
canon, black literary, 7, 8–9
canon, eighteenth-century, 8–9, 20–21
Carey, Brycchan, 231n13
Caribbeanness, 68
Carretta, Vincent, 120–130, 131–132
CBeebies, 211–212
Certeau, Michel de, 29, 49, 55–56
Chatterton, Thomas, 48
Chavanelle, Sylvie, 86
Chivallon, Christine, 28
Chodhury, Mita, 201
Circum-Atlantic, the, 20
Clarke, Warren, 110, 140
Clarkson, Thomas, 163, 164
coevalness, 54–55
Colston, Richard, 45, 53, 61–63
    statue of, 61
complicity, African, 152
Conquergood, Dwight, 29, 54
Conrad, Joseph
    Heart of Darkness, 77, 97
Cook, Pam, 128, 141
Coombes, Annie E., 38
Corn Exchange, Bristol, 63
costume drama:, 128, 141, 143
Coward, Roz, 2
Coxall, Helen, 33, 34, 35
Cribb, T. J., 198

Dabydeen, David, 8–9, 68, 148
    A Harlot's Progress, 104–123
        commodification, 108, 115–116
        pederasty, 115–117
        representation of history, 121
        sexual relations, 117–119
        writing, 122
D'Aguiar, Fred, 11
    "The Last Essay on Slavery," 21, 94
    Feeding the Ghosts, 80–84
        binary oppositions, 82–83
        hybridity, 82
        representation of history, 81

The Longest Memory, 89–93
    black characters, 91–92
    representation of history, 93–94
    representation of slavery, 93–94
diaspora, 181
    definition of, 14
diorama, the, 35
documentary film, the, 148, 149, 156
Dream Works Studio, 139
Dresser, Madge, 26, 47–48, 52, 57, 58, 61, 148
Durrans, Brian, 220n45

Ebron, Paulla, 204–205
Edwards, Paul, 8, 129
einfuhlen, 94
Elmore, Jenifer, 238n29
Elton, Julia, 151–152
enslaved Africans, terminology of, 34
Equiano, Olaudah, 9, 87
    biography, 129–134
    birth, 131
    canon, place in, 129–130
    cosmopolitan identity, 132–134
    diasporic identity, 130–131
    naming, 130, 135
    religious identity, 134–135
    traveler, as, 130
ethnography, 29–30, 37, 38–39, 41, 54

Fabian, Johannes, 220n38, 222n78
family as metaphor, 152–160
Fergus, Jan, 233n60
Ferguson, Moira, 125
Ferriar, John, 186
Fielding, Emma, 110, 140
Forbes, Tony, 43, 44, 62
Fox, William, 79, 176
Fraiman, Susan, 162, 164
Froude–Durix, Carole, 225n47
Fryer, Peter, 7–8
Future of Multi–Ethnic Britain: The Parekh Report—See *Parekh Report*

Garrick, David, 201
Gates, Henry Louis, 129
Gentleman, Francis, 186
Georgian House—See *Pinney House*
Gerzina, Gretchen, 215n26
Gilroy, Paul, 12–14, 180, 181
goneness, 60
Gregory, Phillipa, 68, 105–106
    A Respectable Trade, 67–68
    commodification, 109–111
    representation of Africa, 105, 108
    representation of romance, 112–115
Gronniosaw, James, 82, 87
Guardian (Manchester) *The*, 1–2, 210
Guptara, Prabhu, 10

Hall, Catherine, 14–15
Hall, Stuart, 3, 11–12, 69, 70, 83, 134–135
Hartman, Saidya, 84, 174–175
Hawkesworth, John, 186
heritage, English, 141
Higson, Andrew, 141, 144
History Teacher, The, 139–140
holocaust, African, 27
holocaust, Jewish, compared to African, 27, 59–61, 120
hybridity, 68–70, 71, 78, 153–155

identity, black British, 10–11, 13
identity, British, 1, 4
illness as metaphor, 171, 176–177
Imperial War Museum, 42
infection, 176–177
Iser, Wolfgang, 202
Isert, Paul Erdmann, 81–82
Iwanisziw, Susan, 238n31

Johnson, Samuel, 152, 164
Jolly, David, 153
Jordan, Caletta, 26, 52

Kae-Kazim Hakeen, 135
Kaeppler, Adrienne, 220n38
Karp, Ivan, 33
Kirshenblatt-Gimlett, Barbara, 35
Kolawole, Mary E. Modupe, 36
Kureishi, Hanif, 70–71
Kwei-Armah, Kwame
   Fix-Up, 210–211

Lawrence, Stephen, Inquiry Report, 3
Ledent, Bénédicte, 67, 68, 87, 94, 103
Lee, Spike, 184
Leigh, Mike, 157
Levy, Andrea, 209
   Small Island, 209–210
Lewis, Richard Jeffreys, 61
Liverpool, city of
   slave trade in, 30–32, 151
livery, 144
Living History, 45–46
Low, Gail, 88, 223n2

Manning, Peter, 36–37
Mansfield Park (film), 125–126
   allegory, 168–169
   Fanny as heroine, 125–126, 164, 166
   Maria Bertram, 167–169
   Mary Crawford, 169–170
   representation of slave trade, 126, 165–166, 170–171
   Tom Bertram, 171–172
Martin, S. I.
   Incomparable World, 67, 68
Massey, Anna, 140
McDonalds, 182, 204–205
Merseyside Maritime Museum, 26, 27, 33
   See also *Transatlantic Slavery: Against Human Dignity*
Middle Passage, representation of, 39–43
Millennium, the, 2
Mintz, Stephen, 22, 139
Monu, Nick, 179, 180, 203, 236n6

Moores, Peter, 26, 32
More, Hannah, 48
Morrison, Toni, 22, 40, 68
Munns, Jessica, 238n32, 241n74

Nichols, Bill, 156
Notting Hill Riots, 3
Nowak, Helge, 10
Nussbaum, Felicity, 183, 185

O'Callaghan, Evelyn, 86
Oostindie, Gert, 23
Othello, 147, 184, 202

Parekh Report, The, 1, 2–4, 15–16, 17
pastiche, 86, 95, 160
Patraka, Vivien, 27, 59–61
Pearce, Susan, 218–219n14
Pennant Family, 150, 151
performance paradigm, 29, 55, 59–61, 202
Pero, 48–49, 50
Pero Footbridge, Bristol, 50–51, 148
Perry, Ruth, 161
Peters, Julie Stone, 180, 181, 202
Phillips, Caryl
   The Atlantic Sound, 30–31
   Cambridge, 68, 85–89
      narration, 87–88
      pastiche, 86
      representation of history, 88
   Crossing the River, 68, 95–104
      biraciality, 102
      pastiche, 95
      representation of history, 99
      representation of race, 100–102
Phillips, Trevor, 3–4, 148–149
Pidduck, Juliana, 230n3
Pinney House, Bristol, 49–50
Pinney, John, 48–49, 150–151
plurivocality, 94–95
pornography, 78–80, 175–176
Portsmouth (New Hampshire) Black Heritage Trail, 54

postcolonialism, 14
   and the novel, 68, 70
Postlethwayt, Malachy, 177
presence, 59–60
Pringle, Thomas, 107
Prior, Jayne, 153

Queen Square, Bristol, 56–57

race, history of, 183–184
race relations, American, 22
racism, 12–13
Radway, Janice, 112
Rendall, Janet, 154
Renov, Michael, 149
resistance, African, 36
Respectable Trade, A (film), 50, 140–147
   costume film as, 143
   Frances, 146–147
   Mehuru, 144–147
   representation of slavery, 142–43
   screenplay for, 147–147
Respectable Trade, A: Bristol and Transatlantic Slavery (exhibit), 45
restored behavior, 55
resurrectionary moments, 46
Richardson, Alan, 48
Richardson, David, 31–32, 47, 148
Rigby, Graeme
   The Black Cook's Historian, 67
Roach, Joseph, 182–183, 216n61
Robertson, Roland, 182
Rosenthal, Laura, 235n10
Royal Shakespeare Company, 179, 180
Rozema, Patricia, 164
   Jane Austen, and, 164
Runnymede Trust, 213n2
Rushton, Edward, 32

Said, Edward, 160–161
Samuel, Raphael, 4, 45–46, 141
Savage, Kirk, 28
Schechner, Richard, 29, 55
Secrets & Lies, 157–160

Sharp's Revolt, 155–156
Shyllon, F.O., 7
Slave History Trail, The, Liverpool, 27
Slave Trade Trail Around Central Bristol, The, 26, 30, 45–65
slavery, American, representation of, 28–29
slavery, Dutch, 23
slavery, representation of, 84–85, 174–175
   See also *A Son of Africa, A Respectable Trade, Britain's Slave Trade*
Small, Stephen, 28, 217n3, 220n45
Smethurst, Paul, 87
Smith, Valerie, 114
Smollett, Tobias xi, 176
Society of Merchant Venturers, 26
Son of Africa, A, 134–140
   cosmopolitanism, 137
   diaspora, 136–137
SOSKAN, 217n63
Southam, Brian, 162, 234n68
Southerne, Thomas, 186–187
Southey, Robert, 48
Spencer, Jane, 187, 196
Sterne, Lawrence
   A Sentimental Journey, 168
Stewart, Maaja, 163–164, 166
Stocking, George, 38
structure of feeling, 64
sugar boycott, 79, 176
Sypher, Wylie, 180, 215n30

Taylor, Doreen, 26, 52
Thistlewood, Thomas, 107
Tibbles, Anthony, 36, 39, 42, 217–218n5
Thomas, Hugh, 214–215n26
Tobin, Beth Fowkes, 183
Tomalin, Claire, 161
Toxteth Riots, 25
Transatlantic Slavery: Against Human Dignity
   Transatlantic Slavery: Against Human Dignity, 26
   artifacts, exhibition of, 36–37, 39
   dioramas, 35

exhibition text, 33
representation of African history, 37–38
representation of Middle Passage, 41–42
representations of torture, 39
sideboards, 34–35
transnationalism, 182–183
Trooboff, Rhoda, 238n31
Troost, Linda and Sayre Greenfield, 230n4

Unsworth, Barry, 68

Sacred Hunger, 68, 72–80, 176
anachronism, 76
authorial presence, 75
relation to Conrad, 77
representation of history, 76–77
representation of sugar, 78–80

Vaswani, Ratan, 219n31, 221n52
Victoria and Albert Museum, 210

Walcot Nation Day, Bath ix–x
Walker, John, 32

walkers, trail, 52–65
walking in the city, 55–56
compared to linguistic speech act, 56
Wallerstein, Immanuel, 182
Walvin, James, 6
Warner, Marina, 151
Waters, Malcolm, 182
Werbner, Pnina, 154–155
Werner, Sollers, 129, 130
Wheeler, Roxann, 183
Whitbread Prize, 209
wild zone, 169
William Wilberforce Museum, 40–41
Williams, Raymond, 64
Williamsburg, Colonial, Virginia, 28–29, 218n13
Windrush, the, 3–4
Wood, Marcus, 27, 28, 30, 39, 40, 99, 125, 172–174, 175–176

Yearsley, Anne, 48
Young, Robert, 69

Zong Incident, 80, 83